SHANGHAI
1937

Shanghai
1937

Stalingrad on the Yangtze

BY PETER HARMSEN

CASEMATE
Philadelphia & Oxford

Published in the United States of America and Great Britain in 2015 by
CASEMATE PUBLISHERS
908 Darby Road, Havertown, PA 19083
and
10 Hythe Bridge Street, Oxford OX1 2EW

Copyright 2013 © Peter Harmsen

ISBN 978-1-61200-309-2
Digital Edition: ISBN 978-1-61200-168-5

Cataloging-in-publication data is available from the Library of Congress and
the British Library.

10 9 8 7 6 5 4 3 2 1

Printed and bound in the United States of America.

For a complete list of Casemate titles please contact:

CASEMATE PUBLISHERS (US)
Telephone (610) 853-9131, Fax (610) 853-9146
E-mail: casemate@casematepublishing.com

CASEMATE PUBLISHERS (UK)
Telephone (01865) 241249, Fax (01865) 794449
E-mail: casemate-uk@casematepublishing.co.uk

Contents

··

Acknowledgments

NO ENDEAVOR IS A ONE-MAN UNDERTAKING. THIS ALSO GOES FOR *Shanghai 1937*. The information needed to tell the untold story of the great battle on the banks of the Yangtze had to come from numerous sources, some less obvious than others. I have depended on the help of acquaintances, and the occasional kindness of strangers, without whom this book would never have made it into print.

I wish to acknowledge the following institutions for their generous assistance: Academia Historica, Taipei; the National Central Library, Taipei; the Department Military Archives, Freiburg im Breisgau; and Columbia Center for Oral History. The willingness of the Asahi Shimbun Photo Archives and of the American Geographical Society Library, University of Wisconsin-Milwaukee Libraries, to share their rich and unique holdings of historical images was essential in putting together a pictorial record of the momentous events described in this book.

Among individuals who have contributed, I would particularly like to mention Kashiwagi Kazuhiko, editor at Asahi Shimbun Photo Archives, and Fang Jun, a Beijing-based amateur historian who shows by his own personal example that the memory of the Sino-Japanese War is very much alive in China today. Thanks should also go to my colleague Sam Yeh in the Taipei office of the French news agency AFP for his help in giving this book an Internet presence.

I am extremely grateful for the help provided by the staff at Casemate

Publishers, including editorial director Steven Smith, for his enthusiastic support during the entire process of preparing this publication; designer Libby Braden for ensuring that the book ended up as visually appealing as it did; and editor Anita Baker for polishing the manuscript with a keen eye for both the big picture and the small, but important, detail.

The patience of my wife Hui-tsung was crucial. Finally, thanks to my children, Eva and Lisa, for putting up with all the evenings and weekends Dad had to spend in front of the computer.

TAIPEI, FEBRUARY 2013

....

Prologue

IN THE EARLY PART OF 1937, THE CONCEPT OF URBAN WARFARE WAS still new to the world. Three months of battle in Shanghai in the fall of that year changed all that. The struggle between China and Japan demonstrated what happens to a major city when it becomes the arena for two vast armies, fielding hundreds of thousands of men and an array of destructive weapons. There had been other instances of war in an urban setting—indeed, earlier in the decade Shanghai was an example of that—but never on such a massive scale. The scenes of flattened housing complexes and gutted factories that were later to captivate and horrify the global public during the battle of Stalingrad had in fact already been played out more than five years earlier in China's largest city.

In a sense, the struggle for Shanghai in 1937 was a dress rehearsal for World War II. Or more correctly, perhaps, it *was* part of World War II. Arguably, it could be considered to be the first major battle in a conflict that divided mankind into two major camps—one consisting of Fascist regimes in various guises, the other a motley group of democratic and totalitarian nations. To westerners it is natural to see World War II as starting in earnest with Hitler's invasion of Poland in 1939. For Asians, it is just as logical to think of it as beginning two years earlier on the north Chinese plain and along the banks of the Yangtze.

Even if the battle of Shanghai is considered isolated from the larger context of World War II, it was undeniably an event that would leave an indelible mark on the two ancient civilizations caught up in it. It was the biggest clash between nations that East Asia had seen since the Russo-Japanese War of 1904 and 1905.[1] It turned localized, and possibly manageable, Sino-Japanese friction into a full-scale war that would continue for eight bloody years. In fact neither side, Chinese or Japanese, has ever really found closure, and to this day, nearly 80 years later, they remain locked in mutual suspicion. Much of this is due to the appalling brutality exhibited by the Japanese Army in China, which was epitomized in the infamous Rape of Nanjing—a direct result of the Shanghai campaign.

Shanghai was Asia's most cosmopolitan city and home to citizens from a range of nations, as well as a large number of stateless people. Although they lived in areas left mostly untouched by combat, they were often just yards away from scenes of carnage where men and women fought and died in their thousands. These foreign inhabitants became the unwilling witnesses of the battle that raged all around them, and in that way they helped write history themselves. Rarely before had so many civilians seen so much bloodshed at such close range. The analogy would have been if a district of Stalingrad had miraculously been left unharmed by the battle, allowing the residents to take in all of the fighting that devoured the rest of the city. Or, in the words of American correspondent Edgar Snow: "It was as though Verdun had happened on the Seine, in full view of a Right Bank Paris that was neutral; as though a Gettysburg were fought in Harlem, while the rest of Manhattan remained a non-belligerent observer."[2]

Verdun and Gettysburg are apt comparisons. These battles had been momentous events, and the battle that consumed the Yangtze River delta in the latter half of 1937 was, too. The rest of the world understood this and the fighting regularly occupied the front pages of major newspapers around the globe. Shanghai seized the imagination then for much the same reasons as it does so again today. It was a place of excitement and exotic adventure, and the public wanted to be informed when its fate was hanging in the balance.

Therefore, it is ironic that so little has been written in any language other than Chinese about the battle of Shanghai in past decades. Not a single monograph on this crucial encounter is listed among the hundreds of thousands of volumes dealing with World War II and its antecedents. In a time when academic and popular writers must use all their imaginative powers to think up uncovered angles on the war in Europe and the Pacific, the battle of Shanghai and many other battles of the 1937–1945 Sino-Japanese War constitute a gaping hole in the historiography. It is my hope that this book can make a modest contribution towards rectifying this imbalance.

―――――――

In what follows, almost all Chinese names are spelled using the pinyin system of transliteration introduced in China after 1949 and now increasingly adopted elsewhere. Traditional spelling has only been kept in a few instances where the use of pinyin would confuse rather than enlighten. China's supreme leader is referred to as Chiang Kai-shek rather than Jiang Jieshi. In addition, in bibliographical references, authors' spellings of their own names are maintained, even if they do not follow the conventions for the use of pinyin, for example, Hsin Ta-mo instead of Xin Damo.

Geographical names are generally given in their modern rendering rather than the way they were described in 1937, e.g. Beijing instead of Beiping and Taiwan instead of Formosa. Here, too, exceptions have been allowed for the sake of clarity. Manchukuo is not spelled Manzhouguo, and Marco Polo Bridge is not called Lugou Bridge.

It is generally the custom to give the full names of Chinese persons in the first reference, and later refer to them by their family names only. I have frequently departed from this convention so that it is possible to make the necessary distinctions between people with the same family names, e.g. Zhang Zhizhong and Zhang Fakui, who were both pivotal commanders. My aim is also to make it easier for the reader to commit the often unfamiliar names to memory. For Japanese persons, family names are put before given names.

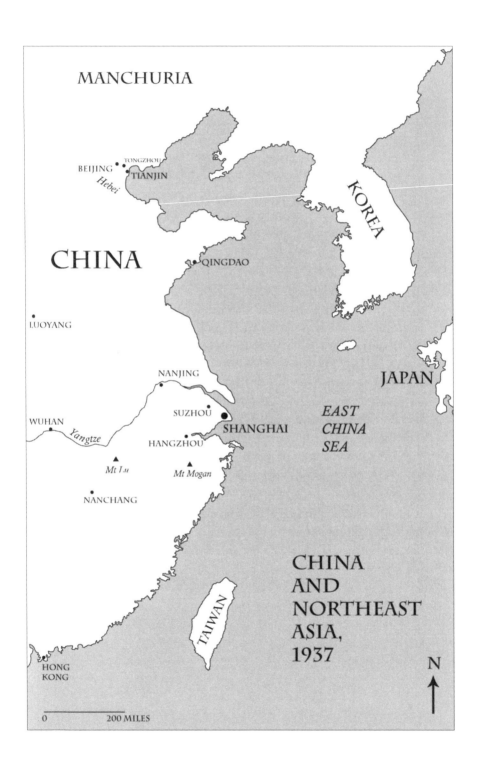

MANCHURIA

BEIJING • TONGZHOU
Hebei • TIANJIN

CHINA

• QINGDAO

KOREA

• LUOYANG

NANJING •
SUZHOU •
• WUHAN
Yangtze
• SHANGHAI
HANGZHOU •

▲
Mt Lu
▲
Mt Mogan

• NANCHANG

JAPAN

EAST
CHINA
SEA

TAIWAN

HONG
KONG

CHINA
AND
NORTHEAST
ASIA,
1937

N
↑

0   200 MILES

CHAPTER

1

....

Three Corpses

JULY 7–AUGUST 12

THE BULLET-RIDDLED SEDAN HAD SCREECHED TO AN ABRUPT HALT at the entrance of the airfield. Nearby, the two men who had been inside lay sprawled on the ground. Their blood-soaked uniforms identified them as members of the Japanese Navy's elite Special Landing Force. The brains splashed across the dashboard showed that one of them had died inside the car. He had then been dragged out to be slashed, kicked and pounded into a pulp. Half his face was missing and his stomach had been cut open, the sickly pallor of his intestines gleaming faintly in the night. The other man had escaped the vehicle but had only managed a few paces before being gunned down. A little distance away lay a third body, dressed in a Chinese uniform.[1]

It was several hours before dawn on Tuesday, August 10, 1937. Darkness still engulfed Hongqiao Aerodrome eight miles west of Shanghai, and the investigators had to work under automobile headlights and using electric torches. They were a diverse group. There were Chinese, of course, but there were also Japanese, British, French and American detectives—representatives of foreign powers that felt quite at home in China's largest and most prosperous city after nearly a century there. Also present was a group of reporters from the cutthroat world of Shanghai's English- and Chinese-language press. Despite the antisocial hour, they had to be here. This could be big, very big.

The investigators quickly determined that the badly mangled body belonged to 27-year-old Sub-Lieutenant Oyama Isao, while the other dead Japanese was his driver, First Class Seaman Saito Yozo. The identity of the Chinese fatality was a mystery. The scene looked like the result of a simple shoot-out. However, too many questions remained unanswered: What were the Japanese doing at a military airfield miles away from their barracks? Who had opened fire first and why had he decided to shoot? The Chinese investigators and their Japanese counterparts didn't see eye to eye on the answers to any of these questions. As they paced up and down the scene of the incident, scouring the ground for evidence, loud arguments erupted again and again. Shortly before sunrise, they wound up their work having reached no agreement on what had actually happened. They got into their cars and headed back to the city.

The acrimony that the Chinese and the Japanese detectives displayed towards each other surprised no one. Tensions between the two nations had risen dramatically over the preceding five weeks, in Shanghai and beyond. These tensions were the result of distant events as hundreds of miles to the north an undeclared war was raging. It had started in early July, when a series of misunderstandings had caused Japanese and Chinese soldiers to clash near Beijing in a hectic night of confused skirmishing. Very soon events had taken on a seemingly unstoppable momentum of their own, as more and more areas around the old imperial capital were sucked into a conflict that still had no name. So far Shanghai, in the middle of China's economic heartland, had successfully avoided any hostilities, but everyone knew that the peace might not last.

China's future was uncertain. What were the intentions of the Chinese government in Nanjing, the Yangtze River city from which it had ruled the vast country for the past decade? What plans were being prepared by military and political decision makers in Tokyo? Would the Beijing turmoil expand into a general war engulfing all of China? The answers to these questions would also affect thousands of Japanese—soldiers, diplomats and businessmen—who were residing in Shanghai and other large cities along the Yangtze River. They knew that if war were to break out there, deep inside what would then be enemy territory, they would all be in great danger, surrounded by millions of hostile Chinese. In the present circumstances, all that was needed was a single spark. The incident at the aerodrome might be just that spark.

The investigators were keenly aware of the consequences if they failed to handle their delicate task with the necessary finesse. But even if they were hoping for peace, it was clear that Shanghai was a city preparing for war. As they drove through the still dark suburbs on their way from Hongqiao back to their downtown offices, their car headlights fell on whitewashed trees, interspersed with sandbag positions and the silhouettes of lone Chinese sentries. Officially, these sentries were members of the Peace Preservation Corps, a paramilitary outfit that, due to an international agreement brokered a few years earlier, was the only Chinese force allowed to stay in the Shanghai area. However, rumors were circulating that they were in fact disguised members of the 88th Division, one of the best-trained units of the entire Chinese Army.

Having entered the city, the vehicles passed first the French Concession and then the International Settlement, both parts of Shanghai where foreigners lived in comfortable isolation away from the din and dirt of the Chinese neighborhoods. Some districts were indistinguishable from London, Paris or Boston. The maple-lined streets housed businesses with names such as Ambassador Cinema, Vienna Ballroom and Café Bonheur. Surroundings such as these seemed almost designed to give a false sense of security. This was not Europe or America, but very much Asia. The deceptively peaceful veneer could dissolve any time and unveil an uglier and much more violent reality underneath, as had happened only too recently.

The incident took place in Zhabei, a rough working-class neighborhood not far north of the Art Deco facades of the International Settlement. Since the start of the boom years early in the century, Zhabei had attracted tens of thousands of migrants from the countryside with its promise of work, food and shelter. This had led to overcrowding with many people living in too little space, and Zhabei had become a leprosy-ridden slum area normally shunned by Shanghai's expatriates. They could mostly afford to pretend it did not even exist. Mostly, but not always. Five years earlier Zhabei had been the scene of fierce, house-to-house fighting between Chinese and Japanese soldiers who had been killing each other with gusto in a brief unofficial war. For five weeks in early 1932, the constant, unsettling sound of battle had been carried by the wind into the International Settlement, while swarms of refugees had tried desperately, and mostly in vain, to gain entry into the safety of the foreign quarters.

In the end, the Japanese had scored a Pyrrhic victory, while China, despite its defeat, had arguably gained more. It had won confidence. After nearly a century of humiliation at the hands of foreign imperialists, it now knew that it could strike back and hit hard, even at the most aggressive and merciless of all the hated colonial powers that were encroaching on its territory. Important as it was, this was not the only lesson that China drew from the 1932 war. It was abundantly clear that any new conflict with Japan was likely to be costly. Even five years after the fighting, despite years of busy reconstruction efforts, Zhabei still carried the physical scars of that short, sharp flash of violence. With the threat of conflict now in the air again, the stakes were, therefore, high as the investigators returned to their offices while the day dawned over Shanghai. Mismanage this crisis, and there was no telling what bloodshed might ensue and at what cost to millions of innocent civilians.

In the hours that followed, both sides released their respective versions of the events. According to the Chinese, the Japanese vehicle had tried to force its way through the gate of the airport. When Peace Preservation Corps members posted at the entrance had motioned to Saito, the driver, to stop, he had abruptly turned the car around, while Sub-Lieutenant Oyama had shot at the Chinese guards with an automatic pistol. Only then had the Chinese opened fire, killing Oyama in a hail of bullets. Saito had managed to jump out before he, too, had been gunned down. It was not the first time someone Japanese had tried to enter the airport, the commander of the Chinese guards told a western reporter. It had happened repeatedly in the past two months, and they "obviously were undertaking espionage."[2]

The Japanese account, unsurprisingly, blamed the entire incident on China. It stated that Oyama had been riding along a road skirting the airfield, with no intention of entering. Suddenly, the vehicle had been stopped and surrounded by Peace Preservation Corps troops who, without warning, had opened up a barrage of rifle and machine gun fire. Oyama had not had the slightest chance to shoot back. The two Japanese had every right to drive on the road, the property of the International Settlement, a Japanese statement argued, before labeling the incident as a clear violation of the 1932 peace agreement. "We demand that the Chinese bear responsibility for this illegal act," the statement concluded.[3]

One crucial question remained: who was the dead man in the Chinese uniform and how could he have lost his life if Oyama had not been able to return fire? A Japanese doctor, who had been among the first to arrive at the scene, took special note of the man's appearance, stating that he had rather long hair, and he had allowed his finger nails to grow to almost feminine lengths. This was odd, because neither was permitted in the Chinese military. Even stranger was the fact that the lethal bullet had entered the back of the man's skull. He had been shot from behind, execution-style. The conclusion seemed inevitable: he was not a soldier, and he had not been killed in a shoot-out.[4]

Shanghai—"Paris of the East" to some foreigners with a romantic bent, "Queen of the Orient" to others—was a prize worth fighting for. With about 3.5 million residents in 1937, it was Asia's largest city after Tokyo, the fifth-largest in the world, and the key to the riches of an entire continent. A popular guidebook proudly stated that Shanghai was home to 48 different nationalities. The vast majority of the inhabitants were Chinese, while about 70,000 permanent residents were foreigners. Japanese, citizens of a young and hungry empire undergoing rapid expansion, formed the largest segment and numbered about 20,000. British and Russians, the latter mainly émigrés who had fled the 1917 revolution, accounted for just below 10,000 residents each. The United States and Canada were also represented, as was every European country from Greece and Czechoslovakia to Norway and Poland.[5]

The various nationalities had been drawn to Shanghai by one thing—trade. Commerce was the driving force behind the city's seemingly miraculous transformation. This transformation saw a cluster of poor villages gathered around a small walled town expand into a sprawling modern metropolis in less than 100 years. In 1842, the ailing Chinese Empire had lost the First Opium War to Great Britain, and as a concession to the victors it had declared Shanghai open for foreign trade. In the decades that followed the city prospered as a result of its unique location near the Yangtze estuary. On the one hand, this connected Shanghai to some of the most vital areas of China, situated along its longest river, and on the other it provided direct access to the ocean and global shipping routes. Shanghai got a cut as the produce of China—cotton, wood oil and animal hides—

passed through its docks on the way to the world markets. In the other direction flowed mainly one commodity, opium.[6]

Still, Shanghai owed its rapid progress to more than just geography. It was built on the toil of hundreds of thousands of destitute Chinese peasants. Unlike the foreign residents, they had not entered the city from the ocean side transported by comfortable steamers, but overland, mostly walking on foot while carrying their only possessions on their backs. They came to man the factories and workshops that were transforming Shanghai into an industrial powerhouse. Many had no choice. Nothing was worse than the rural squalor the migrants had left behind. However, by every conceivable measure, life at the bottom of Shanghai society was as bleak and brutal as anything European capitalism had produced in its darkest Dickensian hour. Days spent at exhausting and often dangerous work were followed by nights in cramped and unsafe apartment buildings. The hopelessness of it all turned Shanghai into a fertile recruiting ground for China's nascent labor movement.

Not all new arrivals ended up in industry. The young and the pretty were just as likely to be channeled into the biggest sex industry the world had ever seen. It was a profession capable of catering to every taste, every perversion, and every wallet. At the top were women of immaculate beauty and refined manners, highly skilled in the Oriental art of love, and capable, too, of cultured talk if that was what their customers wanted. At the bottom, one found the "nailers," offering their quick services against dark alley walls.[7] Soldiers and sailors from all corners of the globe formed a considerable portion of the clientele, with the Japanese showing a particular talent for efficiency. "We assemble the men in squads of thirty," an admiral of the Imperial Navy explained, "give them each a bath and a change of underclothing, then march them as units to the comfort headquarters."[8]

Prostitution was inextricably linked to Shanghai's sprawling criminal scene, as were gambling and extortion. It was no surprise that a big city would give rise to organized crime, but Shanghai made "the Chicago of Al Capone appear a staid, almost pious, provincial town," as the Chinese writer Han Suyin remarked.[9] The sinister Green Gang dominated the Shanghai underworld, allowing its members to roam virtually at will. They were the untouchables after they had penetrated deep into the police force. In that capacity, they worked quickly and efficiently to solve all crimes targeting expatriates, prompting the foreign authorities to tolerate their presence, however grudgingly.[10]

On top of all the other hardship that they had to endure, Shanghai's faceless poverty-stricken masses also experienced the violent political storms that swept across China in the first quarter of the 20th century. In 1911, the last dynasty collapsed with startling speed, bringing to an end the two-millennia-old imperial system and setting the stage for long years of chaos. The revolutionaries who brought down the emperor had hoped for a republic in the European mold, but instead the country was plunged into internecine strife by rival warlords. They were the power holders in a corrupt new oligarchy fueled by greed and based on violence, and they coveted Shanghai because of its lucrative opium trade. Consequently, the city changed hands among them several times.

It clearly was not a sustainable situation, neither for Shanghai nor for China. The endless fratricidal wars gave rise in the 1920s to frustrated calls for unification, and as the decade entered its second half, the movement to bring all of China under one government finally gained traction. It found an efficient leader in an ambitious and ruthless officer, who had been educated in Japan but was fiercely patriotic. His name was Chiang Kai-shek. Born in 1887, he exhibited the youth and dynamism that was called for in those turbulent and dangerous times. In 1926, he set out from the south Chinese province of Guangdong at the head of a vast Nationalist army. He headed north with the aim of successively bringing all the provinces under his control as he went along. Shanghai was in his path, and in the spring of 1927 his troops reached the city.

The undisciplined warlord forces holding Shanghai were no real match for Chiang, and they knew it, so they melted away before any serious fighting had even taken place. The Communists were another matter. Despite a tenuous alliance with Chiang, they signaled their intention of taking over Shanghai, using their existing organization in the city to arrange strikes and dispatch armed gangs to patrol the streets. Chiang struck decisively and fiercely, with the help of the feared Green Gang. Labor activists taken prisoner were beheaded or thrown alive into the furnaces of locomotives. One union leader was beaten only half to death, before being thrown into a pit and buried alive.[11] The crackdown was so brutally complete that Communism would not gain a serious foothold in Shanghai again until the late 1940s. The criminal underworld, on the other hand, was as strong as ever.

The 1927 killings had overwhelmingly taken place in the Chinese part of Shanghai, as had the short war with Japan that broke out five years later. In January 1932, maverick Japanese officers who were already busy establishing an informal empire in the northeast of China, now set their sights on Shanghai. They paid Chinese thugs to attack a group of Japanese priests, and then, in "retaliation," sent members of the Special Landing Force, the empire's marines, from the International Settlement to Zhabei to teach the Chinese a lesson. As Japanese motorcycles raced up and down the streets, spraying facades with their mounted machine guns, they were met with fire from Chinese snipers. Some were regular soldiers, others members of the Green Gang, all acting together in loose coordination.[12]

Japan poured in more troops, and so did China. The Chinese reinforcements included the elite 87th and 88th Divisions, equipped with modern German materiel and trained by battle-hardened advisors from Germany. The Germans had brought with them to the East the deadly tactics of the Great War and taught their Chinese apprentices how to prepare near-impregnable defenses consisting of deep trenches protected by thick walls of sandbags and dense forests of barbed wire. These worked to deadly effect. Japan's infantry was caught in the crossfire of machine guns and cut down mercilessly. Its tanks had little room to maneuver in the narrow streets and often found themselves trapped like bleeding bulls in the arena, blinded and waiting for death.

Over more than a month of fighting, the center of the battle remained at Zhabei. Japanese technological superiority, which had initially counted for little, eventually reached a critical mass sufficient to tilt the balance. Shelling by naval vessels anchored in Huangpu River reduced large parts of the district to smoldering ruins. Biplanes finished the job, flying sortie after sortie over the rubble to indiscriminately drop bombs and strafe anything that moved, whether in uniform or not. The targeting of unarmed civilians triggered outrage across a world not yet inured to the harsh reality of terror bombing.[13]

The final blow to Chinese resistance came in late February, when a Japanese division launched a surprise landing on the banks of the Yangtze, north of Shanghai, attacking the defenders from the rear. By early March, when diplomacy took over, half a million residents had been turned into homeless refugees. At least 4,000 Chinese soldiers and hundreds of Japanese had lost their lives.[14] It was the deadliest international conflict involving China since the Boxer Uprising, an anti-foreign rebellion that had shaken the waning empire in the year 1900. Even so, it was only a modest dress rehearsal for much greater horrors that were to follow five years later.

In mid-July 1937, retired Dutch Colonel Henri Johan Diederick de Fremery was holidaying at a resort in the Diamond Mountains in the Japanese colony of Korea. He was taking a break from his job as military advisor to the Chinese government, which preferred Germans but welcomed experienced officers from other western nations as well. One morning he woke up to see the Rising Sun flag flying at his hotel. When he inquired why, the reply was prompt: "Because of the war with China," he was told. The Dutchman's assignment, which had so far been a fairly pleasant sinecure, was about to become much busier. Within a few weeks, the 62-year-old former artillery officer would be spying on the Japanese military on behalf of the Royal Netherlands Indies Army.[15]

That fateful summer, the world's attention was riveted not on Shanghai, but on Beijing, which was directly on the frontline of China's desperate struggle with a Japanese Empire driven by voracious ambitions on the Asian mainland. Since the turn of the century, Japanese military and civilian officials had become convinced that control over north China's plentiful resources, especially coal and iron ore, would offer long-term security in the incessant competition with the older empires of the West. Increasingly, they had also come to consider the area a potential buffer zone against the Soviet threat. Taking Manchuria, China's northeastern provinces that bordered Japan's possessions in Korea, had seemed the logical first step.[16]

The Japanese had struck in 1931, blowing up a railway line that they themselves owned in Manchuria. They used this as a pretext to invade the region and set up a puppet state, which they called Manchukuo. They then gradually pushed their influence further, showing every sign that they planned to devour all of northern China little by little. In 1935 they had wrested control of 22 counties in eastern Hebei province, right at the gates of Beijing, and had established the "East Hebei Autonomous Government." Meanwhile, Japanese officers had begun making public statements suggesting that China's five northernmost provinces ought to be separated from the rest of the country and placed under Japanese control.[17] One of the justifications was that China had ceased to exist as a functioning state and, therefore, was little different from the resource-rich areas of Africa and Asia that the western colonial powers had divided among them.

Chiang Kai-shek, the leader of most of China since 1927, had adopted a strategy of yielding to Japan until he was strong enough to offer serious resistance. It was a policy he felt he was forced to adopt. China was poorly developed and not ready for war, and he himself enjoyed only imperfect control of his own country, having entered into tenuous alliances with local warlords in regions where his own influence was limited. His weakness was further emphasized by his inability to stamp out the Communist rebel movement. Despite the ferocity of the crackdown in Shanghai, pockets of Red resistance remained throughout the countryside. Chiang wanted to eradicate this threat before taking on Japan. He held the view that he couldn't go to war if he had to constantly watch his back too.

However, he was under growing pressure from powerful north Chinese leaders who felt the threat from Japan in a much more immediate fashion than he did and longed to put an end to the island empire's continued territorial expansion. In late 1936, the most prominent of these leaders took advantage of a visit by Chiang by kidnapping him and keeping him under house arrest until he committed to a more serious effort at reining in Japan. Chiang later imprisoned his kidnapper, but he kept his promise to stand up to the Japanese challenge, sensing that public opinion could no longer stomach appeasement. As a result, it was a more determined Chiang who led China as the situation gradually deteriorated in the first half of 1937.

Japan was no less determined. In the summer of that year, Japanese soldiers stationed in Hebei province along the border of Tokyo's informal Chinese Empire performed frequent maneuvers, mostly after sunset. They did so even in the vicinity of Chinese-controlled Beijing, where they, like the militaries of other major foreign powers, were allowed to maintain a limited presence. The maneuvers marked a routine meant to both maintain their level of military preparedness and at the same time intimidate anyone who might be bold enough to defy them. By late June, the Japanese drills had become nearly nightly occurrences, and the Chinese authorities had felt compelled to impose a curfew on the civilian population to avoid any unmanageable incidents.[18]

Therefore, no one took any particular notice when on the evening of July 7 a Japanese company garrisoned at the town of Fengtai near Beijing set out for a night of exercises near the Marco Polo Bridge, named after the Venetian merchant who had mentioned it 600 years earlier in his memoirs. As the Japanese soldiers moved around warily in pitch-black darkness, a number of shots rang through the warm air. Apparently, they were fired by a group of Chinese soldiers camped nearby. Apprehension among the Japanese grew when the officers carried out a count and found one soldier missing.

The Japanese assumed the soldier was being held captive in the Chinese camp and went searching for him. As tense soldiers fanned out into the night, fingers on triggers, incidents were bound to happen. Scattered fighting erupted around the bridge, and the Japanese reinforcements that arrived in the following hours began shelling the nearby walled city of Wanping. In the meantime, the missing soldier had turned up, apparently having made an unauthorized visit to a brothel. By then it was too late. The battle had started. There were dead and injured on both sides. A dangerous line had been crossed.

Chinese and Japanese officers started negotiations to contain the crisis. After four days, they eventually managed to hammer out a truce. It was a wasted effort. The ceasefire was undermined from the start by mutual loathing and suspicion, and both sides took measures that could only escalate the conflict. On the same day that the truce was signed in China, the Japanese cabinet decided to reinforce the troops in the area around Beijing with units from Manchukuo, Korea and the home islands. The intention, abetted by Emperor Hirohito, was, in language that had already become well known, "to teach China a lesson" by subduing Chinese forces around Beijing and the nearby port city of Tianjin. The day after, Chiang Kai-shek sent a cable to the 19th Army, one of the main units stationed in the north, stating that "I am now determined to declare war on Japan."[19]

Once the Japanese reinforcements were in place at the end of July, an imperial order was issued instructing the local commander to "chastise the Chinese Army in the Beijing-Tianjin area."[20] The well-equipped Japanese units unleashed a series of coordinated attacks, with extraordinarily bloody results in some places. Chinese soldiers manning a barracks south of Beijing were nearly wiped out, and when a thin column of survivors tried to escape north through the fields towards the city, they were chopped to pieces by Japanese heavy machine guns placed in advance along the escape route. The injured soldiers were left to die slow agonizing deaths under the scorching sun, as unfeeling peasants collected bayonets and other equipment useful for their work.[21]

East of Beijing, along the road to Tianjin, an incident occurred that served as an ominous forewarning of the kind of war that had now started. The setting was Tongzhou, an ancient town surrounded by thick brick walls and protected by heavy wooden gates. Recently, it had become the seat of the puppet "East Hebei Autonomous Government." Although the town was officially run by Chinese administrators and protected by an indigenous auxiliary police force, they were not the real rulers. The Japanese Empire was represented both by regular soldiers and by members of the feared secret police, the Kempeitai. In addition, there were nearly 400 Japanese and Korean civilians, some of them prostitutes servicing the garrison, others businesspeople with their families. This foreign presence was resented by the Chinese. Even members of the auxiliary police, who were ostensibly allies of Japan, secretly loathed their masters.

As Japanese commanders prepared for their offensive around Beijing and Tianjin, they pulled out the bulk of the troops stationed at Tongzhou, planning to deploy them in the upcoming assault. This was the opportunity two officers of the auxiliary police, Chinese loyalists at heart, had been waiting for. In the early hours of July 29, they sent their men spilling out into the streets. Long swords glimmered in the faint moonlight as the chilling chant of "Kill! Kill!" echoed down the narrow alleys. Most Japanese men had departed, and what followed was not so much a battle as a massacre. Years of pent-up anger was released in an orgy of blood. The Chinese police officers cut off the arms of old women and raped the young ones, before stabbing their genitals with bayonets. They decapitated others and lowered their heads in wicker baskets from the parapets.[22]

Japanese soldiers rushing to Tongzhou after the massacre encountered a horrific spectacle. "I saw a mother and child who had been slaughtered. The child's fingers had been hacked off," said one of them, Major Katsura Shizuo. He went on to describe the grisly scene at a Japanese store near the south gate of the city: "The body of a man, probably the owner, who had been dragged outside and killed, had been dumped on the road. His body had been cut open, exposing his ribs and his intestines, which had spilled out onto the ground."[23] A survivor told the *Asahi Shimbun* of the torture inflicted on some of the Japanese civilians before they were killed: "I chanced to see a man being dragged along by a wire. At that time I thought that he was only bound with it, but now I know that it was pierced through his nose."[24]

After Tongzhou was recaptured, more carnage followed, but the tables had been turned. Japanese soldiers bent on revenge beheaded all the men they managed to capture, whether rebels or not, and raped the women. When they were done with Tongzhou, they swept the surrounding countryside searching for anyone who looked like a fleeing police officer, hard to determine at a distance, and gunned them down too. Finally, they set the town on fire. It created a dense column of black smoke that could be seen by the horrified residents of Beijing in the following days. Now they knew what life and death under Japanese rule would be like.[25]

Of the 385 Japanese and Koreans residing in Tongzhou, altogether 223 lost their lives. It appears that no one bothered to count the Chinese casualties, but there is little doubt they reached a comparable number. As horrific as it was, the violence in Tongzhou would quickly pale in comparison with the astonishing atrocities Japanese soldiers proved capable of as they entered China's great population centers further down the east coast. However, in Tokyo the massacre was described in detail by a jingoistic press and triggered immense public anger. It made de-escalation of the China incident all the more unlikely, even if some in the Japanese hierarchy might still have hoped for a last-minute reversal of the descent into chaos.[26] "The mood in the army today," Hirohito's brother, Prince Takamatsu, wrote in his diary, "is that we're really going to smash China, so that it will be ten years before they can stand up straight again."[27]

As the Marco Polo Bridge skirmish set northern China ablaze with the rapidity of a prairie fire, Nationalist General Zhang Fakui was attending a routine training course for senior military personnel at Mount Lu in the southeastern province of Jiangxi. Short and small of build, even by the

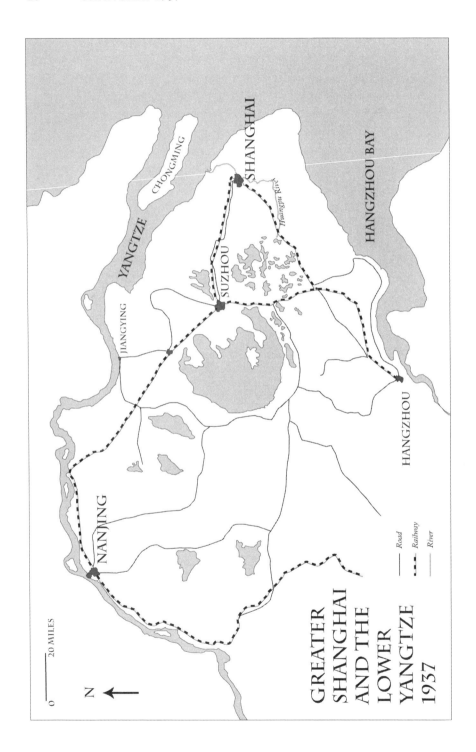

GREATER
SHANGHAI
AND THE
LOWER
YANGTZE
1937

Road
Railway
River

N

0   20 MILES

SHANGHAI
Huangpu River
HANGZHOU BAY
CHONGMING
YANGTZE
SUZHOU
JIANGYING
HANGZHOU
NANJING

standards of the time, and with "a tapering pointed face" that made it impossible to call him handsome, Zhang did not stand out in any group. Indeed, when among fellow senior officers, he could easily be confused for an orderly. His physical courage, however, was legendary and had earned him the nickname "Zhang Fei," after an ancient half-mythical general famous for taking a stand on a bridge and single-handedly facing down an entire enemy army.[28]

Approaching 41 years of age, Zhang Fakui had spent more than half his life in uniform, fighting first warlords, then Communists and, in a sign of the unpredictable and fast-changing nature of alliances in China, even the Nationalists. It was only a few years before that he had thrown in his lot with rebels campaigning against Chiang Kai-shek. Chiang, who wielded supreme power in the armed forces as chairman of the National Military Council, had forgiven him, and he was put in charge of weeding out Communist strongholds in a large area spanning several provinces south of Shanghai. But it was fast becoming clear that the enemy had changed. The Japanese threat loomed large as the summer activities at Mount Lu got underway. With war having broken out in the Beijing area, Zhang watched officers from the northern armies abruptly cut short the training and hastily return home.[29]

Mount Lu was also Chiang Kai-shek's summer residence and there, on July 16, he gathered together 150 members of China's political and cultural elite to discuss strategies for dealing with the Japanese.[30] The savvy general-turned-statesman, who had only one year earlier preferred a cautious approach, now advocated staunch determination. "This time we must fight to the end," Chiang told the participants. Two days later, the first period of the summer training was over, and Chiang met each of the graduating officers, explaining the duties and responsibilities they could expect to assume once the war spread southwards from Beijing, as seemed increasingly likely. Zhang Fakui was told to prepare for operations in the Shanghai area.[31]

Meanwhile, Chiang's spy chief, Dai Li, was busy gathering information on Japanese intentions for Shanghai. It was not an easy matter. Dai, one of the most sinister figures of modern Chinese history, had spent vastly more energy and resources in the preceding years suppressing the Communists than spying against the Japanese. As a result, in the critical summer of 1937, he only had a thin network of agents inside "Little Tokyo," the Hongkou area of Shanghai dominated by Japanese businesses.[32] One was a pawnshop owner and the rest were double agents employed as local staff in the Japanese security apparatus. They could provide nothing but tidbits, rumors and hearsay. Some sounded ominous in the extreme, but there was almost nothing in the way of actual actionable intelligence. One of the double agents reported back a conversation he had carried out with an inebriated Japanese officer in July. "It's only going to take a few days before Shanghai is going to be ours," the officer had told the double agent, believing him to be on the same side. "Then your work is going to really get busy all of a sudden."[33]

While Chiang was groping in the dark, deprived of the eyes and ears of an efficient intelligence service, he did have at his disposal an army that was at least somewhat better prepared for battle than in 1932. Chastised by the experience of fighting the Japanese, Chiang had set in motion a modernization program that aimed to equip the armed forces with the skills and materiel needed to not just suppress Communist rebels, but also face a modern fighting force supported by tanks, artillery and aircraft.[34] He had made headway, but not enough. Serious weaknesses remained, and now there was no time for remedial action.

While in sheer numbers China seemed to be a power to be reckoned with, the figures were deceptive. On the eve of war, the Chinese military consisted of a total of 176 divisions, in principle divided into two brigades of two regiments each.[35] However, only about 20 divisions had a full peacetime strength of 10,000 soldiers and officers, while 5,000 men was the norm for the rest. What's more, Chiang exercised personal control over a mere 31 divisions,[36] and he could not count on the allegiance of the others. In order to resist Japan successfully, Chiang would have to rely not just on his skills as a military commander, but also as a builder of fragile coalitions among maverick generals with fierce local loyalties.

Equipment was another issue. The modernization drive was not scheduled to have ended until late 1938, and it showed.[37] In every weapon category, from rifles to field artillery, the Chinese were inferior to their Japanese foe, both quantitatively and qualitatively. Domestically made artillery pieces had a shorter range, and substandard steel-making technology caused the gun barrels to overheat adding the risk of explosion to the mix. Some arms even dated back to imperial times.[38] A large proportion of the Chinese infantry had received no proper training in basic tactics, let alone in coordinated operations with armor and artillery. There was one important exception to this sorry state of affairs. The 20 full-strength divisions, all under Chiang's control, were considered a roughly equal match for the Japanese foe as they had been through rigorous training designed by Chiang's German advisors, a group of highly skilled professionals, who had attended the Prussian military academies before being steeled in the battles of the Great War less than a generation earlier.[39]

Chief of the German advisory corps was General Alexander von Falkenhausen, and it is hard to think of anyone more qualified for the job. True, the 58-year-old's narrow shoulders, curved back and bald vulture's head lent him an unmilitary, almost avian appearance, but his exterior belied a tough character that in 1918 had earned him his nation's highest military award, the Pour le Mérite, while assisting Germany's Ottoman allies against the British in Palestine. Few, if any, German officers knew Asia as he did. His experience with the region stretched right back to the turn of the century. As a young lieutenant in the Third East Asian Infantry Regiment he had taken part in an international coalition of colonial powers that put down the Boxer rebellion in the year 1900. Ten years later, he had been an observant and curious tourist, traveling through Korea, Manchuria and northern China with his wife. From 1912 to 1914, he had been the German Kaiser's military attaché in Tokyo.[40] He was to put his knowledge to good use in the months ahead.

———————

If China's ground forces were of uneven quality, this was even truer for its air arm. It was the pride of the Chinese military, and a resource considered so valuable that Chiang avoided sending any of the planes to the north after the Marco Polo Bridge incident. They were a key asset and as such not to be squandered. The hostilities in 1932 had proved to him and his generals that a modern air force was necessary. They had concluded with considerable prescience that leaving the skies to the enemy was simply too dangerous.[41] The Chinese government had initiated an ambitious procurement program and set up the Central Aviation School outside Hangzhou, a little more than 100 miles west of Shanghai. Built on an American-inspired philosophy of rigorous training, its relentless pace winnowed down the aspiring pilots, leaving only the best.

China had more than 600 military aircraft by the middle of 1937, on paper at least.[42] The figure was as impressive as it was misleading. The expansion of the air force had mainly been overseen by Italians, which was a mixed blessing. Mussolini's Fascist government had sent a large number of pilots to China as advisors and had seen to it that its military aircraft manufacturers controlled a major part of the market. This enabled the Chinese to build up its air force at a rate it could not have achieved on its own, but it also gave rise to a number of startling inefficiencies. For starters, the Italian influence had triggered a practice in the Chinese Air Force of adding aircraft to the roster even if they had in reality been reduced to wrecks. This meant that of the 600 aircraft officially forming the air force at the start of the hostilities, only 91 were actually ready to fight. When a senior air force commander told Chiang Kai-shek this unwelcome truth, Chiang threatened to have him executed.[43]

The training of Chinese pilots provided by the Italian advisers was a disaster of equal magnitude, according to retired U.S. Army Air Force Captain Claire Lee Chennault, who was in China in the summer of 1937 to conduct a survey of the Chinese capabilities. The Italians had set up a separate flight school near the city of Luoyang in central China which, Chennault said, "graduated every Chinese cadet who survived the training course as a full-fledged pilot regardless of his ability." This had deadly consequences. The American airman watched how "fighter pilots supposedly ready for combat spun in and killed themselves in basic trainers." "The Chinese Air Force," Chennault wrote in his diary after a visit to Luoyang, "is not ready for war."[44]

The pilots trained at Hangzhou were in a different league. One of them was Gong Yeti, a 22-year-old lieutenant with the Fourth Air Group, who spent the summer of 1937 in intensive training. In the daytime, he would practice flight maneuvers in his Curtiss Hawk III, a modern biplane recently delivered from the United States and mainly used by the Chinese as a dive bomber. At night, he would read *Fighting the Flying Circus* by Eddie Rickenbacker, an American ace who flew in the skies over France during the Great War less than 20 years earlier. The prospect of finally facing the Japanese enemy filled Gong with boyish excitement. Sweeping down over mock targets near his airfield, he imagined they were Japanese battleships. "War cannot be avoided. The time for revenge has come," he wrote in his diary on July 13.[45]

However, a shadow was hanging over Gong's youthful thirst for adventure. One of his best friends during 18 months of training at aviation school had been killed the same month in a flying accident. It had been the saddest day of Gong's life.[46] Leafing through Rickenbacker's war memoirs, he found advice that helped him out of the stupor caused by his friend's death. "One of the greatest horrors of the war," the American ace wrote, was the pilots' "callous indifference upon the sudden death of their dearest chum." And yet, Rickenbacker added, a certain emotional numbness was a simple necessity. Fighter pilots had to keep fit and clear-minded, and they could not allow themselves to be dulled by thoughts over lost friends. "I must learn from Rickenbacker," Gong declared in his diary.[47]

Despite considerable holes in China's military preparedness, at some point in July Chiang Kai-shek decided that it was the time to openly resist Japan. Furthermore, he believed that Shanghai was the place where the first battle had to take place. It was a decision heavily influenced by Falkenhausen, and it made strategic sense. By initiating new hostilities in the Shanghai area, Japan would be forced to divert its attention from the north China front, thus forestalling a Japanese thrust towards the important city of Wuhan. It would also prevent any interruption of potential supply routes from the Soviet Union, the most likely source of material assistance given Moscow's own enmity with Japan.[48] It was a clever plan, and the Japanese did not anticipate it. Rather, intelligence officers in Tokyo were convinced that Chiang would send his troops to the north of China.[49]

One afternoon in late July, a group of high-ranking officers gathered at Chiang's official residence in the capital Nanjing. Zhang Fakui, the officer who had taken part in the summer course, was among the attendees. Also in attendance was Zhang Zhizhong, the 46-year-old commander of military forces in the pivotal area stretching from Nanjing to Shanghai. Meetings such as this one happened on and off, and clearly they were much more than just social events for Chiang, an extreme ascetic who neither drank nor smoked and, despite being married, was said to never engage in sex. In order to achieve results, the gatherings always followed the same set procedure. First Chiang would raise an issue, then every person present would explain his view in turn, and in the end Chiang would draw the final conclusions. Afterwards, there would be dinner. The topic on this hot summer day was no surprise: Japan. After everyone had spoken, Chiang summarized the opinions that had been aired. Since China had decided to resist, he said, it should take the initiative in Shanghai. There was no turning back.

Zhang Fakui already knew that Shanghai was where his services would be required. The same afternoon, Chiang gave him more detailed instructions, putting him in charge of the right wing of the army, which was being prepared for action in the metropolitan area. He was given responsibility for the forces east of the Huangpu River in the part of Shanghai referred to as Pudong, an area of warehouses, factories and rice fields. Zhang Zhizhong, a quiet-spoken and somewhat sickly-looking man who had previously headed the Central Military Academy,[50] was to command the left wing west of the Huangpu. The officers all welcomed the plan, immediately seeing the intuitive logic of taking on the Japanese in Shanghai, rather than around Beijing. There were not only strategic but also tactical benefits. The wide open north Chinese plains were ideal tank country and would give the Japanese armored columns a crushing advantage. The Shanghai area, by contrast, abounded in rivers and creeks, all favoring defensive operations. Logistically, too, the Chinese would benefit from a well-developed network of highways and railways radiating out from Shanghai. "We wanted to open a second front, to launch an offensive to split the enemy's forces in China," Zhang Fakui said many years later. "I approved of it. Everyone approved of it."[51]

Zhang Zhizhong seemed to be an ideal pick to lead the troops in downtown Shanghai, where most of the fighting was likely to take place. The job as commandant of the military academy was a coveted position that enabled its holder to form links with junior officers earmarked for fast-track promotion. This meant that he personally knew the generals of both the 87th and 88th Divisions, which were to make up the core of Zhang's newly formed 9th Army Group and become his primary assets in the early phases of the Shanghai campaign.[52] Besides, he had the right aggressive instincts. Zhang Zhizhong felt that China's confrontation with

Japan had come in three stages. In the first stage, the Japanese invasion of the northeast in 1931, Japan had attacked and China had remained passive. In the second stage, the first battle of Shanghai in 1932, Japan had struck, but China had struck back. Zhang Zhizhong argued that this would be the third stage, where Japan was preparing to strike, but China would strike first.[53]

It appears that Zhang Zhizhong did not expect to survive this final showdown with the Japanese arch-foe. He took the fight very personally and even ordered his daughter to interrupt her education in England and return home to serve her country in the war.[54] Even so, he was not the strong commander that he seemed to be. He had one important weakness. He was seriously ill. He never disclosed his actual condition, but it appeared that he was on the brink of a physical and mental breakdown after years in stressful jobs. He had in fact recently, in the spring of 1937, taken a leave of absence from his position at the military academy. When the war broke out, he was at a hospital in the northern port city of Qingdao and was preparing to go abroad to convalesce. He canceled his plans in order to contribute to the struggle against Japan. When his daughter returned from England and saw him on the eve of battle, it worried her to see how skinny he had become.[55] From the outset, a question mark hung over his physical fitness to command.

Liliane Willens, a nine-year-old girl born in Shanghai to Russian Jewish émigré parents, was vacationing in July 1937 at Mount Mogan—a cool inland retreat that was favored by Shanghai's well-to-do after a popular seaside resort up north near Beijing had become unsafe due to the escalating conflict in the region. One day, Liliane's four-year-old younger sister told her she had met Chiang Kai-shek, who sometimes spent time in the area. The Chinese leader had been strolling along a mountain path, and although surrounded by numerous guards, he had smiled at the small girl and said "Hello" in English. Her curiosity awakened, Liliane arranged an expedition to Chiang's villa, but the children were stopped by a group of armed soldiers barking at them to leave immediately.[56]

After this brief brush with power, Liliane returned to Shanghai with her parents. It was a city subtly transformed by rumors of war. On the surface, an appearance of peaceful normalcy prevailed with even the Japanese behaving as if nothing had changed, and engaging in friendly competition with representatives of the other foreign powers in the city. The visiting baseball team of Tokyo's Meiji University inflicted a resounding defeat on a team of Shanghai-based American marines.[57] On France's Bastille Day, July 14, the armored Japanese cruiser *Izumo*, moored in the Huangpu River, joined the flagship of the French fleet in offering up a searchlight display.[58] Everyone was complaining about the unbearable heat and worrying about the upcoming typhoon seasons. It was almost as if the weather was the main concern.

Still, underneath it all was a constant lingering tension fueled by contradictory military and diplomatic news. Unfounded reports in the local press about great Chinese victories on the northern front often caused patriotic crowds to set off fireworks.[59] However, the mood could change overnight. Carroll Alcott, a correspondent for the Associated Press, developed an ability to gauge public sentiment by looking out of his window every morning. If thousands of civilians were heading towards the supposed safety of the International Settlements, "then the men on the floors of the Shanghai Stock Exchange and the gold bar market were talking war."[60] People in Shanghai had learned a lesson from the hostilities five years earlier. They realized that it was vital to escape the combat zone before fighting broke out. Once the first shot had been fired, it would be too late. They also knew that Zhabei was the area to avoid.

There were a few scares. On the evening of July 24, a Japanese sailor was reported missing, setting off a frantic search throughout the city. Grim-faced Japanese soldiers with steel helmets and fixed bayonets deployed in the streets, checking rickshaws and vehicles. Obvious parallels were drawn between this event and the Marco Polo Bridge incident, where the temporary loss of one Japanese soldier had set the entire north of China ablaze. It did not take long for large numbers of residents to leave Zhabei, pushing their most precious belongings in wheelbarrows or carrying them in bundles over their shoulders. The panic subsided almost as quickly as it had erupted, and four days later, after most Chinese families had returned to their homes, it emerged that, very much like at Marco Polo Bridge, the sailor had gone AWOL after a visit to a local brothel.[61]

Despite the unsettling political news, Shanghai remained first and foremost a place where business was done and fortunes were made. As war approached, residents with investments to protect thought up ingenious ways to see their assets through the coming storms. One ship owner carried out a paper transfer of his company to a German firm, equipping each of his vessels with a swastika flag and a token German captain who did nothing but show up occasionally on the bridge in full uniform. The Chinese entrepreneur figured that the Japanese Army would not seize any ship sailing under the flag of Nazi Germany, a powerful nation that had recently shown signs of wanting to improve relations with Japan. His deception worked. As his steamers plied their Yangtze routes, suspicious Japanese Navy officers monitored them through their binoculars, obviously believing something was not right, but they were not stopped.[62]

Everyone felt the war coming, regardless of nationality and occupation. In the French Concession, Father Robert Jacquinot de Besange, a Jesuit priest, was watching events with a sense of foreboding. Very much a practical man—he had lost his right arm in a failed chemical experiment at the concession's Aurora University—he was widely recognized as a champion of the disadvantaged. He had been in Shanghai in 1932 and knew from personal experience about the suffering that modern war in urban areas brought to the civilian population. He feared that the suffering was about to start all over again and his dark premonitions found expression in a poem:

God, please renew our hope!
The Future is Yours alone: the shadow
Is spreading more thickly this evening,
Make it a little less dark for us.[63]

———————

At 8:30 a.m. on Tuesday, August 10, a motley group of officers left the Japanese Consulate on the banks of the Huangpu River. Some were easily recognizable as Chinese officers with their peaked caps, others were Japanese with colonial-style pith helmets; a large number were in western suits, making it harder to determine their nationality. All were members of a hastily composed Sino-Japanese joint investigation team charged with quickly wrapping up the case of the shooting at the Hongqiao Aerodrome the night before. They knew that they would have to reach agreement fast,

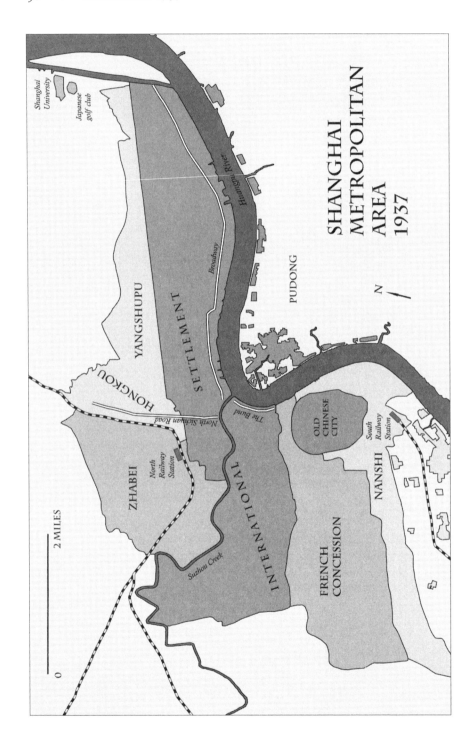

SHANGHAI
METROPOLITAN
AREA
1937

Shanghai
University

Japanese
golf club

Huangpu River

Broadway

YANGSHUPU

SETTLEMENT

HONGKOU

North Sichuan Road

PUDONG

The Bund

ZHABEI

North
Railway
Station

OLD
CHINESE
CITY

INTERNATIONAL

Suzhou Creek

NANSHI

South
Railway
Station

FRENCH
CONCESSION

N

2 MILES

0

or risk losing control of events. On both sides there were people, whether in uniform or not, who were spoiling for a fight, and this incident could be all the pretext they needed.

As they drove to the airport, they passed armed guards of the Chinese Peace Preservation Corps standing at sandbag barricades that had not been there just a few hours earlier. Once at Hongqiao, they paced up and down the scene of the incident under a blazing sun, seeking to agree on what had happened. It was all but impossible. The evidence did not add up to a coherent narrative both sides could accept. The Japanese were not convinced there had been a shoot-out at all. Oyama, the officer who had been in the car, had left his pistol at the marine headquarters in Hongkou and had been unarmed the night before. Whoever shot and killed the man in the Chinese uniform, it could not have been him, they maintained.[64]

At 6:00 p.m. the investigators returned to the city. Foreign correspondents eager for information knew exactly who to look for. Shanghai Mayor Yu Hongjun, less than two weeks in the job, had already become a darling with the western journalists. Little, sharp-witted and English-speaking, he was the city's cosmopolitan face to the outside world.[65] That evening, uncharacteristically, he had nothing for the reporters, apart from a plea addressed not only to the Japanese, but also the Chinese. "Both sides should maintain a calm [demeanor] so that the situation may not be aggravated," he said.[66] Thirty-nine-year-old Yu was in a difficult situation. He was responsible for millions of civilians, and he was prepared to go to great lengths to prevent open war—greater lengths than any of his foreign sympathizers were aware of at the time.

Mayor Yu was in fact at the center of an elaborate act of deception that almost succeeded. It is unlikely that the world will ever know exactly what happened at Hongqiao Aerodrome on the night of August 9. However, nearly eight decades later, the balance of the available evidence suggests that the two Japanese soldiers were lured into a Chinese ambush.[67] Zhang Fakui, the commander of the Chinese right wing, attributed the act to members of the 88th Division, led by General Sun Yuanliang. "A small group of Sun Yuanliang's men disguised themselves as members of the Peace Preservation Corps," Zhang Fakui said years later, when he was an old man. "On August 9, 1937 they caught two Japanese servicemen on the road near the Hongqiao military aerodrome. They accused the two of forcing their way into the aerodrome. A clash took place. The Japanese were killed."[68]

This left their superiors with a delicate problem. Two dead Japanese were hard to explain away. Mayor Yu, who must have been informed about the predicament by members of the military, consulted with Tong Yuan-liang, who was chief of staff of the Songhu Garrison Command, a unit set up after the 1932 fighting. They agreed on a quick and cynical measure to make it look as if the Chinese guards had fired in self-defense. On their orders, soldiers marched a Chinese death convict to the gate of the airport, dressed him in the uniform of the paramilitary guards, and shot him dead.[69] It was a desperate ruse, and it might just have worked, if it were not for all the questions raised by the way the Chinese body looked. The Japanese did not believe the story, and the whole plan was falling apart. What little mutual trust was left was evaporating fast. Rather than preventing a show-down, if anything the cover-up was hastening the descent into war.

Late on August 10, Yu sent a secret cable to Nanjing, warning that the Japanese had stated ominously they would not allow the two deaths at the airport to have been in vain.[70] The following day, the Japanese Consul General Okamoto Suemasa paid the mayor a visit, demanding the complete withdrawal of the Peace Preservation Corps from the Shanghai area, as well as the dismantlement of all fortifications erected by members of the corps.[71] It was almost impossible for the Chinese to acquiesce, since from their point of view, it appeared that the Japanese wanted to render Shanghai defenseless at the same time as they strengthened their own presence in the city.

The Chinese suspected that Japan was preparing reinforcements following its launch on August 11 of what the *North China Daily News* called "one of the most imposing displays of naval might" in Shanghai's history. Twenty vessels, including cruisers and destroyers, sailed up the Huangpu River and moored at wharfs close to "Little Tokyo." Japanese marines in olive-green uniforms marched ashore down gangplanks, while women from the local Japanese community, dressed in kimonos, bowed with delighted smiles to the flags of the Rising Sun which were hanging proudly from the sterns of the battleships.[72]

In fact, Japan had planned to dispatch additional troops to Shanghai even before the shooting at Hongqiao Aerodrome. They had deemed it

THREE CORPSES • 39

necessary in order to bolster the meager contingent of 2,500 marines posted permanently in the city. More troops were required to aid in the task of protecting Japanese nationals who were being hastily evacuated from the big cities along the Yangtze River.[73] These were defensive maneuvers, and the Japanese military seemed to shy away from opening a second front in Shanghai, for the exact same reasons that the Chinese favored an extension of hostilities to the area. Japanese troops would be diverted away from the strategically crucial north and the Soviet threat looming across China's border and they would be sucked into fighting in a claustrophobic urban environment where their technological superiority, especially in tanks and planes, would have less impact.

While officers of the Japanese Navy believed it was becoming harder by the day to prevent the war from spreading to Shanghai, they wanted to give diplomacy a last chance. The Japanese Army, meanwhile, was more than eager to wage war in the north of China, but in the Shanghai area it showed little of that belligerence. If worse came to worst, the Army favored pulling all Japanese nationals out of Shanghai. When in the end it agreed to draw up plans for dispatching an expeditionary force to the city, it did so only reluctantly and in order to escape charges that it was shirking its responsibilities.[74] "Why on earth would the Japanese even consider fighting in Shanghai?" Sascha Spunt, the son of Shanghai's wealthiest cotton merchant asked an acquaintance, a Chinese general. The general grinned as he replied: "They don't."[75]

"Japan had no wish to fight at Shanghai . . . It should be simple to see that we took the initiative," said General Zhang Fakui, the commander of the Chinese right wing at Shanghai told his post-war interviewers.[76] Taking the initiative and opening a new front was not, however, a rash decision, and it was implemented with deliberate caution. The political leaders, fearing to move too fast, had to constantly keep their military officers on a tight leash, lest their yearning to see Japanese blood got the better of them and the situation at the frontline spun out of control. Zhang Zhizhong, the commander of the left wing, was one of the top brass longing for a quick showdown with Japan. Still, by the end of July he was waiting impatiently with his troops in the Suzhou area west of Shanghai, wondering if a unique chance was being squandered. On July 30, he cabled Nanjing for permission to strike first. If Japan were allowed to launch an attack at Shanghai, he argued, he would have to waste precious time moving his troops from their current position more than 50 miles west of the city.[77] Nanjing replied with a promise that his wish would be granted, but urged patience for now: "We should indeed seize the initiative over the enemy, but we must wait until the right opportunity arises. Await further orders."[78]

That opportunity came on August 11, with the Japanese show of force in the Huangpu River, and the Japanese demand, made in public, for the withdrawal of China's paramilitary police. Japan had exposed itself sufficiently as the aggressor in the minds of the domestic and overseas public, making it safe for China to act. At 9:00 p.m. on that day, Zhang Zhizhong received orders from Nanjing to move his troops to the vicinity of Shanghai.[79] He obeyed the order with lightning speed, taking advantage of the extensive transportation network in the Shanghai area. The soldiers of the 87th Division mounted 300 trucks, which had been prepared in advance.[80] Meanwhile, civilian passengers aboard trains where unceremoniously ordered off to make room for the 88th Division, which boarded the carriages and headed for Shanghai. Altogether, more than 20,000 motivated and well-equipped men were heading into battle.

On the morning of Thursday, August 12, residents near Shanghai's North Train Station, also know as the Zhabei Station, just a few blocks away from "Little Tokyo," woke up to an unusual sight: thousands of soldiers dressed in the Chinese Nationalists' khaki colors, with German-style helmets and stick grenades swung across their chests. "Where do you come from?" the Shanghai citizens asked. "How did you get here so fast?"[81] A foreign correspondent visiting the troops reported back that he had sensed an unmistakable "air of tense expectancy," as the soldiers, smart-looking by Chinese standards, took up positions behind barricades and emplacements built the night before.[82] They were soldiers of the 88th Division, arguably the best trained and equipped unit in the entire Chinese Army. They had been in Shanghai in 1932 and now they were back, determined to put up a better show than last time.

In fact, they were not supposed to have moved so close to the Japanese lines. Prior to the departure from Suzhou, Zhang Zhizhong had issued detailed orders to each individual unit under his command, including specific instructions for the 88th Division to go by train and deploy in a line from the town of Zhenru to Dachang village, both located a couple of miles west of Shanghai. Only later, the division was to continue towards a line that stretched from Zhabei district to the town of Jiangwan, placing it closer to the city boundaries.[83] However, the 88th Division was the same unit that allegedly orchestrated the Hongqiao incident. Its soldiers were gung-ho. They were in Shanghai to fight. Sun Yuanliang, the division's commander, confirmed in his memoirs that his orders were to get off the train at Zhenru. "However, based on the situation there," he wrote, "I made the decision single-handedly to continue straight to Zhabei train station."[84] Sun Yuanliang could afford a bit of initiative. He had been one of Chiang Kai-shek's favorite students known as the "thirteen guardians of the heir apparent."[85]

Zhang Zhizhong was belligerence personified, but he was faced with even more pugnacious officers down the ranks. On the morning of August 12, he was approached by Liu Jingchi, chief of operations at the Songhu Garrison Command. The battle of 1932, Liu argued, had gone badly for the Chinese because they had hesitated and not struck first. This time ought to be different, and Zhang should order an all-out assault on the Japanese positions that same evening, he said. Zhang countered that he had clear and unmistakable orders from Chiang Kai-shek to let the Japanese shoot first, for the sake of China's image in the world. "That's easy," retorted Liu. "Once all the units are deployed and ready for attack, we just change some people to mufti and send them in to fire a few shots. We attack, and at the same time, we report back that the enemy's offensive has begun." Zhang Zhizhong did not like the idea. "We can't go behind our leader's back like that," he said.[86]

Zhang Zhizhong's position was not an enviable one. Forced to rein in eager and capable officers, he was acting against his own personal desires. Eventually, he decided to seek a free hand to act as he saw fit. In a secret cable to Nanjing, he requested permission to launch an all-out attack on the Japanese positions in Shanghai the following day, Friday, August 13. This was a one-off opportunity to exploit momentum already created with the movement of the troops, he argued. Wait much longer, and torpor would set in. He suggested a coordinated assault that also involved the Chinese Air Force. The reply from Chiang Kai-shek was as short as it was unwavering: "Await further orders."[87]

Even as Chiang's troops were pouring into Shanghai, Chinese and Japanese officials continued talking. Ostensibly this was in the hope of reaching a last-minute solution, but in reality it was a show. Both sides wanted to be able to claim the moral high ground in the battle that now seemed inevitable. They knew that whoever openly declared a decision to abandon negotiations would automatically be seen as the aggressive party. During talks at the Shanghai Municipal Council, Japanese Consul General Okamoto argued that if China had really wanted peace, it would have withdrawn troops to a point where clashes could be avoided. Mayor Yu responded by pointing out the growing numbers of Japanese forces in the city. "Under such circumstances, China must adopt such measures as necessary for self-defense," he said.[88]

In the streets outside, Shanghai was reduced to chaos. The appearance of entire divisions of Chinese troops overnight had been welcomed by the city's residents, but it had also convinced them that this was no false alarm as was the case with the incident of the missing sailor a few weeks earlier. This time was for real. Thousands of families left their homes, especially those in Zhabei. Some hoped to gain entry into the International Settlement, others headed straight for the countryside. It was the largest exodus in Shanghai's history, bigger even than the one triggered by the fighting in 1932.[89]

Amid the civilian stampede, the small Japanese garrison prepared feverishly for battle as the situation grew more threatening by the hour. To outside observers, there seemed to be little order to the Japanese soldiers' activities, as if they had been taken aback by the sudden, massive Chinese deployment around them.[90] The garrison's commanders rushed to hire about 1,000 local workers to hastily clear out shrubbery and flatten bunkers at the Japanese Golf Club, transforming the greens into a workable airfield.[91] Meanwhile, the Chinese kept pouring in well-trained troops, and in the Huangpu River, south of the Shanghai city center, they sank two old steamers and a dozen junks, limiting the access of the mighty Japanese Navy further upriver.[92] Then the sun set, on Shanghai's last day of peace.

As the darkness thickened in the streets, Admiral Hasegawa Kiyoshi, commander of the Third Fleet moored near the city, sent an ominous message back to Tokyo: "The situation in the area around Shanghai could explode at any moment." In the imperial capital, top cabinet ministers in charge of conducting the war met at the prime minister's residence, agreeing that the time had come for the Army to send troops to Shanghai. Emperor Hirohito, the nominal head of one of the most powerful military forces on the planet, no longer felt he was master of the situation. "Perhaps," he told an aide, "nothing can be done at this juncture."[93]

CENTRAL SHANGHAI, AUGUST 1937

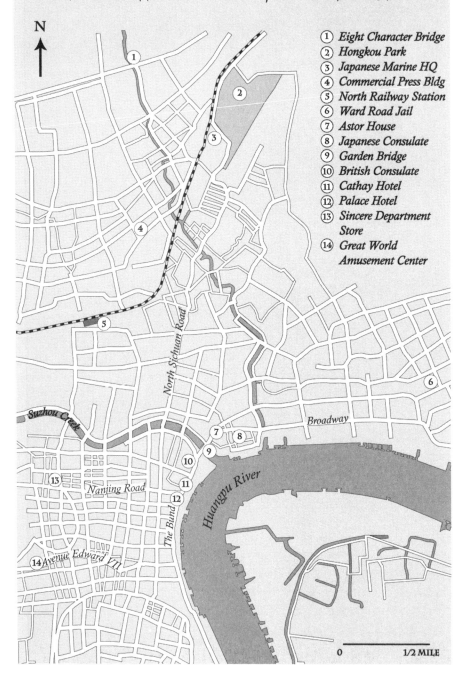

N

1. Eight Character Bridge
2. Hongkou Park
3. Japanese Marine HQ
4. Commercial Press Bldg
5. North Railway Station
6. Ward Road Jail
7. Astor House
8. Japanese Consulate
9. Garden Bridge
10. British Consulate
11. Cathay Hotel
12. Palace Hotel
13. Sincere Department Store
14. Great World Amusement Center

North Sichuan Road

Suzhou Creek

Broadway

Huangpu River

Nanjing Road

The Bund

Avenue Edward VII

0   1/2 MILE

CHAPTER

2

· ·

"Black Saturday"

AUGUST 13–15

EARLY ON AUGUST 14, THE 66-YEAR-OLD CHRISTIAN MISSIONARY Frank Rawlinson had gone to his office at the Mission Building, behind the British Consulate General, as was his wont on Saturdays.[1] It was only a quarter mile from the Japanese cruiser *Izumo*, the Third Fleet's flagship anchored in the Huangpu River in front of the Japanese Consulate. This made his workplace one of the most dangerous spots in Shanghai. The *Izumo* had assisted the Japanese marines inland with its heavy artillery—especially its four eight-inch guns and 14 six-inch guns—and had made itself an obvious target for Chinese attack.

Shortly before 11:00 a.m., five Chinese planes emerged over the rooftops, heading for the river and the Japanese vessels.[2] The aircraft released their bombs, but all missed, and several of them exploded in the wharfs, pulverizing buildings and sending shrapnel cascading through the air. The guns of the Japanese battleships responded with a massive barrage, further endangering those unfortunate enough to live or work in the area, as shell fragments whirled towards the ground with deadly abandon. At 11:20 a.m. yet another Chinese air raid took place. This time it was carried out by three planes, and again the *Izumo* was the direct target.[3]

When it was time for lunch, Rawlinson drove to his home in the French Concession. He passed the Garden Bridge over Suzhou Creek, a stream that cut through Shanghai and was the end station for much of the city's sewage. Mercifully sheltered from its foul smell inside his car, he picked a route along the Bund, the landmark waterfront area, navigating through unusually thick crowds. They were mostly refugees from the Chinese districts, seeking a sanctuary from the hostilities north of the creek. Rawlinson knew well that Shanghai was a city that could change its appearance overnight under the influence of great political events. After all, it had been his home for 35 years, ever since he had arrived as a young missionary. China had still been an empire back then, and he had become infatuated with its ancient culture. He had even adopted a Chinese name, Yue Lingsheng. Gradually, he had become a respected member of the foreign establishment. Among his many titles were editor of the periodical *The Chinese Recorder* and co-founder of the Shanghai American School. China was his destiny.

As he approached old age, he had witnessed how his beloved China was coming apart under the iron heel of aggressive Japanese imperialism. "I do not like war. I think it is un-Christian," he had written in a letter to acquaintances in the United States less than two weeks earlier. "Yet I don't know what else China can do but resist Japan unless she wants to become practically a Japanese colony."[4] However, after many years of patiently biding its time, China was finally fighting back, and as a result, on this Saturday, the nation's most prosperous city was being exposed to modern war at its most lethal.

Under normal circumstances, Rawlinson would have returned to his office in the afternoon for quiet work, but the intense fighting along the Huangpu River made it advisable to depart from the routine of more peaceful days. Instead, he spent some hours at home, before going out to fetch the evening newspaper shortly before 4:00 p.m. He made it a small family outing. He got into his car with his wife Florence and his 13-year-old daughter Jean. It was not a long trip, and on the way back, he drove his vehicle along Avenue Edward VII on the border between the International Settlement and the French Concession. It was packed with people.

Huangpu was several hundred yards away, but even so the sky above them was filled with smoke puffs from anti-aircraft guns showing that the battle over the *Izumo* had continued into the afternoon. Rawlinson, always a keen observer of life around him, eagerly took in the scenes passing by outside the car window while still trying to steer his vehicle through the mass of automobiles, bicycles and pedestrians jamming the street. As the car approached the Great World Amusement Center, a Chinese theater where rice was being distributed to war refugees, the mob outside became even denser. Driving and watching was by that point downright hazardous with the very real possibility that someone might get hurt. Florence Rawlinson urged her husband to stop the car. You'll get a better view from outside, she told him.

The moment Rawlinson stepped out of the car there was a flash of light and then a deafening explosion. After long seconds of stunned silence, Florence Rawlinson peeped apprehensively out of the car window and felt her heart sink when she saw her husband lying on his back, sprawled across the curb. She stumbled hurriedly out of the car and took his lifeless head in her arms. In dazed shock she noticed a large hole in the left part of his chest. Blood was gushing out in a thick stream. Jean had also got out and was standing nearby, watching in quiet disbelief.

Around them, people were getting up and trying to find their bearings, moving around with the groggy aimlessness of sleepwalkers. Large pieces of debris covered the asphalt. Some of the debris was brick and concrete, broken and distorted. Other debris was human and too horrible to look at. Several automobiles had burst into flames. Down the street a cloud of thick smoke enveloped the spot where the Great World Amusement Center had been. Chaos had struck the heart of Shanghai, and amid it all, Rawlinson died. He was one of four U.S. citizens who lost their lives in Shanghai on the same day, within minutes of each other. Together, they had become the first American casualties of World War II.

———

Hundreds of civilians were killed when a series of stray bombs dropped by Chinese Air Force aircraft exploded in densely packed areas on what was almost instantly described as "Black Saturday" or "Bloody Saturday." By the time the tragedies happened, the battle of Shanghai had already entered its second day. Since Friday, August 13, the city's residents had been listening to rifle fire and machine gun salvoes, interrupted by the occasional muffled boom of artillery. Even the most optimistic souls could no longer brush events off as just isolated incidents. It was war. The frontline that emerged roughly followed the northern boundary of the International Settlement, stretching for about eight miles from the North Railway Station via Hongkou and Yangshupu to the Huangpu River, with a salient extending from the settlement north to Hongkou Park in the Chinese part of Shanghai.

Friday the 13th had indeed lived up to its reputation and been an unhappy day. The first shot in what was to become a three-month battle was fired in the middle of the morning. Members of the Japanese marines, who had put on civilian clothes and posed as thugs—boisterous *ronin*—had turned up at barricades manned by the Peace Preservation Corps at the northern edge of Yangshupu at about 9:15 a.m. They proceeded to provoke the Chinese guards with loud taunts and jeers. When the Chinese let off a warning shot into the air, the Japanese fired back, aiming to kill. The Chinese responded in kind, and a deadly exchange followed. From that point on, the situation could no longer be reined in. This, at least, is the version of events given by the head of the Peace Preservation Corps to an interviewer many decades after the war was over.[5]

Other Chinese officers, including Zhang Zhizhong, said that the battle of Shanghai started with a clash on the western edge of "Little Tokyo," near the Commercial Press, a building only recently reconstructed after having been destroyed during the 1932 battle. Sporadic shooting dragged on for 20 minutes before petering out. Mayor Yu promptly issued a statement to the Associated Press and Reuters blaming the Japanese for having fired first. The Japanese maintained that they had been targeted by a Chinese machine gunner hidden inside the Commercial Press building before returning fire themselves.[6] The truth about who started the battle, and where and when it started, will probably forever remain obscured in claims and counterclaims.[7]

No matter the exact circumstances under which the battle erupted on August 13, it had quickly become unstoppable. As the day progressed, nervous small-scale activity continued throughout the northern part of Shanghai. Chinese commanders dispatched patrols to make probing attacks, hoping to find weak points in the Japanese defenses and to push them back wherever possible,[8] while their Japanese counterparts rushed to occupy key positions outside their main line of defense, so as to be in a more advantageous position once their adversary launched a larger offen-

Asia's Stalingrad: Japanese infantrymen cautiously advance down an alley left completely in ruins.
By early October 1937, when this photo was taken, this part of Shanghai, the working class
neighborhood of Zhabei, had been a battleground for nearly two months. *Courtesy Asahi Shimbun*

上海戰線
〇〇に於ける我陸戰隊の猛射　　　　　　　　　　檢閲濟

Japanese infantry man a barricade in downtown Shanghai, early in the battle. In 1937, Shanghai was China's most cosmopolitan and westernized city. *Author's collection*

A group of Japanese marines visit a brothel in Shanghai. Japan and other foreign countries often behaved like semi-colonial powers in China, causing widespread anger in the local population. *Author's collection*

A Japanese unit has its picture taken before leaving for the Shanghai front. *Author's collection*

Two Japanese officers south of Wusong. Both have their helmets fastened with intricate knots applied to the chinstraps, all according to detailed military regulations. *From the American Geographical Society Library, University of Wisconsin-Milwaukee Libraries*

A tense situation on August 12, 1937, the eve of battle. Japanese marines have rolled up their vehicles, British-made Vickers Crossley M25 armored cars, in expectation of Chinese attack. *Courtesy Asahi Shimbun*

The Japanese cruiser *Izumo* had seen action since the early 20th century. In Shanghai, it seemed to live a charmed life, never once taking a direct hit from Chinese artillery or aircraft. *Author's collection*

Two Japanese marines, or "bluejackets," as the contemporary press often nicknamed them. During the first difficult days of the Shanghai campaign, they held out against a numerically vastly superior Chinese force. The soldiers here are wearing the winter issue blue wool uniform, suggesting the photo was taken in late 1937. *Author's collection*

The Japanese marine headquarters in northern Shanghai was a veritable fortress and could accommodate thousands of soldiers at a time. *Author's collection*

Street battle in August 1937. The officer in the foreground is leaning against a Vickers Crossley M25 armored car with the decal of the Imperial Japanese Navy on the side. The vehicle was also in use during the 1932 struggle for Shanghai. *Courtesy Asahi Shimbun*

Japanese marines posted on a rooftop in Hongkou keep an eye out for Chinese snipers in August 1937. The usual Japanese tactics when locating a sniper was to burn down the entire building. *Courtesy Asahi Shimbun*

Rescue workers and journalists step gingerly among human remains left after a Chinese airplane mistakenly releases two bombs over the Palace and Cathay Hotels in the international part of Shanghai on August 14, 1937. *From the American Geographical Society Library, University of Wisconsin-Milwaukee Libraries*

A Lincoln Zephyr left burned out in the middle of Nanjing Road after the twin blasts on August 14, which quickly becomes known as "Black Saturday" or "Bloody Saturday." *From the American Geographical Society Library, University of Wisconsin-Milwaukee Libraries*

6

Top left: Japanese marines defending Hongkou in the middle of August, at the moment of greatest crisis. The footwear is typical for the Japanese army. The soft shoes may be of the "camel foot" kind with a split at the toe. They did not look particularly martial to outsiders, but they were practical. So were the puttees, which could occasionally come in handy when bandages were not available. *Courtesy Asahi Shimbun*

Top right: A pile of used rounds next to the heavy machinegun indicates a battle that has lasted for some time. The low angle and the fatigued expression on the face of the soldier to the right suggest this photo from August 1937 depicts an authentic combat situation. Notice the knots used to fix the chinstrap of the helmet. *Courtesy Asahi Shimbun*

Bottom right: A Japanese motorcycle with a machine gun mounted on the sidecar speeds down a Shanghai street in the frantic early days of the battle. *From the American Geographical Society Library, University of Wisconsin-Milwaukee Libraries*

Above: Japanese marines drive through the deserted streets of Shanghai under a faint August sun. The marines were proud of their naval ties, as reflected in the anchor symbol on the grill of the truck. *Courtesy Asahi Shimbun*

Left: The Railway Bureau near the North Train Station in Zhabei. This area was held by members of China's elite 88th Division and became among the most contested pieces of real estate in the Shanghai region. After Japan had won the battle, and the Rising Sun flag was flying over the bureau's building, it grew into a tourist attraction. Here a number of American sailors inspect the site. *Author's collection*

Above: A Japanese marine officer gives a pep talk to his men before they move into battle, mid-August 1937. Other officers and NCOs appear to be studying a map in the bottom right corner. *Courtesy Asahi Shimbun*

Right: Japanese officers counterattack near the wharf area in mid-August. *Courtesy Asahi Shimbun*

10

Japanese defenders in the early stages of the Shanghai battle. The gate could be leading into
the wharf areas, which were an elusive prize for the Chinese attackers in late August.
Courtesy Asahi Shimbun

A horse is loaded onto a Japanese barge before being transported to a shore near Shanghai. Although the Japanese army was technologically far ahead of its Chinese foe, it still to a large extent was driven by horsepower. *Author's collection*

Japanese soldiers have descended from their transport into the landing craft that will take them into battle. Most are wearing a white bandana, known as a hachimaki. It was traditionally used to create team spirit, similar in purpose to some American paratroopers putting on Indian-style war paint before jumping out of their planes over Normandy in 1944. It was also useful when telling friend from foe during night fighting. *Author's collection*

Japanese troops disembark on the south bank of the Yangtze in early September 1937. Landing troops took longer than expected, mainly due to difficult natural conditions. In most cases during the battle of Shanghai, Japanese amphibious maneuvers met little Chinese resistance. *Author's collection*

Japanese infantry marches inland after successfully disembarking on the south bank of the Yangtze in late August. *Courtesy Asahi Shimbun*

Members of the 3rd Japanese Division prepare to storm Wusong fortress north of Shanghai, early September 1937. Several of the soldiers wield so-called "knee mortars," light weapons capable of throwing grenades up to 150 yards. The man in the foreground gets ready to fire his weapon, apparently a Model 10, by using his right hand to pull a lanyard that in turn will activate the trigger. *Courtesy Asahi Shimbun*

Light Japanese artillery offers support to infantry during the battle for Wusong, early September 1937. *Courtesy Asahi Shimbun*

sive. The small bands of soldiers from both sides moved along narrow alleys to minimize the risk of detection,[9] but whenever they chanced upon each other, the results were deadly.

In the western sector of the frontline, where the Chinese Army's newly arrived 88th Infantry Division was preparing its positions, the center of activity was the headquarters of the Japanese marines near Hongkou Park. It was a virtual fortress, with its massive four-story structure protected from air and artillery bombardment by a double roof of reinforced concrete. The building, which had a large inner courtyard, took up two city blocks, enabling it to hold thousands of troops at a time. Highly visible, it constituted both a real military threat and a symbol of Japan's presence in Shanghai. The Chinese were in no doubt about what they had to do. They had to wipe it out.

The main link between the marine headquarters and the Japanese section of the International Settlement further south was Sichuan North Road. It became the scene of hectic activity from the first day of battle. Japanese armored cars and motorcycle patrols with machine guns mounted on the sidecars sped up and down the otherwise deserted street, while trench mortars positioned along the pavement lobbed grenades into Zhabei to the west. As columns of smoke rose to the sky from the buildings in the Chinese district, Japanese officers, squeezing into a narrow conning tower on top of the marine headquarters, watched the results of the bombardment through field glasses. Reports that Chinese snipers had positioned themselves in the upper floors of buildings along the road prompted Japanese squads commanded by sword-wielding officers to carry out door-to-door searches. Suspects were unceremoniously dragged away to an uncertain fate. Not a single civilian was to be seen in the area. Everyone kept indoors, behind closed windows and pulled curtains.[10]

On the afternoon of August 13, the Eight Character Bridge[11] west of the marine headquarters became the scene of one of the battle's first major engagements. The bridge was just 60 feet long, spanning a minor creek. However, in spite of its modest size it was considered by both sides to have significant tactical importance. The Chinese commanders saw it as a main route of advance into the Hongkou area and they believed that if the bridge ended up in Japanese hands, it would become like a "piece of bone stuck in the throat."[12]

At about noon, Major Yi Jin, a battalion commander of the 88th Infantry Division, led a couple of hundred men of his battalion from the area around the North Railway Station towards Eight Character Bridge. When the soldiers reached their objective at about 3:00 p.m., they spotted a small Japanese unit which had just arrived across the creek and was setting up defensive positions. The Chinese opened fire and managed to take possession of the bridge. In turn, the Japanese launched a brief artillery bombardment that resulted in several Chinese casualties. Shots rang out near the bridge on and off until 9:00 p.m. when a precarious silence descended over the area.[13]

Further to the east, in the 87th Infantry Division's sector, the day was also filled with frantic maneuvering, interrupted by sometimes lengthy bursts of violence. Chinese reconnaissance parties infiltrated into areas held by the enemy and made it all the way to the Japanese Golf Club near the Huangpu River, where they started shooting at the workers busy preparing the makeshift airfield. At the first volleys from the Chinese snipers, clouds of dust filled the air, and the workers hastily ran for cover. Japanese soldiers posted in the club house immediately returned fire, ruining the aim of the snipers.[14]

After about an hour, two Japanese vessels moored in the Huangpu River, the destroyer *Kuri* and the gunboat *Seta*, were called on to assist the Japanese marines facing the 87th Infantry Division on land. Four- and six-inch shells screamed across the sky, exploding in the Chinese districts to the north. Shanghai University was also shelled as the Japanese troops on land believed it to have been occupied by Chinese soldiers. Eventually, the last remaining staff members, two Americans, were forced to flee the campus.[15] The naval artillery had come to the rescue of hard-pressed infantry on shore in a scene that would be repeated over and over again in the coming days and weeks.

The moment of battle had arrived too soon for the Chinese Army. It had not had time to transform itself into a first-class fighting force of 60 modern divisions, which was Chiang Kai-shek's dream and could probably have been achieved if peace had lasted longer. Even so, Alexander von Falkenhausen was confident that his highly motivated, thoroughly trained and expensively equipped Chinese soldiers could perform well in the struggle with the Japanese that was getting underway. The key question, Falkenhausen thought, was whether the Chinese were prepared to abandon their dated practices and follow German instructions. Most importantly, they were to seek an *Entscheidungsschlacht*—the decisive battle of Prussian doctrine that could eliminate their adversary in one fell stroke.

"If the Chinese Army follows the advice of the German advisors, it is capable of driving the Japanese over the Great Wall," the self-assured officer told a British diplomat. Perhaps drawing implicit comparisons with the way a series of victorious wars in the 1860s and 1870s had helped unite the German nation and forge it into the greatest power in continental Europe,[16] Falkenhausen considered the upcoming cataclysm a welcome opportunity to bring the Chinese people together after years of internal strife. "War on a national scale," he said, "is a necessary experience for China and will unify her."[17]

The German general's optimism had rubbed off on Chiang Kai-shek, who had internalized the German way of war and insisted on a strong stand against the Japanese in the early stage of the battle of Shanghai. During the night between August 13 and 14, he finally sent orders to Zhang Zhizhong, the commander of the left wing, to launch the all-out attack on the Japanese positions that the field commanders had been craving for. Zhang was to throw all troops at his disposal into one bold effort to knock out the Japanese once and for all, the way the Germans recommended. The plan had one weakness. The assault was to concentrate on the marine headquarters and the rest of the Hongkou salient, while avoiding battle with the Japanese inside the formal borders of the International Settlement. This was meant as a sop to international public opinion, and was sound politics. However, militarily it approached suicide and significantly raised the risks of the entire operation. The Hongkou area was the most heavily fortified position of the entire front. The marine headquarters was at the center of a dense network of heavy machine gun positions protected by barbed wire, concrete emplacements and walls of sandbags.

After preparations that lasted most of the day on August 14, Zhang's forces launched their attack late in the afternoon. Intense fighting took place in the few hours left before sunset, and it was evident almost immediately that the 88th Infantry Division had run into resistance that was even tougher than expected. In addition to the direct fire from the entrenched Japanese, the attackers were bombarded by the Third Fleet's powerful artillery, which was awe-inspiring even when it used only a fraction of its total strength of 700 pieces.[18] As during the Great War, artillery was the queen of the battlefield. The Chinese infantry, by contrast, lacked proper training in the use of heavy weaponry against fortified enemy positions.[19] Their heavier guns, which could have made a difference, were held too far in the rear, and all too easily missed their targets as inexperienced crews followed the flawed coordinates of observers not placed near enough to the targets.[20] In addition, some of the Japanese positions had such thick defensive walls that it was questionable whether even the most powerful weaponry on the Chinese side, 150mm howitzers, could do more than just dent them.[21]

Such tactics led to extraordinarily heavy losses on the Chinese side, even in senior ranks. Towards 5:00 p.m. Major General Huang Meixing, the 41-year-old commander of the 88th Infantry Division's 264th Brigade, was leading an attack in the vicinity of the marine headquarters. His divisional commander Sun Yuanliang tried to contact him on the field phone, but was forced to wait. When he finally got through to Huang, he cracked a rare joke. "It took so long I thought you were dead," he said. Just minutes afterwards, as if fate wanted to punish Sun Yuanliang for this bit of black humor, Huang Meixing's command post was hit by an artillery grenade, killing him instantly.[22] Shock spread through the ranks as the news became known, recalled Wu Ganliao, a machine gunner in the 88th Division. "Brigade commander Huang was a fair-minded person, and he showed real affection for his troops. It was sad news."[23]

Huang was by no means an exceptional case. Chinese officers died in large numbers from day one. One regiment lost seven company commanders in the same short attack.[24] There were several explanations for the high incidence of death among the senior ranks. One was an ethos among some officers to lead from the front in an attempt to instill courage into their men. However, even leading from the rear could be highly risky in urban combat, where the opposing sides were often just yards removed from each other and where the maze-like surroundings provided by multi-story buildings and narrow alleys could lead to a highly fluid situation, so that the enemy was just as likely to be behind as in front. In addition, soldiers on both sides deliberately targeted enemy officers, perhaps more so than in other conflicts, because stiff leadership hierarchies placed a premium on being able to decapitate the opposing unit.

First and foremost, however, the massive fatality rates among officers and, to an even larger extent, the rank and file were the result of Chinese forces employing frontal attacks against a well-armed entrenched enemy. The men who, as a result, were dying by the hundreds were China's elite soldiers, the product of years of effort to build up a modern military. They formed the nation's best hope of being able to resist Japan in a protracted war. Nevertheless, on the very first day of battle, they were being squandered at an alarming, unsustainable rate. After just a few hours of offensive operations with very little gain to show for them, Chiang Kai-shek decided to cut his losses. "Do not carry out attacks this evening," he commanded Zhang Zhizhong in a telegram. "Await further orders."[25]

In the weeks preceding the outbreak of war in Shanghai, Chiang Kai-shek had received a parade of leaders from the provinces who were anxious to join in the upcoming fight. After years of civil strife a new sense of unity was tying them together for the first time. "Lead us against the Japanese, and we pledge our troops and loyalty for the duration of the war," was the message they all conveyed.[26] As a sign of his sincerity to the provincials, Chiang decided to appoint one of his longest-standing rivals—a man who years earlier would happily have seen him killed—to the position of overall commander in the Shanghai area.

His name was Feng Yuxiang, but to foreigners, he was better known as the Christian General. He had risen to prominence as a warlord in China's tumultuous north and become famous for his missionary zeal after converting to Christianity. He was reported to have carried out mass baptisms of his soldiers with fire hoses and ordered them to march to the tunes of "Hark the Herald Angels Sing."[27] This was all very well for Chiang Kai-shek, himself a converted Christian, but he was more concerned about the 54-year-old Feng Yuxiang's advocacy of a lenient line towards the Communists. Besides, he could hardly forget that Feng Yuxiang had participated in an open rebellion against his rule early in the decade. Even so, he was prepared to shelve these differences for the time being.

Tall and bulky and perennially cheerful, Feng Yuxiang did not hesitate when offered the command. "As long as it serves the purpose of fighting Japan," Feng told Chiang, "I'll say yes, no matter what it is." His appointment was announced as the first shots were fired in Shanghai.[28] Feng was about a decade older than his direct subordinates, which was an advantage, Chiang thought. He wanted someone possessed and prudent who could counterbalance the fiery tempers at the next level down the chain of command. "The frontline commanders are too young. They've got a lot of courage, but they lack experience," Chiang said.[29]

Feng moved his command post to a temple outside Suzhou in the middle of August. Almost immediately afterwards, he went to see Zhang Zhizhong, who had set up his command right by the Suzhou city wall. At that time, Zhang had just begun to realize how tough the Japanese resistance in Shanghai really was. His staff was beginning to pick up disconcerting signs of his illness, sensing that sickness and exhaustion meant he was physically struggling to stay upright and lead the battle.[30] Perhaps a feeling of being overwhelmed was why he failed to undertake basic tasks such as providing adequate protection from air attack.

Feng, by contrast, had an infantryman's healthy respect of aircraft and had noticed how his own motorcade had seemed to attract the attention of enemy airplanes. "You better move," he told Zhang Zhizhong's chief of staff. "Otherwise you'll get bombed." Shortly after his visit, Feng left for Shanghai in a car. He had not even got two miles before a swarm of Japanese planes appeared over his head, flying in the direction of Suzhou. Seconds later he saw clouds rise over Zhang Zhizhong's command post. Zhang survived the bombing, but he had received a lesson. "The Japanese knew right from the start where Zhang's headquarters was," Feng said.[31]

———————

For Sascha Spunt, the scion of the wealthy cotton-trading merchant dynasty, Friday, August 13 was an exciting day, but it had nothing to do with the war. He was getting married. After a civil ceremony at the French Consulate, the family had an informal luncheon at their luxurious home near the Bund. When a friend of the family was about to raise his glass for a toast, he was interrupted by the muffled boom of guns in the distance, then the sharper sound of the naval artillery just outside on the river.

"Nobody can say this wedding isn't getting started with a bang," the friend said.[32]

Expatriates picnicking in the Yangshupu area when the fighting started greeted the new turn of events with similar sangfroid. They were spectators and saw the fighting with the amused aloofness of onlookers forced to witness a drunken bar brawl. As shells from the naval artillery started flying over their heads, they agreed the time had come to withdraw south to the International Settlement. However, their mood remained excellent. It was the kind of adventure that had brought the thrill-seekers to Asia in the first place. One of them called it "the most exciting three hours since my own war days."[33]

Just north of Suzhou Creek, a group of political scientists from American universities were watching the evolving battle from the roof of their hotel, the Astor House. They were on a study tour of Asia and had avoided Beijing because of the fighting there. Now they found themselves in the middle of the action, noticing how the fires in Zhabei colored the sky an unnatural, but strangely beautiful, hue of red. They were due to leave on a ship for Japan on Sunday, two days later, but had started wondering if the rapidly evolving events might upset their plans. "We were a little concerned, but not seriously concerned at that point," said William Verhage, a 37-year-old professor from Minnesota State Teachers College.[34]

For the foreigners of Shanghai, visitors and residents alike, the war was a rather violent diversion, but nothing truly dangerous, or so they thought. For the Chinese, life was falling apart. As the fighting intensified around the Japanese district, thousands of refugees fled through the streets, heading for Suzhou Creek and the Garden Bridge, which was the only link to the International Settlement that remained open. It was a mad and merciless stampede where the weak had little chance. "My feet were slipping . . . in blood and flesh," recalled Rhodes Farmer, a journalist for the *North China Daily News*, who found himself in a sea of people struggling to leave Hongkou. "Half a dozen times I knew I was walking on the bodies of children or old people sucked under by the torrent, trampled flat by countless feet."

Near the creek, the mass of sweating and panting humanity was almost beyond control, as it funneled towards the bridge, which was a mere 55 feet wide. Two Japanese sentries were nearly overwhelmed by the crowds and reacted the way they had been taught—with immediate, reflexive brutality. One of them bayoneted an old man and threw the lifeless body into the filthy creek below. This did not deter any of the other refugees, who kept pushing towards the bridge and what they believed to be the safety of the International Settlement.[35] They could not know it, but they were moving in the wrong direction, towards the most horrific slaughter of innocent civilians of the entire Shanghai campaign.

———————

A typhoon swept over Shanghai on Saturday, August 14. It was terrible weather for flying, but the Chinese Air Force nevertheless sent off its young pilots, 40 altogether, none of whom had been tried in battle. The lack of coordination between Chinese army and air force officers caused the attacks to have only marginal tactical value for the troops on the ground. While a few planes bombed the marine headquarters at Hongkou Park, causing no losses whatsoever to the Japanese soldiers holed up inside,[36] most targeted the Japanese vessels in the Huangpu River, and especially the flagship, the *Izumo*.

A total of six sorties took place over Shanghai during the day, concentrated in the morning and the late afternoon, with a long uneventful lull in between.[37] The same scene was played out in each raid. Chinese aircraft would appear over the dark gray horizon and follow the Huangpu River north towards the Japanese fleet, which was anchored near Huangpu's confluence with Suzhou Creek in a spot easily recognizable from the air. The Japanese vessels in turn would let loose their cannon and fill the air with a dense carpet of exploding shells, never allowing the planes to come close enough to drop their bombs with any degree of precision. "It was their first taste of Archie," said a foreign spectator, who had been an aviator in the Great War, using pilot slang for anti-aircraft artillery. "When the shells began to burst round them they got the wind up and dropped their eggs as quickly as possible."[38]

The results were predictable. Most of the bombs landed in the Huangpu, causing slender white geysers to rise towards the sky, seeming to almost freeze before collapsing back into the river and sending yellow tidal waves rolling towards the Bund. One stray bomb landed on land, hitting a Standard Oil gas tank, which exploded in a sea of flames. The pilots did score one hit against a Japanese target. A shell exploded a little further down the river near the cable-laying vessel *Okinawa Maru*, whose crew was repairing an underwater telegraph line, sending shrapnel whistling across the deck and killing one sailor. However, the *Izumo* itself remained stoically in front of the Japanese Consulate, leading some to start mumbling that the old vessel must have a charmed life.

Despite the lack of success, spectators on the ground watched the show with intense interest. Some were refugees from the battlefields in the north of the city, while others were simply taking advantage of their day off to suck in a bit of real-life drama. Just south of Suzhou Creek, the roof of the Mission Building, where Rev. Rawlinson had spent the morning busy at work, was filled with more than a hundred onlookers, until C. L. Boynton, an official of the National Church Council, ordered them down. "I bought a good padlock and locked them off the roof," he wrote.[39] Elsewhere, there was no one to warn the crowd of the dangers, and the corner of the Bund and Nanjing Road, which offered a direct view of the *Izumo*, had attracted thousands.

Shortly after 4:00 p.m. yet another Chinese raid took place. The sortie consisted of ten aircraft, which, like all the others before them, dispersed as soon as the anti-aircraft guns began barking. The six planes in front vanished into the clouds, but the four in the rear maintained their formation. One of them suddenly veered off course, and moments later four bombs fell from its belly. Two broke through the surface of the Huangpu, but the other two were caught by the heavy typhoon wind and carried towards the riverbank. Thousands stared helplessly as the bombs, already put on their set course by fate, steered relentlessly for the tightly packed space at the eastern end of Nanjing Road.[40]

———————

William Verhage, the young professor from Minnesota, watched the two bombs approach from a balcony on the fifth floor of the Palace Hotel, near the corner of Nanjing Road and the Bund. The members of his tour group had moved there from Astor House earlier in the day, after all foreigners had been ordered to evacuate the areas north of Suzhou Creek. He ducked back into his hotel room and fell flat on the floor, just in time before a large explosion made the entire building shiver. Seconds later, another loud blast erupted, this time even closer.[41]

Verhage found his way to the stairs and started groping his way down through a fog of dust. The main lobby was a scene of carnage. The first bomb had hit the Cathay Hotel across the street, blowing in the front door of Palace Hotel and shattering its large window panes, setting off a hail of glass shards. More than a dozen people were lying in pools of blood, injured or dying. The second bomb had crashed through the roof of the Palace Hotel and exploded on the top floor. "Chinese men, women and children were coming down from the roof," Verhage recalled later. "Their faces were white with plaster, and blood was oozing out through the white."

He immediately started looking for his tour guide, 30-year-old Robert Karl Reischauer, a brilliant political scientist from Princeton University. He went to the front of the hotel. Just outside, Nanjing Road was a scene of utter bloody chaos. The ground was littered with broken glass. Scattered everywhere were human remains—mostly nondescript lumps of flesh covered in tattered clothing. A new Lincoln Zephyr was engulfed in tall flames. However, there was no sign of Reischauer. Verhage turned around and headed to the reception. There he found the tour guide, one arm on the counter and the other over the shoulder of a wounded Chinese. His leg was a bloody mess. "Take me out of here," Reischauer said calmly.

The two bombs released by the Chinese airplane had struck at exactly 4:27 p.m. The attacks stopped the arms of a clock at the entrance of Cathay Hotel, freezing in time the moment of the twin blasts. The shock waves and the debris had both taken a toll on the mass of people who had been crammed into the street. To Percy Finch, a foreign correspondent, it was as if a giant mower had pushed through the crowd, chewing it to bits. "Here was a headless man, there a baby's foot, wearing its little red-silk shoe embroidered with fierce dragons," he wrote. "One body, that of a young boy, was flattened high against a wall, to which it clung with ghastly adhesion."[42]

A sickening stench of burnt flesh filled the air. As the wounded came to, they started moaning. Some were screaming. Part of the façade of the Palace Hotel had been blown away. On the fourth floor, a man clung desperately to the remains of the wall with one hand, waiting for help. It came too late, and he eventually let go, crashing through the glass awning of the hotel's entrance before hitting the pavement. Others attempted to crawl to safety, scrambling with fumbling limbs over mangled bodies and slipping in the blood that covered the sidewalk.

Sascha Spunt, who had been married the day before and was on the way to a party celebrating his own wedding, jumped out of his car and helped the injured and dying. He was followed by his younger brother Georges, who watched as a truck pulled up. "Rescue workers started tossing in the mangled remains—half of a human torso, arms, legs, heads," Georges wrote later. He tried to keep calm by reminding himself he had seen pieces of flesh before, on butchers' wagons. Then he noticed a worker holding up a bleeding bundle. It was a disemboweled infant. Georges started sobbing uncontrollably.[43]

While the bombs exploded in Nanjing Road, police officer Jules le Rouzic was on duty at Mallet police station on 151 Avenue Edward VII inside the French Concession. From his guard booth near the entrance he had had a good view of everything that went on in the sky this afternoon. Shortly after the explosions on Nanjing Road, he noticed two airplanes approaching from Huangpu River and observed as one of them seemed to be losing height. Moments later, two heavy bombs detached themselves from the aircraft, disappearing out of sight behind nearby buildings. Then a cloud of thick smoke rose from the area around Avenue Edward VII's intersection with Boulevard de Montigny. Seconds later came a loud blast. Behind him, inside the office of the guard on duty, le Rouzic heard a voice shouting, "The Great World has been bombed!"[44]

The Great World Amusement Center was a six-story building dominated by a tower in the style of a wedding cake. In times of peace, it had offered a large variety of diversions ranging from fortune-telling to gambling, and from sex to removal of earwax. The menus of its small food stalls had included anything from dried fish to stewed intestines. A wide sample of the city's population had milled around inside, and street performers and pickpockets had vied for space outside. After hostilities had broken out, the building had hastily been transformed into a makeshift shelter and distribution center for rice. The crowds were larger than ever. Now, however, they sought not entertainment, but mere survival.

On the afternoon of August 14, the throngs gathered around the amusement center were predominantly Chinese. Some were refugees from across the Garden Bridge, who had found temporary homes here on the edge of the French Concession and the International Settlement. Others were simply curious onlookers and as was the case on the Bund, the main show was the drama in the sky. The sight of Chinese aircraft displaying the signature white star on a blue background was accompanied on the ground by triumphant giggling and pointed fingers.

The mood was excited once more at about 4:45 p.m. when two Chinese aircraft seemed about to make another run on the Japanese positions. Cheers and applause rose from the street. Then sharp-eyed individuals noticed two small dark dots drop from one of the planes—the same bombs that M. le Rouzic had seen.[45] They fell with deadly haste, hitting the busy street before anyone had time to react, let alone escape. One left a huge crater near the traffic control tower in the middle of the road. The other exploded a few feet above the ground, causing shrapnel to fly over a large area.[46] The explosions were so powerful that they killed a servant at the building of the Y.M.C.A., nearly 700 feet down Boulevard de Montigny.[47]

The casualties included several foreigners. On Avenue Edward VII, Rev. Rawlinson was dying in his wife's arms, while his teenage daughter was watching. Just yards away two other Americans, Hubert Honigsberg and his wife, were killed in their car. It was the same type of carnage as in Nanjing Road, just larger. Death on the most massive scale was at the entrance of Great World Amusement Center, where the fatalities were piled five feet high.[48] The victims—men, women and children—had been thrown up against the walls of the buildings. Many were stripped completely naked after the intense gas pressure from the bombs had torn off their clothes.[49]

"Any of you lose this?" a member of the Russian émigré community asked as he stood up from behind the dust-covered bar at the Cathay Hotel, where he had been sifting through the debris. He was holding a severed thumb in his hand.[50] Outside on Nanjing Road, medical personnel were forced to prioritize among the injured, picking the ones most likely to survive. With grim faces they ignored the low-key mumblings and pleas of help from those destined to die. They needed all the help they could get from volunteers as they tried to disentangle bodies and save those still alive. For a brief period, nationality did not seem to matter. A Japanese girl in high heels stepped carefully among the injured, alongside a Chinese nurse in a snow-white dress that gradually turned a deep scarlet.

The injured were carried into the first floor of the Palace Hotel. The bomb had destroyed the elevator and debris blocked the stairs, making it harder to reach the many who had been injured at the top of the building when the bomb broke through the roof. The hotel's manager yelled for someone to call for an ambulance to help save six people who lay dying in rooms upstairs. It was in vain. Two disasters happening at the same time had stretched the city's resources beyond the limit, and most ambulances were dispatched to the Great World. The foreign military forces were also slow to react. It was 35 minutes before a British armored car battalion arrived and gradually restored order to the street.[51]

With no help forthcoming, friends of Reischauer, the injured political scientist, decided to take matters into their own hands. One of them commandeered a motorcycle and asked an American marine who happened to be standing nearby to drive the bleeding scholar to the General Hospital, past Japanese sentries north of Suzhou Creek. Reischauer was fully conscious the whole time, and heard when a doctor said that he would have to amputate his leg. "All right," Reischauer said. "I don't mind . . . I don't mind losing a leg." The hospital staff cleaned his injuries and put him to bed. Shortly afterwards, he died. "He went easily," said Verhage, "never suspecting I think that his life was at stake."[52]

Back on Nanjing Road, Rhodes Farmer, the journalist with the *North China Daily News*, spotted one of his colleagues lying in the street, staring at the sky with vacant eyes. As he helped carry him into a waiting truck by grabbing his shoulders, the injured man's guts spilled out. Despite the horrors surrounding him on all sides, Farmer's professional instincts took over, and he walked around the scene to get details for a story. After seeing enough, he went to work at the newspaper. In the daily's offices, the journalists were sitting at their typewriters all reporting the same event. They would finish part of their reports, head for the lavatory to vomit, and then return to finish their work.[53]

Evening was approaching, and firemen were hosing down the sidewalks outside the bombed-out hotels. The intellectual post mortem had already begun. Journalists and officials alike wanted to make sense of the tragedy. However, in the beginning much remained unclear. For starters, the exact number of casualties was a matter of contention. Initial reports referred to as many as 5,000 killed and injured.[54] As the months passed, the figure was gradually downgraded, and the most reliable figure, cited in an official report prepared by police in the French Concession, reported 150 dead at the hotels and 675 dead at Great World.

Even the lower numbers were horrific. R. Jobez, the vice chief of French police who signed off on the report, called it "a catastrophe without precedent in the history of the French Concession."[55] News of the disaster was reported around the world. *The New York Times* described a "terrific" slaughter. *Le Figaro* called it "a tragic day for Shanghai." It had special resonance, because the German terror bombing of the village of Guernica in the Spanish Civil War had only taken place a few months earlier, in April. Now death was again raining from the sky, on a larger scale than ever. The era of airpower had arrived. No one could be truly safe any longer, no matter how far removed from the frontline.

———————

Claire Chennault had been in the air since the early hours of August 14. He had slept for only a few hours at his base in Nanjing before jumping into a lone, unarmed fighter to observe the Chinese air raid as a neutral. He had a good reason to be curious. The day's attack was his brainchild. It was a mere coincidence. The previous night he had been at the Nanjing Military Academy in the company of Chiang Kai-shek and China's First Lady, known abroad simply as Madame Chiang Kai-shek. "Madame," as Chennault called her, had captivated the American warrior with her youthful charm and perfect English from the first time he met her. "She will always be a princess to me," he had written in his diary.[56] That night, as war approached, she had been in tears. "They are killing our people," she had said, sobbing. "What will you do now?" Chennault had asked. "We will fight," she had answered, throwing back her head proudly.[57]

Chennault had suggested bombing the ships in the Huangpu River because of the support their artillery provided to the Japanese infantry. Since there was no Chinese officer with the expertise to prepare an operation like this, the First Lady had asked Chennault to take over. Chennault was completely unprepared for this new role, but already feeling a certain sense of affinity with China and goaded by excitement at the prospect of trying his hands at a real air war, he had agreed. He had stayed up until 4:00 a.m. with his old friend Billy McDonald looking at maps and planning the day's missions. "Unknowingly, we were setting the stage for Shanghai famous Black Saturday," Chennault wrote with remarkable frankness in his memoirs.[58]

After taking off the following morning, Chennault had run into low clouds and had evaded rainstorms down the Yangtze valley in the direction of Shanghai. As he approached the city, he got a first inkling that the attacks had not gone according to plan. He spotted six Chinese planes, and far below them, a warship with guns blazing. The aircraft had just dive-bombed the vessel, apparently without success. Chennault made a run past the ship and discovered to his chagrin that it had a huge Union Jack painted on the afterdeck. It was the British cruiser *Cumberland*.[59]

After he returned to base, Chennault was informed about the tragedy that had taken place that day. Much later, in his memoirs, he was able to tell the world his version of how and why the attack went so horribly wrong. The Chinese crews had been trained to bomb at a fixed speed from an altitude of 7,500 feet. Since it had been overcast that day, the pilots had decided to dive below the clouds and bomb from 1,500 feet instead. They not only failed to adjust their bomb sights to the new speed and altitude, but also ignored strict orders to steer clear of the International Settlement. Ultimately, therefore, hundreds were dead due to human error.[60]

In the days after the tragedy, there were also other explanations as to why Chinese pilots had ended up killing so many of their own compatriots. According to Chinese press reports, the pilot of the plane over the French Concession had tried to release his bombs over a race course nearby, but they fell short by about 300 yards.[61] An air force captain interviewed in his hospital bed by the *Shanghai Evening Post and Mercury* claimed that he had been the pilot of the plane, and offered yet another version. He explained that he had been on the way back to his base in his twin-seat aircraft from a raid against the Naval Landing Force headquarters when he was attacked from above by a Japanese fighter who killed his observer and wounded him. Somehow, the bullets from the Japanese plane damaged the bomb racks, causing the disaster to take place, he said.[62]

Eleanor B. Roosevelt, married to former U.S. President Theodore Roosevelt's son, was in Shanghai at the time of the bombing and was horrified by the loss of innocent life. She sent a letter to Japan's premier, Prince Konoye, urging him to seek ways to minimize the risk of Chinese air raids, which she argued was caused by the presence of Japan's military in the Shanghai area. The Japanese did not reply. However, the day after, the *Izumo* was removed from its anchorage near the Japanese Consulate to the middle of the Huangpu River. The cruiser was close enough to still be able to contribute its artillery to the fight inland, but far enough away to significantly reduce the danger to civilians in the city.[63]

What no one knew at the time was that the twin tragedies could very well have been prevented—by Japan. The Japanese had broken the Chinese Air Force codes, which consistently kept them one step ahead. On August 13, the Third Fleet had intercepted a Chinese telegram revealing the plan to attack the vessels anchored in the Huangpu. As a result of this intelligence, the Japanese had prepared a preventive air raid to be carried out by naval aircraft on the morning of August 14.[64] Bad weather intervened. One ship-based air unit arrived too late to its designated point, while another warned that high waves had made takeoff and landing nearly impossible. The Japanese commanders had reluctantly canceled the day's operation, with severe consequences for the people of Shanghai.[65]

———————

The day after "Black Saturday," August 15, the weather remained poor, but the air war continued, with a more intense Japanese effort. Sergeant Hosokawa Hajime was on one of 20 Mitsubishi G3M medium bombers that took off from Omura Air Base on the southern Japanese island of Kyushu. Their targets were air bases near Nanjing. It was a risky undertaking. On their way to the Chinese capital, they were attacked by Chinese Curtiss Hawk fighters and on their return flight, after they had bombed their targets, they were pursued once more. This time, the more maneuverable Chinese aircraft went in for the kill.

Sergeant Hosokawa observed how a plane in the formation took a hit to one of its wing tanks and soon was engulfed in flames. The seven-member crew squeezed into the front cabin, and the pilot thrust open the top hatch to provide relief from the heat of the blaze that was consuming the aircraft. As the flames approached, the airmen were stretching their torsos out of the narrow opening, but could not jump as they had no parachutes—a matter of honor. All they could do was to wait for the inevitable. Suddenly, the plane turned into a fireball and plunged to the ground. Shortly afterwards, another plane in the formation was hit, and again the crew rushed to the front cabin, opening the top hatch with no hope of actually escaping. Hosokawa watched the pilot in the second plane hug his crew members before it dropped out of the formation and shot to the ground like a fiery comet. By the time the battered formation landed on the Japanese-controlled Korean island of Cheju, it had lost four aircraft.[66]

The G3Ms were part of the newly formed First Combined Air Group,[67] which had been placed under the command of Hasegawa Kiyoshi's Third Fleet. As the hostilities in Shanghai broke out, the 54-year-old vice admiral had displayed little hesitation when it came to deploying his planes far beyond Shanghai, even though this entailed expanding the war beyond a few localized incidents. On the same day that Sgt Hosokawa's formation was battered by Chinese fighters, a total of 14 other G3M bombers took off from their airfield in the north of Taiwan, which like Korea was a Japanese colony. Having targeted air facilities in the Chinese city of Nanchang, all planes returned.[68] Hasegawa was able to order these raids as his nominal political masters in Tokyo provided little guidance and overall showed limited interest in being involved in events at the front.

It was a surreal situation. Even after thousands had been killed in battle, the fighting in China remained an undeclared war as far as the Japanese government was concerned, and it committed forces only in a piecemeal fashion. The Japanese Cabinet kept referring to events in Shanghai and further north near Beijing as "the China Incident."[69] However, euphemisms were not enough to disguise the fact that Shanghai was becoming a problem. In the early hours of August 15, a Japanese Cabinet meeting decided to send army reinforcements to the hard-pressed marines in Shanghai, and the 3rd and 11th Divisions were deployed.

The two divisions were to form the Shanghai Expeditionary Force, a unit resurrected from the 1932 hostilities. Many of the soldiers who were to be sent off to war were reservists in their late 20s and early 30s who had long since returned to civilian life from military service and were poorly disciplined.[70] In their habitual disdain for the Chinese, the Japanese leaders figured that this would be more than enough to deal with the nuisance across the sea. Underestimating the foe was a mistake they were to repeat again and again in the coming weeks and months.

To head the force, the Japanese leaders fetched out of retirement 59-year-old General Matsui Iwane, a veteran of the 1904–1905 Russo-Japanese War. Matsui, a wisp of a man weighing no more than 100 pounds with a large 19th-century moustache and a palsy affecting his right face and right arm, was not an accidental choice. He knew China well and had been an acquaintance of Sun Yat-sen's, the revolutionary who had been the driving force in establishing the Republic of China in 1912 after the fall of the empire. Intellectually, Matsui ranged well beyond mere military matters, and it was well known among Japanese officials that he had indulged a "political hobby" after leaving the army, promoting his special idea of Asian unity and how to bring it about.[71]

Matsui mixed strident Japanese nationalism with a pan-Asian outlook, thus embodying much of the contradiction that characterized imperial Japan and its views about its role in Asia. In 1935, he had helped establish Dai Ajia Kyokai, or Greater Asia Society, an organization working to overcome divisions among the peoples of the continent and strengthen them to better resist western imperialism. He had toured China in the mid-1930s and had met Chiang Kai-shek repeatedly. If the encounters had established any rapport, that had soon disappeared. By the summer of 1937, Chiang was not Matsui's favorite Chinese at all. A staunch anti-communist, the Japanese general had been gravely dismayed by Chiang's decision to make peace with his Red rivals in order to coordinate and concentrate their efforts in a bid to defeat the Japanese threat.[72]

Matsui channeled his disaffection with Chiang into an extremely pro-active approach to the command of troops in the field. He exhibited an aggressive bent from the moment he got his assignment, before he had even set foot in Shanghai. The city must be taken, he believed, but it was not the ultimate prize. That was the Chinese capital Nanjing. After being named commander of the expeditionary force, he explained to Army Minister Sugiyama Hajime that there was no choice but to break Chiang Kai-shek by taking the Chinese seat of government. "That is what I must do," he said.[73] Shortly afterwards, Matsui told his chief of staff Major General Iinuma Mamoru that Japan ought to declare war on China.[74]

The central government in Tokyo had little clear idea about its ultimate goals in Shanghai, leaving local commanders free to set the agenda. By default, they were placed in a situation where they could wield disproportionate power. The problem was that they liked the power too much and did not shy away from using it. Vice Admiral Hasegawa had demonstrated this by launching air attacks on a wide range of targets along the Chinese east coast immediately after the outbreak of hostilities. Matsui was of the same mold. In the existing circumstances, this made them dangerous men.

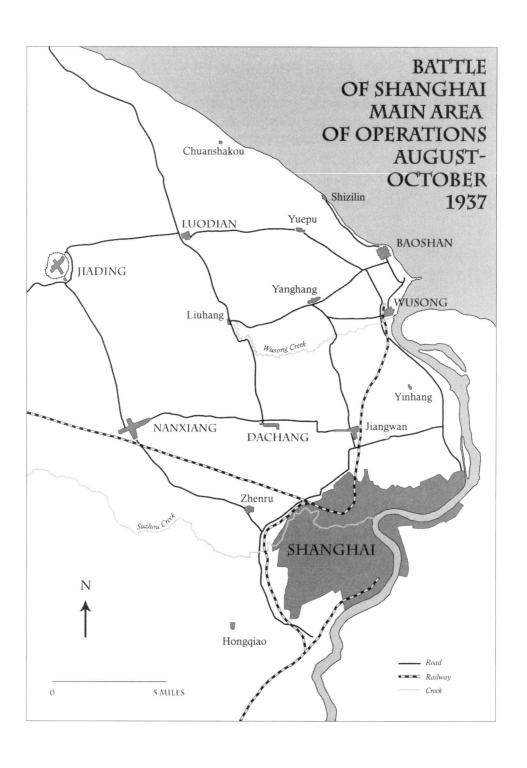

BATTLE
OF SHANGHAI
MAIN AREA
OF OPERATIONS
AUGUST-
OCTOBER
1937

Chuanshakou

Shizilin

Yuepu

LUODIAN

BAOSHAN

JIADING

Yanghang

WUSONG

Liuhang

Wusong Creek

Yinhang

NANXIANG

DACHANG

Jiangwan

Zhenru

Suzhou Creek

SHANGHAI

N

Hongqiao

0   5 MILES

———— Road
▪▪▪▪ Railway
———— Creek

3

. . . .

Flesh against Steel
AUGUST 16–22

"LITTLE TOKYO" HAD BECOME AN AREA UNDER SIEGE. SURROUNDED by hostile Chinese troops on three sides, its only link to the outside world was the dock district along the Huangpu River. From the first day of the battle, the area was showered with Chinese mortar shells, setting off an exodus among the Japanese residents, some of whom had lived in Shanghai for years. An increasingly common sight was kimono-clad women carrying heavy loads on the way to the wharfs where they would board ferries taking them home to Japan. Hongkou, said visiting Japanese correspondent Hayashi Fusao, "was a dark town. It was an exhausted town."[1]

Those who remained in "Little Tokyo," mostly men and mostly forced to stay behind to look after their businesses, tried to get on with their lives with as little interruption to their normal routines as possible. However, it was not easy given the constant reminders of the war around them; the rows of barbed wire and piles of sandbags, the soldiers marching from one engagement to the other, the sound of battle often taking place only a few blocks away. "Every building was bullet-marked and the haze of gunpowder hung over the town," wrote Hayashi. "It was a town at war. It was the August sun and an eerie silence, burning asphalt, and most of all the swarm of blue flies hovering around the feet."[2]

Smashed shop windows bore witness to widespread looting, while charred buildings were the result of Japan's primary tactic against snipers—burning them out. The snipers favored targeting cars as they sped down the avenues of the Japanese districts. Medical crews had recovered the drivers, mostly dead, but their vehicles remained, crashed into the building facades where their occupants had lost their lives. Littering the narrow alleys were the uncollected bodies of Chinese shot out of hand for the simple crime of looking suspicious. Floating down Suzhou Creek were the bodies of suspected spies—coolies with bashed-in heads, their toes beaten into a pulp by rifle butts.[3]

No one knew how many of the Chinese had been executed by regular Japanese soldiers, and how many were the victims of the *ronin*, the civilian thugs who followed the army everywhere and played an important role in the early stages of the battle. "They are the devil dogs of Japan at war and peace," wrote correspondent Rhodes Farmer, who came across them on a trip to Hongkou, and noted how revolvers and knives were strapped to their waists. "They were without exception little men, tough, long-haired, sly as snakes, dressed flashily like hoodlums the world over."[4]

Journalists touring the area were inevitably taken to the marine headquarters at the end of Sichuan North Road. The courtyard was crammed with trucks, armored cars and motorcycles. The marines gave the impression of being "immensely fit, alert, vigorous and scrupulously clean." Inside, there was an almost surreal calm. The walls of the rooms were covered in dark timber, while the decorations had a decidedly unmilitary character. Visitors were astonished to find flower arrangements, goldfish and two small grass-green Australian love birds in a painted cage.[5]

Although the marines were acting as infantry, they were extremely conscious of their naval background. A large number of them were sons of fishermen, and it was with obvious pride that they carried their uniforms, with anchors embossed on the buttons and the distinct olive drab color that set them apart from the army's khaki. "Fish have been fighting land fowl, and the result has been most interesting," the chief of staff told visiting journalists as they were served sake, Japanese rice wine. "Even if we are fish on land we have not lost the spirit of sailors in warships and have fought very vigorously. Fighting on land has proved to be so much more interesting than fighting on sea. There are so many more angles to it."[6]

It seemed increasingly likely that Vice Admiral Hasegawa Kiyoshi, the commander of the Japanese Third Fleet, had bitten off more than he could chew when aggressively expanding the operations in the Shanghai area. August 16 was the crucial day. Repeated Chinese attacks put the Japanese defenders under severe pressure and stretched their resources to the limit. Rear Admiral Okawachi Denshichi, who headed the Shanghai marines, had to hastily throw in precious reserves, including irreplaceable tanks, to prevent a Chinese breakthrough.[7] It was a crisis situation, and for the first time the marines had to think the unthinkable. If they did not get help from the outside, they might actually lose the battle.[8]

Three times during the course of August 16, Hasegawa himself sent telegrams to his superiors, each more desperate-sounding than the previous one. After his second telegram, sent at about 7:00 p.m., warning that his troops could probably only hold out for six more days, the Naval Command issued an order to the marine barracks at Sasebo Naval Base in southern Japan to dispatch two units of 500 marines each to Shanghai. After Hasegawa's third telegram later that night, the navy opted for yet more reinforcements. Two units of the marines, consisting of a total of 1,400 soldiers, waiting in Manchuria for deployment at Qingdao, were ordered to immediately embark for Shanghai.[9]

The Chinese, however, did not feel that things were going their way. The battle continued to be much bloodier than anyone had foreseen. Throwing infantry en masse against fortified positions was perhaps the only feasible tactic available to an army rich in manpower confronting an adversary with an obvious technological edge. Yet, it turned the battle into a contest of flesh against steel. The result was a tremendous loss of life. Chiang Kai-shek was losing patience. After several days of fighting, his troops had still not succeeded in dislodging the Japanese from the streets of Shanghai. The Japanese marines entrenched in the Hongkou and Yangshupu areas had proved to be a harder nut to crack than he or any of his generals had expected. At a meeting with his divisional commanders, he ordered a massive attack to be launched in the early morning of August 17. The troops were to field more firepower, and be better prepared than they were for the assault three days earlier. Codenamed Operation *Iron Fist*, it was the most ambitious Chinese offensive in the first crucial week of the Shanghai campaign.[10]

Although the initiative was Chiang's, in its actual execution the operation was mainly a German undertaking. Colonel Hans Vetter, the advisor
assigned to the 88th Division, played a key role in planning the offensive.
He wanted to use the *Stosstrupp*, or shock troop tactics that the Germans
had introduced to much effect in the trenches towards the end of the Great
War. After intensive artillery bombardment, a small, elite group of determined, well-armed men was to punch through the Japanese lines and fight
its way deep into the enemy camp before the defenders had even had a
chance to recover from the initial surprise. The procedure was to be followed both by the 88th Division moving in from the west, targeting the
area south of Hongkou Park, and by the 87th Division carrying out a parallel operation from the east.[11]

Plans for the attack came at a critical time. Zhang Zhizhong knew that
he faced a window of opportunity while he was still enjoying a significant,
but probably only temporary, advantage against the Japanese. The window
had to be utilized before reinforcements arrived. However, the odds were
not good. Urban combat with modern weaponry of unprecedented lethal-
ity was a costly affair, especially when the enemy had the upper hand in
the sky. Japanese airplanes were a constant menace, carrying out incessant
sorties against the Chinese positions at all times of the day. The Chinese
Air Force remained a factor, but it was a question how much longer it
would hold out against the more experienced Japanese pilots and their better and more maneuverable aircraft.

The growing Japanese presence overhead, maintained by both ship-
borne planes and planes based on airstrips on Chongming Island in the
Yangtze Delta, greatly complicated any major movements on the ground.
"The transport and deployment of Chinese units met significant obstacles
due to the busy activity of the Japanese naval aircraft," German advisors
recalled later.[12] Even so, the Chinese Army continued its troop build-up in
the Shanghai area. The 98th Infantry Division arrived on August 15 and
placed one brigade, half its strength, at the disposal of 87th Infantry Division, keeping the division's rear area covered during Operation *Iron Fist*.

As the countdown to the planned final strike continued, morale remained high in the Chinese camp. Despite the lack of progress in the days
since the battle had broken out, and despite the heavy casualties, a feeling
of relief permeated the ranks. After civil wars that in effect had lasted a

quarter century, all Chinese were at long last fighting on the same side. Many officers rushed to write their wills, expecting to die for their country. Few wanted to be killed. Still, they felt that if they had to give their lives, this was a worthy cause. "I was very happy and excited," said Zhang Fakui, the commander of the right wing in the Pudong area, east of Huangpu, which had been designated as the 8th Army Group. "This was the first and only national war I fought in."[13]

Iron Fist kicked off as planned at 5:00 a.m. on August 17. With the expenditure of all available firepower, the 87th and 88th Infantry Divisions launched simultaneous assaults against stunned and bewildered Japanese. In line with the *Stosstrupp* approach of rapid penetration, Zhang Zhizhong introduced a new tactical principle, prompted by the severe losses during the first few days of fighting. Forces under his command were to identify gaps in the Japanese defenses and exploit these, rather than launch massive, costly and most likely futile attacks on heavily fortified positions. Once an enemy stronghold was spotted, the main forces would evade it and leave just enough troops to keep it pinned down.[14]

Chen Yiding, a regimental commander of the 87th Infantry Division, was a pivotal figure in the assault. His soldiers, each equipped with provisions for two days, made good progress during the first hours of *Iron Fist*, taking advantage of their local knowledge and moving with the slippery dexterity of alley cats. They would enter into a building on one street, knock down the wall inside and exit onto the next street, or they would throw down beams from rooftop to rooftop, sneaking as quietly as possible from one block to the next without being noticed by those on the ground. They proved elusive targets for the Japanese, who would expect them to come from one direction, only to be attacked from another.[15]

Nevertheless, changing the tactical situation of the previous days was not enough. The attackers encountered well-prepared defenses that sometimes could not be circumvented, and losses started piling up from early in the assault. An entire battalion of the 88th Division was wiped out trying to take a single building.[16] Despite the sacrifices, there was no major breakthrough anywhere along the Japanese defense lines. This was partly a result of strong support from Japanese naval artillery in the Huangpu River, and partly a reflection of poor coordination between Chinese infantry and artillery.[17]

Equally detrimental to the Chinese cause was their careful avoidance, during the first days of combat in Shanghai, of fighting inside the International Settlement, or even in the predominantly Japanese part of the settlement, in order not to anger the outside world and swing international opinion against them. This approach frustrated their German advisors. "It was obvious that the attacking troops had been told to only take on enemies standing on Chinese territory, not the ones inside the international areas," the Germans wrote with an almost audible sigh of regret in their after-action report.[18]

Their frustration was shared by several Chinese officers at the frontline. "We are much handicapped by the demarcation of the foreign areas," the adjutant to a divisional commander told a western reporter. "We could have wiped out the enemy if it had not been for orders from the Central Government and our commander to avoid causing damage to foreign lives and to give them adequate protection."[19] The existence of the large foreign community mainly played into Japanese hands. Many of Chiang Kai-shek's officers believed that if the Chinese had been able to move through the French Concession and the International Settlement and attack the Japanese from the rear, they could have won easily. "Without the protection provided by the foreign concessions they would have been wiped out," said Zhang Fakui.[20]

At the same time, the Chinese commanders had only hazy ideas about conditions at the frontline and were sometimes misled by exaggerated claims made by officers in the field. At 9:00 a.m. on August 17, the commander of the 87th Infantry Division reported to Zhang Zhizhong that the Japanese Navy Club, a key position, was in his possession. However, when Zhang sent his own people to the spot to investigate, it turned out a four-story building right next door was still occupied by the Japanese who were determined to defend the building to the last man. The divisional commander's self-assured claim was further undermined later that afternoon, when Japanese troops carried out two counterattacks from a nearby naval drill ground.[21] It was, therefore, understandable that not all officers trusted reports that their own units sent back to them. One regiment of the 87th Division was under specific orders to document any advance it made. Every time it had taken a key objective along its predetermined route of advance, it was to pull down a street sign and send it back as evidence that it indeed was in control of the position.[22]

At the end of the day, the Japanese won. Defense had proved stronger, as it had for four long years on the Western Front during the Great War. The challenge the Japanese faced was tough, but at least it was straightforward and uncomplicated. They had to hold on to Hongkou and Yangshupu and wait for reinforcements to arrive.[23] They proved themselves adept at this job. In many cases, Chinese soldiers found themselves fighting for the same objectives they had been targeting when the battle for Shanghai began several days earlier. Pan Shihua, a soldier in the 88th Infantry Division, took part in a harsh seesaw struggle around the Eight Character Bridge, where lax preparation caused casualties to run unnecessarily high. "Because we hadn't done reconnaissance well enough beforehand, we found ourselves surrounded by Japanese armor on all sides," he said.[24] The Chinese forces were getting bogged down. Zhang Zhizhong's window of opportunity was closing fast.

————————

Operation *Iron Fist* was the main German contribution in the initial stages of the Shanghai campaign, but it was far from the only one. German advisors were present both on the staffs and at the frontline. Their pivotal role was no secret, and even the newspapers regularly reported about them. Wearing the uniforms of Chiang Kai-shek's army, the German advisors not only provided tactical input, but gave the Chinese troops an invaluable morale boost, showing them that they were not on their own in the struggle against the mighty and ruthless Japanese Empire.[25] The "German War" was the name that some Japanese gave to the battle of Shanghai, and for good reason.[26]

When war with Japan broke out in the summer of 1937, the German advisory corps consisted of nearly 70 officers, ranging from newly graduated second-lieutenants to five full generals. It was a major asset for the Chinese, and one that they were free to exploit. Even though most of the Germans were in China on short-term contracts and could have left once the shooting started, they felt an obligation to stay at a key moment when their host nation's survival was at stake. "We all agreed that as private citizens in Chinese employment there could be no question of our leaving our Chinese friends to their fate," Alexander von Falkenhausen, the top advisor, wrote later. "Therefore I assigned the German advisors wherever they were needed, and that was often in the frontlines."[27]

The situation was the culmination of a relationship that had evolved over a period of several years. Germany had started playing a role in China's military modernization in the late 1920s, with initial contacts facilitated by Chiang Kai-shek's admiration for German efficiency. The German government's decision to abandon all extraterritorial privileges in 1921,[28] followed seven years later by the diplomatic recognition of Chiang's government, also created a benevolent atmosphere. In addition, as a result of its defeat in the Great War, Germany was a relatively safe bet for China. It was, in the 1920s and early 1930s at least, the only major power unable to resume its imperialist policies of the years prior to 1914.[29] Germany and China were in fact in similar situations, Chiang once mused. "They were oppressed by foreign powers," he said, "and had to free themselves from those chains."[30]

Yet another factor behind the expanding Sino-German military ties was the lack of suitable employment for officers in Weimar Germany, whose military, the *Reichswehr*, was severely curtailed by the demands of the post-war Versailles Treaty. The shadow existence they led at home contrasted starkly with the prestige they enjoyed in China. By the mid-1930s, the Germans had a status among the Chinese that no other westerners had ever experienced. When Chiang met with his generals, his chief German advisor at the time, Hans von Seeckt, would sit at his desk, giving the signal that the foreign officer's place in the hierarchy, while informal, was near the top. When Seeckt had to go by train to a north Chinese sea resort for health reasons, he traveled in Chiang's personal saloon carriage and was saluted at every station by an honorary formation.[31]

Seeckt visited China the first time in 1933, and immediately set about salvaging bilateral ties strained by German condescension towards the Chinese. As the host nation and employer, China was to be shown respect, was his order to the German officers stationed in the country, and being a traditional German, he expected to be obeyed. When he arrived in China for his second tour the year after, he was accompanied by Falkenhausen. No novice to Asia, Falkenhausen hit it off with Chiang Kai-shek almost immediately. It helped that both knew Japanese, the language of their soon-to-be enemy, and could converse freely without having to go through an interpreter.[32] It was an additional advantage that Falkenhausen's wife was on superb terms with Madame Chiang.[33] Falkenhausen's break came when Seekt, suffering from poor health, returned to Germany in early 1935. From then on, he was the top German officer inside China.[34]

It is likely that Falkenhausen felt a deep sense of relief to be posted abroad. His mission removed any immediate obligation to return to Germany and work with the Nazis. "In the 30s we could have in good conscience stayed in China," one of Falkenhausen's subordinates later rationalized. "China was in much greater danger than Germany."[35] Falkenhausen had a very personal reason to adopt that rationale. His younger brother, Hans Joachim von Falkenhausen, a war veteran and a member of the Nazi Party's paramilitary Sturm-Abteilung, was executed in a bloody showdown among rival factions inside the party's ranks in the summer of 1934. He was 36 when he died.[36]

Falkenhausen's unhappy relationship with Berlin's new rulers put him on one side of a political generation gap that divided most of the German advisors in China. Among conservative officers of his age and background, feelings about Hitler, a mere corporal in the Great War, ranged from skepticism to adoration; in between was quiet acceptance of an overlap of interests with Germany's new Nazi rulers, who wanted rapid rearmament and the creation of a vast new army. The younger German officers serving in China were far less ambivalent. They were often ardent Nazis.[37] The racist ideology the young Germans brought with them from home may have contributed to lingering tension with the Chinese. Since most of them expected to leave within no more than a few years, virtually none bothered to change their lifestyles in order to fit into their new surroundings. Rather, in the traditional way of Europeans in Asia, they lived in their own enclave in Nanjing, a small piece of Germany in the heart of China. If they paid any attention to local mores, it was with a shrug of the shoulder. Brought up on austere Prussian ideals, they considered, for example, the Chinese habit of elaborate banquets a costly waste of time and resources.[38]

The Chinese, too, looked at the foreign advisors in mild bewilderment. The German habit of wearing monocles was a cause of wonder and led them to ask why so many were near-sighted on only one eye.[39] A few Chinese did not just puzzle at the behaviour of the strange foreigners, but had attitudes bordering on hostile. Zhang Fakui, for one, appears to have had a particularly delicate relationship with the German advisors. He did not trust them, did not share any secrets with them, and did not take any advice from them. "I had always had a bad impression of the Germans," he told an interviewer decades later.[40]

Falkenhausen's own outlook underwent profound change. At the time of his arrival, he had been somewhat indifferent to China, but he gradually grew fonder of the country, and in the end he was very close to accepting an offer of Chinese citizenship from Chiang.[41] As time passed, he even showed signs of divided loyalties between his old and new masters, ignoring pleas from Germany to favor its weapon producers when carrying out arms procurements abroad. Instead, he bought the arms he thought would serve China best, regardless of where they had been manufactured.[42] Finally, he developed a high degree of resentment of the Japanese foe. "It is sheer mockery to see this bestial machine pose as the vanguard of anti-Communism," he wrote in a report to Oskar Trautmann, the German ambassador in Nanjing.[43]

Once war broke out, Falkenhausen was in favor of an aggressive and all-encompassing strategy against the enemy. He advised that the Japanese garrison in Shanghai be attacked and wiped out, regardless of the fact that it was located inside the International Settlement. He even urged air attacks on western Korea and sabotage on the Japanese home islands.[44] These steps went much further than almost any of his Chinese hosts was prepared to go. Perhaps they feared setting a task for themselves that they could not handle. Falkenhausen, on the other hand, never seemed to have harbored any serious doubts about China's military prowess. Rather, its army's willingness to make sacrifices appealed to his special German passion for absolutes. "The morale of the Chinese Army is high. It will fight back stubbornly," he said. "It will be a struggle to the last extreme."[45]

———————

Baba Toraji, a 21-year-old employee of the exclusive department store Magasin Franco-Japonais, was growing more nervous for every minute that passed on the morning of August 18. A younger colleague of his, fellow Japanese Sakanichi Takaichi, had left earlier to buy bread for his colleagues, and he had not returned. In the end, Baba decided to go looking himself. It did not take long before he found Sakanichi, caught up in a Chinese crowd that had identified him as Japanese. Both men were mauled severely and left on the street. Baba was pronounced dead by the time medical personnel arrived. His younger colleague was sent to hospital with serious injuries.[46]

Earlier in the month, a group of eight Japanese had unwisely shown up on the Bund, trying to push their way through a dense crowd. Jeers started. Someone picked up a discarded shoe and threw it at them. The Japanese broke into a run, and seven managed to escape. A huge brick went sailing through the air and hit the eighth in the back. He fell to the ground, and the mob was upon him. "Men could be seen jumping in the air to land with both feet on the unfortunate man's body," the *North China Daily News* reported. "Others, with stick and bricks that seemed to come from nowhere, belabored him from head to foot." He was eventually rescued and hospitalized in a critical condition.[47]

Being Japanese in Shanghai in August 1937 was dangerous. By contrast, Shanghai's western residents only came into contact with the horrors around them in an indirect fashion. They watched the dense black smoke rising over Hongkou, and they saw the flotsam drifting down Suzhou Creek—cows, buffaloes, and a steady stream of uniformed corpses.[48] The debris of war served as a warning that the battle was escalating and could soon engulf the foreign enclaves. It was time for the women and children to leave. A total of 1,300 British and American evacuees departed from Shanghai on August 17. The British left for Hong Kong on the *Rajputana*, while the Americans boarded the *President Jefferson* for Manila.[49] On August 19, 1,400 more British citizens, mostly women and children, sailed on destroyers to board the *Empress of Asia* at Wusong.[50] This was part of a scheme to evacuate a total of 3,000 British nationals, including 85 percent of the women and children in the city.[51]

Staying on the fringe of a great battle, as the foreigners did, made life more dangerous. Even so, they were not deliberately targeted, and that made them the envy of the Chinese population. Shanghai shops saw brisk sales of the national flags of major non-belligerent nations, as Chinese residents hung them at their doorways in the hope that the sight of a Union Jack or the Stars and Stripes would ward off enemy fire, very much in the fashion that the images of guardian deities kept traditional Chinese homes safe from evil spirits.[52] However, few had faith that anything they could do would make a difference, except running away. Desperate crowds, many uprooted from their homes in the north of the city, gathered in the International Settlement, clamoring for food. Looting soon became widespread. Crowds attacked trucks transporting rice, or smashed their way to shop supplies. The authorities were merciless in tackling the problem. On at least one occasion, French police opened fire on a crowd that had attacked a food hawker. Law enforcers in the International Settlement handed over dozens of looters to the Chinese police, knowing perfectly well they would be shot within hours.[53]

Violence in many forms, often lethal, was meted out in liberal doses among the Chinese. An atmosphere of intense suspicion permeated the city, and everyone was a potential traitor. On the first day of fighting, six Chinese nationals were executed. All were sentenced to death for spying on behalf of the Japanese or for carrying out acts of sabotage in Zhabei and other areas under the control of the Shanghai municipal government.[54] On another occasion, two women and seven men were decapitated for working for the Japanese. Their heads were placed on top of poles and put on display in the market square, as thousands of men, women and children watched with glee.[55]

Following rumors published in the local press that the Japanese had bribed collaborators to poison the water supply, gangs armed with clubs and other primitive weapons raged through the streets, stopping suspicious-looking individuals. Anyone caught with a powdery substance, even medicine, was severely beaten. Fifteen innocent Chinese were killed and 40 injured that way, according to police.[56] Even having the wrong appearance could be deadly. On the morning of August 17, an unregistered Portuguese man was beaten to death by a mob because he was thought to look Japanese. A Sikh police officer who came to his rescue was in turn badly mangled by the crowd.[57]

One group of Shanghai residents was particularly unfortunate and unable to go anywhere, despite being directly in the middle of some of the worst fighting. They were the inmates of Ward Road Jail, Shanghai's largest prison, located in Yangshupu. Thousands of them, along with their wardens, were trapped when the battle started. On the morning of August 17, a shell struck the prison, killing ten people and causing extensive damage to both the cells and the prison staff's quarters.[58] In the days that followed, the prison suffered several direct hits when Chinese artillery in Pudong or at the North Railway Station misfired.

By August 20, the penal authorities began evacuating the prisoners, starting with the criminally insane, who would pose the greatest danger if a chance grenade were to make escape possible.[59] On August 22, a more comprehensive evacuation was planned to take place, but buses meant to bring 150 juvenile criminals to the Chinese district via the International Settlement were stopped by Japanese guards at the Garden Bridge. The juveniles were young and could be recruited for the Chinese war effort and they were returned to their prison.[60] From then on, the evacuation drive nearly stopped, and weeks later, the Ward Road facility was still brimming with inmates, exposed to the deadly fire from both sides.[61]

The Japanese marine units dispatched from Manchuria on August 16, the day of crisis for their compatriots in Shanghai, arrived in the city during the morning of August 18 and were immediately thrown into the battle.[62] A few hours later, the Japanese Cabinet announced the formal end of a policy of non-expansion in China, which by that time had been a hollow shell for several weeks anyway. "The empire, having reached the limit of its patience, has been forced to take resolute measures," it said. "Henceforth it will punish the outrages of the Chinese Army, and thus spur the (Chinese) government to self-reflect."[63]

On the same day, the British chargé d'affaires in Tokyo, James Dodds, suggested a peace proposal to Japanese Deputy Foreign Affairs Minister Horinouchi Kensuke. The proposal, drafted two days earlier by the British, American and French ambassadors to Nanjing, called for the transformation of Shanghai into a neutral zone based on a commitment by both China and Japan to withdraw their forces from the city. Japan was not excited about the idea, and on August 19, Horinouchi presented the British diplomat with his government's official refusal, stating that China would have to retreat to the boundaries outlined in the truce that ended hostilities in 1932.[64] Japan was gaining confidence.

Meanwhile, there was a growing feeling on the Chinese side that important opportunities had been missed. On August 18, Chiang Kai-shek dispatched Deputy War Minister Chen Cheng, one of his main military aides, to the Shanghai front in order to confer with Zhang Zhizhong about how to carry the battle forward.[65] The two generals reached the conclusion that rather than focusing the attacks on the heavily fortified Hongkou area, they should turn their attention to the Yangshupu district, seeking to push through to the Huangpu River and cut the Japanese forces in two.[66] This was the decision the German advisers and the frontline commanders had been waiting for. The gloves had come off, and the self-defeating reluctance to attack Japanese troops inside the settlement borders was gone.[67]

As the forces that had been in Shanghai since the start of hostilities were beginning to show signs of attrition, the generals decided to place the main responsibility for the attack with the 36th Infantry Division, which had only just arrived, and was being moved to the eastern side of the Hongkou salient. It was an obvious choice, as its soldiers were from the same German-trained elite as those of the 87th and 88th Divisions. Two of the division's four regiments were ordered to attack straight south in the direction of the Huangpu, down streets running perpendicular to the river.[68] In order to reach the wharf area, the soldiers would have to pass five heavily defended intersections. Severe casualties were expected.[69]

The two regiments launched the attack almost immediately, moving out in the early hours of August 19. Sabotage and incendiary bombs resulted in a number of large fires that helped improve visibility during the night fighting.[70] However, the intersections proved a problem. The Chinese soldiers, most of whom were seeing battle for the first time, became defenseless prey to Japanese infantry posted on the rooftops or in windows on the upper floors of buildings along their route. In the absence of any other cover, they often had to duck behind the bodies of those already killed.[71] Even so, for a brief period of time, the Chinese believed they had finally managed to break the back of the hated Japanese. "I thought we could push the enemy into the river and chase them out of Shanghai," said Zhang Fakui, watching the battle from the other side of the Huangpu.[72]

Once they had reached Broadway, the last street running parallel with the Huangpu River, they faced the most formidable obstacle of them all. The Japanese defenders had taken up positions on top of high walls protecting the wharfs. Dislodging them was akin to storming a medieval castle. A large steel gate formed an entrance into the wharves, but it yielded to no weapon that the Chinese had brought; even the 150mm howitzers could not destroy it. Officers and soldiers tried to scale the gate, but were mowed down by enfilading Japanese machine gun fire.[73] Also located near the river were Japanese-owned factories, many of which had been turned into veritable fortresses. One example was the Gong Da Cotton Mill at the eastern edge of the International Settlement. Again, the Chinese attackers did not possess weaponry powerful enough to penetrate the Japanese defenses there.[74]

While the Chinese were short of large-caliber guns, the Japanese had plenty aboard the Third Fleet anchored in the Huangpu. The 36th Infantry Division was subjected to merciless bombardment, which threw several of its units into disarray. The following night, between August 19 and 20, the 88th Infantry Division for the first time showed that its ability to wage war had been so severely compromised it was, temporarily at least, unable to carry out meaningful offensive action. When ordered to attack, it moved in a belated and reluctant fashion, and got nowhere.[75] While the Chinese were getting weaker, the Japanese were growing stronger. The marines dispatched from Sasebo arrived in Shanghai on that same night, boosting the number of marines inside the garrison to 6,300 well-armed men.[76]

Despite a propensity to husband expensive equipment, the Chinese decided at this point to throw major parts of their new tank force into the battle. As was the case with the German-trained divisions and the air force, this was another key asset that had taken years to build up. Following the 1932 incident, when Japan had used its armor to some effect, the Nationalist government had decided to acquire its own tank arm, purchasing tanks from a variety of European nations, including Germany, Britain and Italy. As a result of these efforts, by the outbreak of hostilities in 1937, China was able to deploy the British-built, 6-ton, single-turret Vickers model in Shanghai.

The 87th Infantry Division was given disposal of two armored companies, and it lost everything. Some of the tanks had just arrived from Nanjing, and their crews had not had any time to undertake training in coordinated attacks, or even simply to establish rapport with the local troops. As a result, the tank companies were mostly left to their own devices without infantry support.[77] The Chinese also often neglected to seal off adjacent streets when deploying their tanks, allowing Japanese armor to outflank them and knock them out. To be sure, the Japanese, too, lacked experience in coordination between armor and infantry and frequently saw their tanks annihilated by Chinese anti-tank weapons.[78]

On August 20, Zhang Zhizhong was inspecting the Yangshupu front when he met one of his former students from the Central Military Academy, who was in charge of a tank company that was about to attack the wharves. Some of the tanks under his command had been under repair and hastily pulled out of the workshop. "The vehicles are no good," the young officer complained. "The enemy fire is fierce, and our infantry will have trouble keeping up." Zhang was relentless, telling the young officer that the attack had to be carried through to the end nonetheless. A few moments later the tank company started its assault. The young officer and his entire unit were wiped out in a hail of shells, many of them fired from vessels anchored in the Huangpu River. "It saddens me even today when I think about it," Zhang wrote many years later in his memoirs.[79]

In this battle, modern tank warfare mixed with scenes more reminiscent of earlier centuries. Wu Yujun, an officer of the Peace Preservation Corps, was manning a position in the streets of Yangshupu on the morning of August 18 when a detachment of Japanese cavalry attacked. The raid was over almost instantly, and left numerous dead and injured Chinese in its wake. The Japanese repeated the assault two more times. The third time, Wu Yujun prepared an elaborate ambush, posting machine guns on both sides of the street. As the riders galloped past, they and their horses were chopped to pieces. Apart from four prisoners, all Japanese lost their lives. The 20th century had met the 19th century on the battlefield, and won.[80] It was a typical incident, and yet in one respect also very atypical. In the streets of Shanghai in August 1937, Chinese soldiers were far likelier to confront a technologically superior enemy than the other way around.

Many of the Chinese units arriving in Shanghai had never tasted battle before, and in the first crucial days of fighting, their lack of experience proved costly. Fang Jing, a brigade commander of the 98th Division, one of the units to arrive early in Shanghai, noticed how his soldiers often set up inadequate fortifications that were no match for the artillery rolled out by the Japanese. "Often, the positions they built were too weak and couldn't withstand the enemy's 150mm howitzers," he said. "The upshot was that men and materiel were buried inside the positions they had built for themselves."[81]

No one was surprised that the Japanese soldiers put up a determined fight in Shanghai. Since their 1904–1905 triumph over the Russian Empire, the legend of the "brave little Jap"[82] had become firmly established in the mind of the global public. So widespread was this view that if Japanese soldiers did not fight to the death, it was a source of genuine surprise. However, at moments of absolute frankness, the Japanese themselves could feel a need to add nuance to foreign stereotypes about their countrymen's behavior in battle. "Our soldiers would prefer death to surrender," a Japanese diplomat was quoted as saying, "but the majority secretly hope that they will return honorably to their own country, either wounded or unscathed."[83]

Foreign journalists noticed to their astonishment that there seemed to be little in the Japanese code of honor that prevented them from fleeing from a hopeless situation. One of them remembered seeing a number of Japanese soldiers run back from a failed attack during the battle of Shanghai, with the Chinese in hot pursuit. There were even rare instances of Japanese soldiers raising the white flag. The same correspondent witnessed a party of about 50 Japanese motorcyclists who had become bogged down in a rice paddy near the city and were surrounded by Chinese. They surrendered immediately without making any effort to resist.[84]

These were minority cases. Most Japanese soldiers lived up to the high expectations placed on their shoulders at home and abroad. Physically, they tended to be short by western standards, but they were strong and capable of enduring immense hardship.[85] This was as a result of rigorous training combined with draconian discipline, underpinned by the threat and liberal use of corporal punishment. The training was so efficient that a Japanese soldier entering the reserve never ceased to be a soldier again. In the early months of the war, American correspondent John Goette met a Japanese private in his late 30s who had just been called up from his civilian occupation as a dentist. "Hundreds of thousands like him had made a swift change from civilian life to the handling of a rifle on foreign soil," he wrote. "Twenty years after his conscript training, this dentist was again a soldier."[86]

An added element in the training of Japanese soldiers was indoctrination, which came in the form of repetition of the virtues—self-sacrifice, obedience and loyalty to the emperor—which the soldiers had learned since childhood. The result was mechanic obedience on the battlefield. "Even though his officers appear to have an ardor which might be called fanaticism," a U.S. military handbook remarked later in the war, "the private soldier is characterized more by blind and unquestioning subservience to authority."[87] The downside was that soldiers and junior officers were not encouraged to think independently or take the initiative themselves. They expected to be issued detailed orders and would follow them slavishly. When the situation changed in ways that had not been foreseen by their commanders—which was the norm rather than the exception in battle—they were often left perplexed and unable to act.[88]

It could be argued that the Japanese military had few other options than to train its soldiers in this way, since to a large extent it drew its recruits from agricultural areas where there was limited access to education. It was said that for every 100 men in a Japanese unit, 80 were farm boys, ten were clerks, five factory workers, and five students.[89] Nevertheless, reading was a favorite pastime among Japanese soldiers. Military trains were littered with books and magazines, mostly simple pulp fiction. When the trains stopped at stations, even the locomotive's engineer could be observed reading behind the throttle.[90] Some of them were prolific writers, too. A large number of Japanese in the Shanghai area had brought diaries and wrote down their impressions with great perception and eloquence. Some officers even composed poems in the notoriously difficult classical style.

Many Japanese soldiers grew large beards while in China, but in a twist that was not easy to understand for foreigners, they could sometimes mix a fierce martial exterior with an almost feminine inner appreciation of natural beauty. Trainloads of Japanese soldiers would flock to the windows to admire a particularly striking sunset. It was not unusual to see a Japanese soldier holding his rifle and bayonet in one hand, and a single white daisy in the other. "Missionaries have found," wrote U.S. correspondent Haldore Hanson, "that when bloodstained Japanese soldiers break into their compounds during a 'mopping up' campaign, the easiest way to pacify them is to present each man with a flower."[91]

Many Japanese soldiers also carried cameras into battle, and as was the case with the Germans on the Eastern Front, their snapshots came to constitute a comprehensive photographic record of their own war crimes. Journalist John Powell remembered his revulsion when he saw a photo of two

Japanese soldiers standing next to the body of a Chinese woman they had just raped. He had obtained the image from a Korean photo shop in Shanghai where it had been handed in to be developed. "The soldiers apparently wanted the prints to send to their friends at home in Japan," he wrote. "Japanese soldiers seemingly had no feelings whatsoever that their inhuman actions transgressed the tenets of modern warfare or common everyday morals."[92]

—————

On August 20, five Chinese aircraft were returning after another fruitless attack on the *Izumo*, which was still moored in the middle of the Huangpu, when they encountered two Japanese seaplanes over western Zhabei. A Chinese plane broke formation, went into a steep dive and fired a short machine gun salvo at one of the Japanese. It did not have a chance. It burst into flames and plunged to the ground. The other Japanese plane disappeared in the clouds. The entire encounter had only taken a few seconds.[93] It was one of a series of hits that the Chinese Air Force scored during a brief period in August before it was completely subdued by its Japanese adversary.

In particular, it posed a threat to Japanese bombers, such as the highly flammable Mitsubishi G3M medium aircraft assigned to striking targets in Shanghai and other cities in central China. Japan's First Combined Air Group lost half of its medium attack planes in the first three days of the battle for Shanghai, some missing, some confirmed shot down and others heavily damaged. Their crews were particularly vulnerable, since they did not bring parachutes on their missions.[94] From late August, the air group's bombers were escorted by Type 95 Nakajima A4N biplanes.[95] This action amounted to a humiliating admission that China's nascent air force was a force to be reckoned with.

"In view of the pressing situation in the Shanghai area," said the First Combined Air Group's commander, "our air raids reminded me of that famous, costly assault against the 203-Meter Hill."[96] The battle for 203-Meter Hill had been one of the bloodiest episodes of the entire Russo-Japanese War, claiming thousands of casualties on both sides. The Chinese performance was significant enough that even foreign military observers paid attention. British intelligence, in a report summarizing military events in the middle of August, noted Chinese claims of having downed 32 Japanese aircraft. "This statement appears well-founded," the report's writer added.[97]

Even so, the Chinese airmen had been mostly untested and only partly trained when the war started. Their inferiority, especially against Japanese fighters, began to tell, and they gradually disappeared from the skies over Shanghai. Their compatriots on the ground expressed frustration over the lack of air cover. "We occasionally spotted two or three of our own airplanes, but the moment they encountered enemy anti-aircraft fire, they disappeared," said Fang Jing, a regimental commander of the 98th Infantry Division. "They were no use at all. After August 20, I never saw our planes again."[98]

That may have been hyperbole,[99] but it was undeniable that the evolving Japanese air superiority proved a major handicap for the Chinese. The Chinese commanders soon realized that they had to carry out major troop movements under the cover of darkness. Japan's domination of the skies affected everything the Chinese soldiers did and even determined when they could get food. "We didn't eat until at night," said Fang Zhendong, a soldier of the 36th Infantry Division. "That was the only time we could get anything. In the daytime, it was impossible to transport provisions to the frontline."[100]

Without fighter protection the troops on the ground were dangerously exposed. They had very little in the way of anti-aircraft weaponry, mostly 20mm Solothurn guns produced in Switzerland. However, even these weapons made next to no difference as they were primarily deployed against enemy infantry.[101] Also, the Chinese officers were reluctant to use their anti-aircraft guns lest they reveal their positions to the Japanese aircraft.[102] In late August when Japanese Admiral Hasegawa was asked by a Reuters journalist visiting his flagship if he was in control of the air, his reply was prompt: "Yes," he said. "I believe so."[103]

———————————

By the morning of August 21, the 36th Division had pressed the attack against the wharf area almost without interruption for over 48 hours, and victory seemed as elusive as ever. Individual tanks had managed to break into the wharfs, only to discover to their dismay how extraordinarily robust the Japanese defenses were, and how numerous the troops manning them.

In order to punch holes in the Japanese lines and reach Huangpu River, significant tactical muscle was required, and the Chinese no longer had it.[104]

The commanders had no choice but to acknowledge that the division had moved too fast and had neglected to secure its flanks, while reserves that could have moved up and shouldered that responsibility had stayed in the rear. It was necessary to withdraw. During the course of August 21, the division had to go through the agony of abandoning territory won at the expense of much blood over the preceding days. The 36th Infantry Division's retreat marked the final admission by the Chinese that pushing the Japanese into the river was not going to be a simple maneuver.

Part of the reason for the lack of success was a failure to carry out joint operations involving different service arms. The German advisors complained that the Chinese troops on the Pudong side delivered only limited artillery support for the soldiers fighting in Yangshupu. By contrast, the Japanese naval guns were constantly active, doing their utmost to relieve the hard-pressed marines. This activity resulted in heavy losses, not only for the Chinese units at the front, but also for reserve and support units further to the rear, and contributed to the 36th Division suffering more than 2,000 casualties by late on August 22.[105]

Meanwhile, Japanese naval aircraft tried to prevent the movement of more Chinese troops to Shanghai by bombing the railway from Suzhou. However, despite the destruction of several bridges and damage to some railway stations, there were only minor delays. This was welcome news for the Chinese commanders, who had realized that the available resources were insufficient to bring the Shanghai battle to a successful conclusion. New reinforcements were necessary before further attacks could be launched.[106] The assumption was that there was still time. The fact was that there was not.

While the Chinese officers were standing around their maps making plans for the future, Asano Yoshiuchi was waiting aboard the light cruiser *Jintsu* only a few miles away, in the Yangtze estuary. It was the afternoon of August 22, and the 23-year-old officer of the Imperial Japanese Army knew that very soon he would be part of one of the largest amphibious operations ever attempted. His own 3rd Division would land six miles north of Shanghai, and the 11th Division would get ashore a dozen miles further up the Yangtze. Neither division would be of full strength initially. The advance part of the 3rd Division numbered 3,500 men, while the 11th Division, which was short of the regiment-sized Amaya Detachment posted to northeast China,[107] would land 4,000 men.[108] If the operation succeeded, it would boost the Shanghai garrison by thousands of battle-ready soldiers and might tilt the balance in Japan's favor.[109]

For Asano, the days since the 3rd Division had received orders to depart for Shanghai had passed in a confused and action-filled haze. When they had marched out of their barracks in the city of Nagoya in southern Japan a little more than a week earlier, cheering and flag-waving crowds of civilians had seen them off. Then there had been long days of waiting inside Nagoya harbor, until dawn on August 20, when the division had suddenly embarked on several large steamers and sailed off. They soon found themselves part of a task force headed for China. It was led by *Nachi* and *Ashigara*, heavy cruisers that had been the most powerful of their class when they were built a decade earlier and were still impressive vessels. Asano had felt his chest swell with pride as he watched the cruisers' immense steel hulls plow through the violent waves.

Late at night on August 21, the task force had reached the Yangtze River and the Saddle Islands off the river estuary. The soldiers had to be moved onto smaller vessels that could navigate the shallow waters of the Huangpu River. Asano and his unit transferred to the *Jintsu*, using gangways extended between the vessels. They had practiced this move many times before, and it was easy enough to do in the still waters of a harbor, but in the violent seas off China they had to take care that the ships did not collide against each other. Dozens of sailors were standing with long bamboo poles pushing the two hulls away from each other. Once aboard the *Jintsu*, Asano and his comrades discovered few creature comforts, and they had a hard time resting in the swelling heat of the Chinese summer. They had to find any spot they could on the vessel that offered some draft and get as much sleep as possible.

Asano and thousands of other soldiers were waiting almost within sight of the China coast, and still they went undetected. The Chinese commanders had neglected aerial reconnaissance over the Yangtze, and none of them had any idea about this large force waiting to strike. The intelligence failure was all the more astonishing because there had been speculation aplenty. It was widely assumed that if Japan were to send relief to the beleaguered marines in Shanghai, it would land somewhere outside the city, possibly on the right bank of the Yangtze River. "From these points threats can be developed to Chinese (lines of command) along the Shanghai-Nanjing and Shanghai-Hangzhou railways," reasoned an anonymous British analyst in a weekly intelligence summary on the situation in the Far East.[110]

A landing on the Yangtze, north of Shanghai would also set the stage for a deep thrust south, encircling the Chinese troops inside the city. This was a classic Japanese tactic. The military leaders of Japan were ardent disciples of German strategic thinker Alfred von Schlieffen, who had advocated encirclement as the ideal military operation. Schlieffen had based this on his study of the battle of Cannae in 216 B.C., when the Carthaginian general Hannibal had annihilated a superior Roman army using a much-admired pincer movement. It allowed victory despite numerical inferiority, and nothing could be of greater appeal to Japan, an island nation with a limited population. As a result, flanking movements, as described by Schlieffen, had become fundamental doctrine in Japan and had found their way into all army manuals and directions.[111]

Even for those who had not studied Japanese doctrine, an attack north of Shanghai was not a far-fetched proposition at all. It was exactly what the Japanese had done in early 1932 to eventually gain the upper hand in the first battle of Shanghai. Indeed, the fortress of Baoshan still carried the scars of that small war. Even the press corps suspected a repetition of this action. On the afternoon of August 22, a correspondent visiting the Japanese marine headquarters in Hongkou asked the captain guiding them around if there was any truth to rumors that Japan was in the process of landing troops on the Yangtze riverbank, with the aim of carrying out an encircling operation similar to the one five years earlier. The captain replied this was very unlikely. "We prefer to develop new plans," he said.[112] The exact opposite was true, as the next few hours would show.

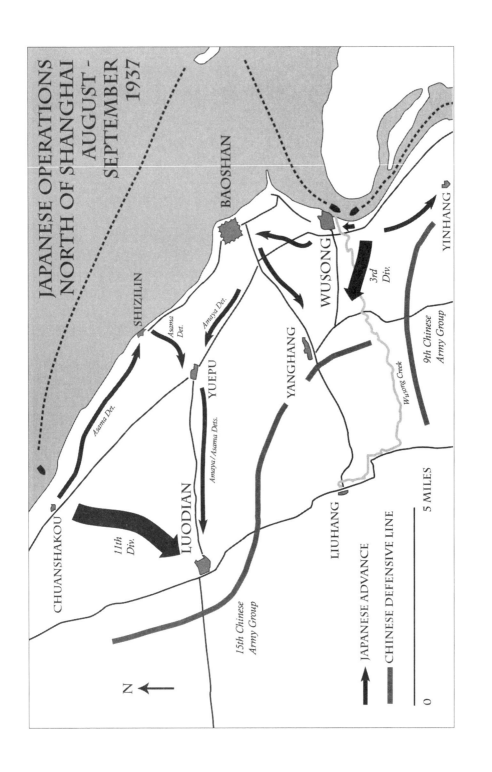

JAPANESE OPERATIONS
NORTH OF SHANGHAI
AUGUST –
SEPTEMBER
1937

BAOSHAN

SHIZILIN

Asama Det.

Asama Det.

Amaya Det.

YUEPU

Amaya/Asama Dets.

LUODIAN

11th Div.

CHUANSHAKOU

YANGHANG

WUSONG

Wusong Creek

3rd Div.

9th Chinese
Army Group

YINHANG

LIUHANG

15th Chinese
Army Group

N

JAPANESE ADVANCE

CHINESE DEFENSIVE LINE

0   5 MILES

CHAPTER

4

....

"Banzai! Banzai! Banzai!"
AUGUST 23–SEPTEMBER 10

AS HE APPROACHED THE LIGHT CRUISER *YURA*, MATSUI IWANE SAW how its gray hull reflected the orange flares on the riverbank as shell after shell tore holes in the velvet curtain that the night had thrown over the Huangpu. The thunder produced by the naval artillery pounding the Chinese positions drowned out all other noises, and it appeared as if the Japanese general's dinghy was moving across the water without the slightest sound. It was 2:00 a.m. on August 23, and the first soldiers were scheduled to jump off their landing barges and wade ashore in just one hour. Only time would tell if the men, many of them in early middle age torn from cozy civilian lives just weeks earlier, still had the fight in them from when they were younger.[1]

The dinghy slowed down and came to a bobbing rest alongside the *Yura*. As Matsui ascended to the cruiser's deck, Rear Admiral Nagumo Chuichi,[2] commander of the 8th Cruiser Division, stood ready to receive him. Nagumo was in charge of the imminent landing, but even though he had his hands full, it was no surprise that he would take time out to personally welcome Matsui on board his flagship. One was an army man and the other a sailor, and they should have been separated by the traditional rivalries between the two services, but they were in fact old acquaintances. Both had been active in the Greater Asia Society. Matsui considered himself lucky that he was able to work with a man like Nagumo at such a critical juncture.

Matsui climbed the ladder to the conning tower. From there he would get a much better view of the action as it unfolded. A dense roar rolled across the river from the town of Wusong, where explosions followed each other in rapid succession. This was where the 3rd Division was to land. From further afield came the fainter sound of the shelling of Chuanshakou, a town on the bank of the Yangtze that had been picked as the 11th Division's landing site. The naval gunners had been at it since shortly after midnight. The previous day, many of the Japanese vessels had sailed as far south as Hangzhou Bay to harass the Chinese troops and force them to spread their attention thinly along the entire coast. However, with so little time left before the landing, there was no point in pretending any longer that it was going to take place anywhere else.

It was less than 48 hours since the decision had been made to launch two amphibious assaults near Shanghai, instead of just one. Matsui had initially favored a plan to land both divisions at Chuanshakou. From there, they would, in one sweeping move, cut through thinly defended countryside far to the west of Shanghai, trapping tens of thousands of Chinese soldiers in and around the city. The Third Fleet had a different and bolder plan, calling for the 11th Infantry Division to stick to the landing at Chuanshakou, but placing the 3rd Infantry Division in a much tougher spot, at Wusong far closer to the massive Chinese troop concentrations at Shanghai. The intention was to apply pressure to both the front and the rear of the Chinese forces. The plan might just work but it could also come to an immensely costly conclusion if the operation at Wusong ran into determined Chinese resistance. The naval officers who had devised the plan were aware of how risky it was, and to sugar the pill and make it easier for their army counterparts to swallow, they offered to put more than 500 elite marines at their disposal.

The discussion for and against the two plans had raged throughout much of the day on August 21, and the army and the navy had seemed incapable of reaching an agreement. In the end, Matsui had taken the decision for them. He was a military man who had spent almost his entire life in uniform, but he also had keen political instincts. He knew it was important to maintain good relations with the naval commanders, and besides, their more aggressive plan could mean speedier relief for the Japanese citizens trapped in Shanghai. Therefore, in the end the navy had carried the day.

Matsui had met with the two divisional commanders on the morning of August 22. He liked them both. Fujita Susumu, commander of the 3rd Division, impressed him with his stoic attitude. The 11th Division's Yamamuro Monetake, on the other hand, was determination personified. He was going to put up a good fight. Still, Matsui did not want them to be rash. The navy's plan, he had explained, would not be easy to implement. Caution was of paramount importance. "Watch out for Chinese soldiers disguised as civilians, and also keep an eye on the mood of Shanghai's population," he had admonished the two. "Soldiers and officers must constantly stay alert to the situation around them. You have to be careful with the water and farm products you requisition. Make sure they are not poisoned by the Chinese."[3]

The day before the landing had been busy. The two divisions had arrived at the Saddle Islands, the small archipelago off the Yangtze estuary, aboard troop transports and had transferred to smaller vessels. Meanwhile, ships of the Third Fleet had sailed up and down the Yangtze and the Huangpu, enjoying a nearly unobstructed view of the landing zones. Summer rains had caused the two rivers to swell, and in many places the water level was above the surrounding countryside, which was protected by high embankments. The Japanese had been able to see large stretches of verdant rice fields, with small canals and creeks running through them in intricate patterns. There were also clusters of farm buildings, some surrounded by solid walls. It was terrain ideally suited for defense.

Matsui had moved from one warship to the next throughout the day. His restless energy had disguised the fact that regardless of what he did now, success or failure was no longer in his hands. However, he could take comfort in the knowledge that he was no stranger to the units he was commanding. When he had been a young second lieutenant nearly 40 years earlier, his first assignment had been in the 6th Regiment, now part of the 3rd Division. Less than a decade earlier, he had been in command of the 11th Division for 28 months. It was as if everything was coming together for Matsui on this warm August night.

Shortly after midnight on August 23, the marines who were to form the bulk of the first attack wave at Wusong arrived in a convoy of steamers from Shanghai. They were a welcome sight as they would spare the 3rd Division from being the first to step ashore. They hastily boarded their landing craft, small vessels especially developed for operations such as this. As the naval artillery barrage reached a crescendo, the boats moved across the waveless water.

With minutes to go before the landing, the ships in the river turned on their searchlights in order to blind the defenders, bathing the riverbank in a ghostly blue. The lights outlined a semicircle around the landing zone and showed the naval artillery where to direct its shelling. Whenever a Chinese machine gun fired, it immediately attracted the attention of the Japanese gunners and was silenced. Trench mortars onshore were aimed at the approaching invaders, but all rounds hit the water with a plop, causing no damage.[4]

At 3:00 a.m., the first landing craft reached the bank. It dropped anchor, the ramp splashed down, and the marines waded ashore. They climbed the dike, which was 15 feet high in some places, and surveyed the terrain in front of them. Suddenly, a burst of machine gun fire ripped through the night, cutting down several of the marines. It was from a Chinese position a mere 50 yards away. The marines attacked with fixed bayonets. As they rushed across the short stretch of open field, they heard an explosion. Someone had stepped on a landmine. More explosions followed. But there was no turning back. They swarmed over the Chinese trench and engaged in a brief hand-to-hand struggle. After a few seconds the position was theirs.[5]

Further ahead were yet more Chinese defenders, but the marines had gained momentum and quickly pushed them back. As the Japanese had hoped, and intelligence had suggested, the soldiers put in charge of guarding that strip of riverbank were poorly performing paramilitary troops. The path was opened to their immediate objective, a military road running parallel with the Huangpu. As the marines set up positions, the 3rd Division disembarked at the water's edge. By 8:00 a.m., the divisional command stepped ashore as the last unit to arrive. Naval pilots were bombing and strafing roads further inland to delay enemy reinforcements. The landing had been a complete success.

The news that Matsui received from the 11th Division was also good.

It had been scheduled to start landing at 2:00 a.m., but moving onto the smaller landing craft had taken longer than expected, and the first soldier from the division did not step ashore at a berth north of Chuanshakou until 3:50 a.m. Even so, as the soldiers moved towards the outskirts of the town, they had discovered only weak enemy resistance. Chuanshakou had been held by a single Chinese company. By 7:00 a.m. most of the first wave had disembarked.[6]

Matsui was pleased. Everything had gone according to plan. Actually, it had gone better than he had allowed himself to expect. Casualties in the two divisions amounted to little more than 40. Matsui credited the spirit of his soldiers. He also quietly thanked the Heavens, which had proven unusually cooperative; it had turned out to be a nearly cloudless morning, making it easy for him to take advantage of his superiority in the air. Once it was clear that the operation had been a success, Matsui called his staff together. This was a cause for celebration. They lifted their glasses of rice wine and shouted a toast for the emperor: "Banzai! Banzai! Banzai!"

———————

Zhang Zhizhong received the phone call at 5:30 a.m. at a small village near Nanxiang, where he had recently moved his headquarters. At the other end was Liu Heding, commander of the 56th Infantry Division, which was in charge of the defenses of the Yangtze riverbank north of Shanghai. Liu informed Zhang that an enemy force of unknown size had landed in the vicinity of Chuanshakou. No other information was available at the time, as heavy bombardment had cut off all phone lines to the landing area. However, Zhang knew more than enough already. It was clear that a new front was opening up. His job had suddenly become immensely more complicated.

As most communications were down, Zhang concluded there was not much that he could do in Nanxiang and so he decided to go to the 87th Infantry Division's command post in Jiangwan, a town north of Shanghai. It was closer to the landing area, and he was likely to get a better idea there of what exactly was happening. He set out in his staff car, but did not get very far. It was a bright summer morning, and Japanese planes filled the sky. His vehicle attracted their constant attention, and his driver was repeatedly forced to take cover. Zhang realized he was getting nowhere and decided to leave the car behind and continue on foot. He soon encountered a private on a bicycle. The soldier got off to salute, and then asked with a snide expression in his face: "What's that? Does the commander have to walk now?" Zhang Zhizhong did not even bother to reply. He snatched the bicycle out of the surprised soldier's hands, jumped on it and steered towards the frontline.[7]

By the time he arrived, it was almost 9:00 a.m. Only then was he informed that the Japanese had landed not just at Chuanshakou, but also at Wusong. The situation was even more critical than he had thought. Wusong was closer, and to put out that particular fire, he immediately dispatched half the 87th Infantry Division and a regiment from the Training Brigade, an elite unit that had just arrived from Nanjing. As for the area around Chuanshakou, it was evident that the 56th Infantry Division alone would not be able to cover the back of the Chinese forces fighting in Shanghai. Therefore, Zhang Zhizhong put the 98th Infantry Division in charge of the defense of most of the Yangtze riverbank that was under threat.[8] Meanwhile, he also sent marching orders to the 11th Division, which had recently arrived in the Shanghai area with Deputy War Minister Chen Cheng. It was to move towards Luodian, a town a few miles from the landing zone at Chuanshakou. The division's commander tried to object. "The moment we raise our heads, we're getting bombed. How are we going to get there?" Zhang Zhizhong insisted. "After all," he said, "I myself made it all the way from Nanxiang to Jiangwan."[9]

The Japanese got there faster. While the main landing force was still fighting for control of the town of Chuanshakou, it dispatched a small unit of a few hundred men down the road to Luodian. The march under a blazing August sun was wearing on the reservists, and once they had arrived in the town and encountered almost no resistance they immediately set up camp, doing little to prepare defenses. That made them easy targets. Advance units of China's 11th Infantry Division arrived south of Luodian in the afternoon and even though it was somewhat shaken by air raids along the way, it decided to attack immediately. It was a short fight. Within an hour the Japanese had been repelled.[10] A map found on a dead Japanese officer had Luodian penciled in. This showed to the Chinese, if they had ever been in doubt, that the town was a major objective.[11]

The Japanese had good reasons for seeking to capture Luodian, just as the Chinese had excellent reasons to try to keep it. The German advisor Falkenhausen insisted that given the overall strategic situation in the Shanghai area as of late August, the town was the key to control of the region. Possession of Luodian would mean control of part of the road south to the town of Dachang and, a little further along the same road, Shanghai proper. Luodian also straddled the road to Jiading, a major town five miles to the west, which in turn was the gateway to the city of Nanxiang, close to the strategically vital railway line connecting Nanjing and Shanghai. "Luodian is the most crucial strategic point at the moment," Falkenhausen wrote in a confidential report.[12]

As if to confirm Luodian's importance, the Japanese reacted to the setback they suffered at the hands of the Chinese 11th Division by hastily organizing a massive counterattack. After securing their right flank against a possible Chinese assault from the north, they sent part of their main force towards the town. They staged a three-pronged attack, with several hundred soldiers in each column. The infantrymen were accompanied by tanks and mountain guns. The Chinese quickly realized that if they faced the assault head-on, they would not stand a chance against the better-equipped Japanese.

Instead, the Chinese defenders set up positions along the roads leading to the town, launching small-scale ambushes to harass the Japanese as they advanced. This slowed down the attack, but did not stop it, and the Japanese were able to enter Luodian for a second time that day. The Chinese reacted quickly, concentrating all available troops inside the town in an effort to intercept the Japanese. Bloody street fighting ensued and lasted well after sunset. It was the type of close combat in which the Chinese were at least the equals of the Japanese, if not their superiors. Eventually, the Japanese columns had to withdraw, leaving behind scores of dead and three burning tanks. Long after dark, shots could be heard in the flat countryside around Luodian as Chinese troops pursued the retreating enemy.[13]

August 23 was Hu Guobing's birthday, but that was the last thing on his mind. It was still early morning when his regiment was ordered to pack up and get ready to move out. The Japanese enemy had landed at Wusong, less than five miles north of the regiment's bivouac near the town of Jiangwan just outside Shanghai, and must be beaten back. War had come quickly to Hu. It was less than a week since he had been in Nanjing, guarding the capital, but not really exposing himself to any danger other than the occasional Japanese air raid. Then suddenly, four days earlier, his regiment had been ordered to board the train for Shanghai.[14]

The first hours of the nearly 200-mile ride from Nanjing to Shanghai had gone fast enough. The troops had been protected by the darkness, and they had not had to worry about air attacks. Once day broke, the ride had become bumpy. Every time a Japanese plane was spotted over the horizon, the train had stopped. It had been 4:00 p.m. by the time they arrived 30 miles west of Shanghai. From there, the Japanese mastery of the air made it inadvisable to go on by train, and the regiment was ordered to march through the night to cover the last distance to Jiangwan. When they reached their destination on the morning of August 21, they dug in and began to wait.[15]

Hu Guobing was a member of the Chinese Army's self-conscious elite. At 23, he was a junior officer in the Training Brigade, a unit set up two years earlier at the urging of Hans von Seeckt, the chief German advisor who had had a defining influence on the formation of the new Chinese Army earlier in the decade. Seeckt had wanted the brigade to function like the *Lehr* or "training" units of the German *Reichswehr*. It was meant to form a nucleus of experienced officers who were to act as instructors of other new units, while also allowing officers from elsewhere in the army to circulate through and acquaint themselves with the most recent developments in tactics and technology.[16] The Training Brigade was the core of China's modernized army, which was to eventually have reached 60 divisions. However, war had intervened, and the brigade had been thrown into battle where it was expected to perform as in peacetime: as an example to others.

Taking pride in doing everything by the rules, Hu Guobing's regiment set off in perfect marching order through the ripening rice fields. A platoon headed by a young lieutenant formed the vanguard, which moved forward at a brisk pace in neat rows, as if on the parade ground. There was nothing discreet about this textbook formation, and Japanese aircraft circling overhead spotted it almost immediately. A shell whistled across the sky and exploded in the middle of the platoon in front, sending tons of moist soil into the air. It left no recognizable piece of the young lieutenant. A squad commander was ripped in half and died instantly. Two soldiers lost legs. Wisely, the regimental commander ordered the platoons to disperse and make their way to the objective individually.

As they came within rifle range of the Japanese line near Wusong, the platoons dispersed further, splitting into squads. Soon the crack and rattle of small arms could be heard all along the regiment's front. Battalion commander Qin Shiquan, a graduate of the Central Military Academy, led two companies towards the enemy positions, taking care not to be seen. When they were close enough, he ordered his bugler to sound the charge. He then raised his Mauser pistol, turned around to face his men and shouted, "Attack! Attack!" The sudden noise caused his position to be fatally exposed. Unseen Japanese observers hiding nearby sent his coordinates to warships offshore. Within minutes shells started raining down on the unit with uncanny precision.[17]

As the Japanese sent a storm of steel over the Chinese formation, all order disintegrated. Soon it was every unit for itself. Hu Guobing spent most of the day evading Japanese aircraft, which circled over the battlefield waiting for targets to reveal themselves. "It seemed as if the enemy could see everything. It was important not to act rashly. There was no other choice really but to take cover in a hole or behind a ridge," he said.[18] The shooting went on throughout the afternoon and did not die down until after the approach of darkness. Only then could the soldiers start breathing more freely, take a few bites of their field rations and relieve their parched throats with a sip from their water canteens. At the same time, they took advantage of the freedom of movement the night offered and rushed to improve their positions. They knew that once dawn broke, it would be too late, and a shallow trench or poor camouflage could mean death.[19]

Hu shared his trench with a young student. They had only known each other for a few hours but they had struck up a fledgling friendship. When darkness gave way to day on August 24, the tense atmosphere returned. Suddenly, Japanese shells started pelting their position. Pressing against the bottom of the trench, Hu was absorbed by one thought, and one thought only—to stay alive. Then it occurred to him that the student next to him had never been in a battle before and that this must be his first artillery barrage. He turned around, intending to say a few comforting words. What he saw was the young man lying prone on the damp soil, eyes closed peacefully as if asleep. Blood was streaming from a gaping injury in his forehead, covering his face in red. He was dead.[20]

For Lieutenant Liu Yongcheng of the Training Brigade, the first two days of battle with the Japanese were not what he had expected. It was a deadly game of hide-and-seek with an invisible enemy who never showed his face, but manifested himself in a sudden hail of bullets or a series of shells which came out of nowhere. Late on August 23, he was leading his men through a small cluster of bombed-out peasant huts near Wusong, when he stumbled across a group of injured Chinese soldiers. Liu did not recognize their faces, but obviously they were the only ones left from their unit. They could not be evacuated, since the route back to the main Chinese line was across wide expanses of open countryside, with no features to offer any protection against the deadly fire of the naval artillery. Liu did not linger long near the injured soldiers but moved on, without a word. He had a job to do.[21]

Later that day Liu was crouching behind a ridge separating two rice fields. He had sent out scouts twice, and they had not returned. He decided to look for himself. He attempted to roll over the top of the ridge, but the moment his silhouette showed, two bullets hit his right leg. He slid back, bleeding profusely from the injuries. One of his squad commanders, a veteran of the 1932 battle, helped him dress the wounds and used the opportunity to broach the tactical situation. He pointed out that his own platoon and the two neighboring platoons had suffered severe losses. "Let's not keep attacking," the squad commander argued. "The enemy knows exactly where we are. But we shouldn't retreat either. Retreating is even more dangerous. Let's just stay here and hold the position behind the ridge." Liu listened in silence. He knew the squad leader was an old hand, and he respected his views. They stayed behind the ridge for the rest of the day.[22]

The following morning, Japanese scouts spotted Liu's position behind the ridge and started raining down rifle grenades. Liu was injured once more, this time in the back. One of his soldiers grabbed a first-aid kit intending to bandage his wound. When he turned Liu around, a bullet hit the wounded officer's shoulder. Bleeding from multiple injuries, Liu was as helpless as the incapacitated soldiers he had seen near the peasant huts the day before. However, when the company commander was informed of Liu's plight, he sent a team of stretcher bearers to evacuate him back to the divisional field hospital. Ahead lay months of recovery, but he was among the lucky ones. Out of 44 officers and soldiers in the platoon that had gone into battle the day before, only 16 remained fit to fight.[23]

Putting Zhang Zhizhong and Feng Yuxiang, the Christian General, in charge of the defense of Shanghai had been Chiang Kai-shek's own decision, in his capacity of chairman of the National Military Council. A week into the battle, he had even consolidated Feng Yuxiang's authority by transforming the Shanghai area into the Third War Zone and putting him in command. Now he was begining to have regrets. In a telephone conversation with Feng Yuxiang shortly after the Japanese landings, Chiang Kai-shek reiterated the need to keep an eye on the younger frontline commanders. "Don't hesitate to give them advice," he said. Feng replied that he would not hold back. Then he went on to tell an anecdote about the Japanese General Nogi Maresuke, who during the Russo-Japanese War of 1904 and 1905 had allegedly left all major decisions to his chief of staff. "The frontline commanders have courage and a belligerent spirit. Their job is to take orders and fight. Mine is to sit behind, like Nogi, write a few poems, and just wait to die." Chiang Kai-shek was insistent: "No matter what, don't be shy. Share some advice with them." "Of course," Feng replied, "if I see something wrong, I'll point it out. I won't hesitate. Don't worry." This was hardly sufficient to reassure Chiang.[24]

Zhang Zhizhong, the scholarly commander of the left wing, was a source of even greater concern to Chiang. All his talk about fighting the Japanese seemed to have been mostly empty rhetoric. Zhang had not shown sufficient will to push through with the attacks against the small Japanese forces in the city at a time when they could have decided the battle. With Japanese reinforcements firmly in place on two locations in the greater Shanghai area, it was too late to seek a quick defeat of the enemy. With little progress on the ground, Zhang added insult to injury by seeming to spend a disproportionate amount of time making grandiose statements to the newspapers. Chiang Kai-shek was frustrated. It was a frustration he shared with his German advisors, who agreed Zhang did not possess the necessary "toughness" in the face of Japanese resistance.

The dispatch of Deputy War Minister Chen Cheng to the front was a first indication, emerging even before the Japanese landings, that Chiang was preparing to replace Zhang Zhizhong. While Zhang had proved to be a weaker leader than expected, Chen Cheng was more a man to Chiang's liking, who advised an all-out battle to challenge the Japanese at Shanghai and divert Japan's attention away from the north.[25] Further confirmation that Chen Cheng was gaining favor followed after the Japanese landings when he was put in charge of the 15th Army Group, which had been hastily formed from seven divisions scattered over a large area west of Chuanshakou.[26] Given its position on the left wing of the Chinese Shanghai Army, the 15th Army Group arguably fell within Zhang Zhizhong's area of responsibility. However, in a humiliating twist, Zhang was not even informed about Chen Cheng's appointment, and only learned about it indirectly from other field commanders.

Fearing that he was being sidelined, Zhang Zhizhong rushed to the Third War Zone headquarters in Suzhou to get a sense of the political situation by talking to the commanders there. While in Suzhou, he also managed to talk on the phone with Chiang Kai-shek in Nanjing and immediately understood how much his standing had declined. Chiang started off by criticizing him for turning up so far behind the frontline. "What are you doing in Suzhou? What are you doing in Suzhou?" Chiang repeated, showing no inclination for dialogue. "Mr Chairman," Zhang replied, "I'm merely back in Suzhou to discuss important strategic issues. Otherwise, I'm constantly at the frontline." Feeling unfairly targeted, Zhang added: "What's the matter with you?" Chiang Kai-shek was incensed at the disrespectful retort. "What's the matter with me?" he yelled. "You ask me what's the matter with me?" His voice transformed to a hoarse shriek, Chiang Kai-shek hung up.[27] At this point, Zhang Zhizhong must have been in little doubt that his days as the chief field commander were numbered.

An undertone of desperation was beginning to spread among the Chinese commanders. The Japanese landings had achieved the immediate objective of relieving the pressure on the small marine forces holed up in Shanghai. The Chinese had been forced to halt their attacks on Hongkou and Yangshupu. Instead they now had to carefully consider where to allocate their resources among various fronts. If the Japanese landing party grew large enough, as was likely, they faced the very real possibility that they could become the object of a Japanese pincer movement. Essentially, within a few days, the Chinese forces had moved from the offensive to the defensive.

It was against this backdrop that Chen Cheng, newly appointed head of the 15th Army Group, arrived in Suzhou on August 24. His presence was intended to help stiffen the resistance, but he was also to acquaint himself with local conditions as he was expected to play a greater role at the front shortly.[28] Chen Cheng's self-assured behavior, and his readiness to overrule the local commander, signaled that real authority already rested with him. He agreed with Zhang Zhizhong's plans from the day before to counter the landings, but considered them insufficient given the threat posed by the fresh Japanese troops. He ordered that more soldiers be moved from Shanghai proper to the landing zones.[29]

Zhang Zhizhong meekly agreed. In fact, he left the other officers assembled in Suzhou, including the Germans, with the impression that he was willing to give up the entire Shanghai front.[30] Just a few days before, he had impressed foreign reporters with his cold-blooded behavior in the middle of a Japanese air attack,[31] but now he came across as downright timid. After ten days of almost no sleep, he seemed to be about to crack. With this kind of leadership in the face of setbacks at the front, it was no surprise that a dangerous defeatist mood was spreading among the generals in Suzhou. To counter this, Falkenhausen proposed a plan that could rekindle the enthusiasm for the offensive among the Chinese. During a long meeting on the night between August 24 and 25, the German general suggested rallying all forces sent to the Luodian area for an attack from all sides against the Japanese landing force. Demonstrating the German predilection for a decisive blow, he wanted to throw the invaders right back into the Yangtze. The assembled officers agreed.[32]

Even so, as day dawned, the optimism that had animated the nightly staff meeting gradually evaporated. It was now 48 hours since the landings, and the Japanese Army had strengthened its foothold at Chuanshakou, rapidly approaching a critical mass that would make it impossible to dislodge it again. Tanks and artillery were lined up on the riverbank, and engineers were building a pier to facilitate unloading men and materiel at an even faster rate. Already they were in possession of a bridgehead that meas-ured 10 miles in length, with a depth of five miles, and they had started constructing a road reaching inland, as an obvious preparation for a major offensive.[33]

In a secret report to Chiang Kai-shek, Falkenhausen described the dif-ficult situation as the Japanese consolidated their material advantage. "It should be noticed that the enemy's army and navy act in close coordination. Even though his land-based artillery is still weak, this is compensated for by strong naval artillery and ship-based aircraft," the German general wrote. He added that airfields on Chongming Island helped underpin Japan's now "complete air superiority" in the area, concluding: "As a result, the main operations on our side should be carried out after dark."[34] The German offi-cer's words marked both a piece of advice and a statement of established fact. From late August, most Chinese movement took place after sunset. Only then could Chinese and Japanese infantry meet on somewhat even terms, without the crushing advantage that air support gave the latter. Night turned out to be the great equalizer in the uneven battle over Shanghai.

In the daytime, the tirelessly active Japanese seemed to be everywhere. They sent rubber boats up small rivers to scout and harass. Their observa-tion balloons were hanging over the horizon, to keep a watchful eye on the Chinese and immediately scramble aircraft when they detected any move-ment.[35] They combined their technological mastery with bravery approach-ing the suicidal. When in danger of being taken prisoner, the Japanese often preferred death. After one pitched battle in the area near Luodian, one of the dead retrieved by the Chinese was a sergeant major who had committed hara-kiri, while a seriously injured private was found to have tried to slit his own throat with his razor-sharp bayonet.[36]

Luodian remained the immediate target of nearly all the Japanese forces in the area, and they faced the same Chinese units that had pushed them out on August 23. The Chinese were firmly entrenched in and around the town, but they were too few to consider offensive operations against the Japanese at Chuanshakou. Instead, they had to do their best to improve their defenses. However, while they were waiting for the Japanese to resume the assault, they were subject to massive and sustained bombardment.[37] Among the Chinese officers, there was a sense of crisis and a very real feel-ing that the line could buckle any time. From their perspective, the Japanese were on a roll. From the Japanese invaders' own perspective, it looked very different.[38]

———————

Gu Qingzhen, a 12-year-old Chinese boy, had nowhere to run when the Japanese arrived. Many inhabitants in the hamlet of Hanjiazhai, near Luodian, had fled ahead of the invasion force, but his parents had been among the ones who had stayed behind to look after their homes. As a patrol of eight infantrymen speaking their strange, toneless language entered the village, they realized they had made a mistake. The small Gu family was among a group of 13 hiding in a building, but they were detected. The Japanese entered with fixed bayonets, and the slaughter began.

Gu was squeezing with his parents into a narrow space behind a stove. It was no use. A soldier found them and stabbed his mother through her heart. Another thrust, and his father was dead. Gu himself escaped detection, but the bayonet that had killed his parents scraped his head and went through his right shoulder. He lost consciousness. When he came to, he could hear the Japanese soldiers talk loudly outside. His head, neck and shoulders were sticky with blood, his own and that of his parents. Gu remained hidden under the bodies of his parents until the following dawn, when was sure the Japanese had disappeared. He walked through countryside littered with murdered civilians until he met the only person left alive from his village, an old women who took him to be reunited with a relative of his.[39]

What Gu had been forced to experience was a Japanese brand of requisitioning-cum-murder. The soldiers of the 11th Japanese Division were running out of supplies and had started to do what armies have done since ancient times—live off the land. While the initial landing had gone exactly according to plan, on the second day it was becoming evident that getting provisions on shore was proceeding at a much slower pace than expected. Soldiers and their equipment were also not being unloaded as fast as scheduled. By noon on August 24, only about 80 percent of the second wave had managed to disembark from their boats. This was a far cry from the impressive invasion force that the Chinese officers believed to be forming on the bank of the Yangtze.

The sluggish movement off the ships was partly because of the natural features of the landing site. The Yangtze was very shallow near its southern bank, and much of the unloading could only take place during a short window of opportunity just before dawn, when the water level was at its highest. The navy had lent a few sailors to help with the onerous task of disembarking the troops. It was not enough. The lack of provisions caused the offensive towards Luodian to slow down. "It's a terrible pity," Matsui wrote in his diary. "The main reason is that insufficient men and materiel have been prepared for landing and provisioning."[40]

Japanese casualties were gradually increasing as the Chinese reinforcements that had been sent to the Luodian area started making a difference. Two days after the landings, the number of killed and injured from the 11th Division had reached more than 400, and from then on kept rising. Among those who had lost their lives was one of the division's senior staff officers. He was killed when he stepped off his landing craft at Chuan-shakou, by a Chinese airplane that had slipped through the Japanese fighter cover. The number of bodies grew so fast that not all could be cremated, the way the Japanese preferred to dispose of their dead, and all privates and junior officers had to be hastily buried instead.[41] For an army claiming to honor its dead soldiers more than those who remained alive, it was a blow to morale.

The 3rd Division faced different challenges in its sector. It was attacked relentlessly on the first day of the landing, and on the second day it had to repel two further major enemy assaults. Also, it was harassed by occasional shelling from Chinese artillery on the Pudong side. However, the biggest danger came from the division's right flank. North of the landing zone was Wusong fortress, which had been guarding the approach to Shanghai since the wars against the British and French imperialists in the mid-19th century. From their safety behind concrete walls, Chinese infantry and artillery continuously aimed at the Japanese as they disembarked from their boats and moved inland. They also targeted small vessels sailing up the Huangpu River with supplies for the division.[42]

As the 3rd Division expanded its bridgehead in the days that followed the landing, the Wusong fortress remained a menace, slowing down the build-up of Japanese forces on the shore. Adding to the Japanese sense of being hemmed in, the village of Yinhang to the south was also under Chinese control. This, combined with the steady increase of Chinese defenders in front of the landing zone, made for a difficult tactical situation. The Japanese casualties, which had initially been considerably lighter than the planners had feared, began to rise. As of August 25, the 3rd Division, or the "Lucky" Division as it was often called, recorded an accumulated total of more than 300 casualties. Two days later, the number had risen to 500, the majority of them killed in action.[43]

The first thing many Japanese soldiers noticed when disembarking at Wusong was the strange stench that filled the air. It was, they would soon find out, the smell from large pyres near the river where the army was burning its dead.[44] As in the 11th Division's sector, it was difficult to process the bodies fast enough. Sergeant Miyoshi Shozo recorded how he arrived at Wusong a few days after the initial landing to discover heaps of unburied Japanese soldiers who had been killed in action. "All the bodies were swollen with putrefaction, due to the decay of the internal organs," he wrote in his memoirs, "and the soft part of the bodies had burst through from the pressure. Even the eyeballs bulged six or seven centimeters out from their faces."[45]

Four days after the landings, both divisions seemed close to being bogged down. What eventually tilted the balance in their favor was the Japanese Navy. In the days immediately before and after the landings, it steadily built up its fleet in the Yangtze and Huangpu Rivers. This added extra artillery and, crucially, it boosted the air power available to the Japanese. On August 26, Japanese planes flew 16 individual sorties over the Chinese positions, on August 27, that number grew to 29 sorties, and on August 28, a total of 68 sorties were flown.[46]

This reinstated momentum into the Japanese attack. On August 28, the 3rd Division was finally able to take the village of Yinhang and extricate itself somewhat from the tactical straightjacket it had experienced so far. On the same day, following intense naval bombardment, the 11th Division stormed Luodian. In the vanguard of the attack was Wachi Takaji, a 44-year-old regimental commander who led his men with his sword drawn, personally killing several of the enemy on the way. The Chinese defenders were pushed out of the town and fled down roads leading inland. By noon, Luodian was in Japanese hands. It was not, however, to be the end of the battle for the village. The Chinese would be back. It was after all a prize that Falkenhausen had said must be kept at all cost.[47]

Guo Rugui was chief of staff of the Chinese Army's 14th Infantry Division, part of the newly formed 15th Army Group, and nominally he was one of the highest-ranking officers in the unit. Yet, he had one problem: He was a recent arrival and knew no one. That was a severe handicap in the Chinese Army, where personal networks always counted for much, and having no close allies could be fatal.[48] Thus, when he tried to propose his plan for retaking Luodian, he faced an uphill struggle. Even though his superiors eventually decided to adopt his plan, those lower down the hierarchy procrastinated. That might be what doomed the attack in the end.[49]

Up until the Japanese landings, the 14th Infantry Division had been involved in guarding the banks of the Yangtze further upriver. That remained the division's primary responsibility, so when the order to march for Luodian arrived, it could only spare two of its regiments, the 79th and 83rd, while the other two stayed on guard duty. Guo Rugui arrived with the troops in Jiading, west of Luodian, on August 29. Learning that Luodian had just fallen, Guo suggested to his divisional commander that no time should be wasted and that they should strike that very night while the Japanese were still not fully settled in their new positions, catching them off balance. The 83rd Regiment was to launch a frontal attack, while the 79th was to march in a long arc around Luodian and attack the enemy from behind.

The division chief agreed, but Guo Rugui still had to persuade the officers who were to carry out the attack. The 79th Regiment's commander made excuses, asking for clear boundary lines to be specified between his regiment and the 83rd. The deputy commander of the division shrugged off the request, arguing boundary lines were completely unnecessary, since the two regiments were not going to attack alongside each other anyway. It was an obvious attempt to delay the operation, or perhaps to have it canceled altogether. It did not work, and the 79th Regiment set out into the night, with its disgruntled commander at the head.

The 83rd Regiment had to cross a bridge over a creek in order to enter the western part of Luodian. The Japanese had placed light and heavy machine guns at the far end of the bridge, and despite several attempts the Chinese regiment was unable to cross, mainly due to their lack of artillery. Meanwhile, the 79th Regiment's commander followed his instruction halfheartedly. Approaching the town from the east, his soldiers encountered a creek. They constructed a floating bridge from pieces of wood requisitioned from farm buildings nearby, but only one of the regiment's three battalions was ordered across, while the other two stayed on the safe side. The soldiers of the lone battalion sent into the town could hear intense shooting where the frontal attack was taking place. Their officers decided against moving forward and instead ordered them to take cover in a bamboo grove on the edge of the town.

The 14th Infantry Division had set up its forward command post in a Daoist temple not far from Luodian. When 15th Army Group commander Chen Cheng arrived he was not happy. "This command post is way too far in front," he said. "The Japanese planes are no joke. By dawn, they'll see you and smash you to pieces. You should pull back at once." The divisional commander saw no other option but to call off the attack. He phoned the 83rd Regiment performing the frontal assault, ordering it to withdraw, but he was unable to get in touch with the 79th. Ignoring pleas from his staff not to abandon the unit, he got into a vehicle with his deputy and rode off, heading for Jiading. After the commanders arrived at Jiading they again called the frontline for news about the regiments. It was bad. The 83rd Regiment had lost 200 men. The 79th Regiment reported two battalions had withdrawn, while the third, the one that had crossed the creek, was still missing.

Only around midday did they hear from the missing third battalion. It had spent the night in the bamboo grove, but by daybreak it had been spotted by the Japanese. A fierce artillery bombardment had commenced, followed by air raids. Finally, machine gun crews had deployed outside the grove and fired into the dense bamboo. Those of the Chinese soldiers who were still able to move had run for the creek, but there they had discovered to their dismay that the floating bridge had started falling apart, planks and boards floating down the stream. With the enemy in hot pursuit, a mad rush for the other side had followed. Some had been cut down by enemy bullets. Others had drowned because they could not swim or because they were dragged down by their equipment. Less than half the battalion had survived.

All Quiet on the Western Front—in the first days after the Japanese had landed at Wusong and Chuanshakou, Liu Jingchi, one of Zhang Zhizhong's top aides, was reminded of the title of the famous novel. After seeing so much bloodshed at the start of the battle, an eerie, almost surreal silence had fallen over downtown Shanghai. The opening up of new fronts north of the city had put the Chinese on the defensive everywhere, and as they had to allocate more troops to the new threats emerging in the countryside, they were no longer able to sustain their offensives inside the urban area.[50]

As the days passed, the fighting picked up, but the tables had been turned. Only the 88th Division, half of the 36th Infantry Division, and an independent brigade remained at the old Shanghai front, while the rest of the Chinese troops were dispatched to face the enemy outside the city.[51] These units now came under severe pressure as they were targeted by repeated Japanese attacks. However, the tactics were surprisingly similar to before. China often had to make up for its inferiority in material terms by relying on its superiority in sheer numbers, and its soldiers' willingness to sacrifice themselves.

Xiong Xinmin, a staff officer with the 36th, witnessed the bloody battle that erupted when a column a Japanese tanks approached the division's positions near the ruins of a university campus. "This means trouble," was all he had time to think before a tall soldier next to him grabbed a cluster of hand grenades and ran straight for the tanks. Seconds afterwards there was a loud explosion, and a dense cloud of smoke spread from under the lead tank. The Chinese soldier had blown himself up in order to stop the attack. It had worked. The other tanks made a U-turn and retreated to their lines.[52]

It was only at this time, after the battle in central Shanghai was already past its first frantic peak, that Zhang Fakui was able to make a difference from the 8th Army Group's positions east of Huangpu River. The fact that his men had played next to no part in the battle up till this point had been criticized vehemently by the German advisors, but in retrospect it is hard to imagine how they could have joined the fight much earlier. During the initial days after the outbreak of hostilities Zhang had spent time inspecting the Pudong side of the river searching for good artillery positions. Then the dreary work of transporting the artillery pieces followed. Mountain guns were cumbersome, but they could be disassembled and carried by small groups of men. Horses were needed to draw field guns. Heavy guns were out of the question because there were no good roads in Pudong. When the Chinese were finally able to fire their artillery, the war in Shanghai was already a week old.[53]

Even after his artillery was in place, Zhang Fakui had to use it sparingly to avoid detection and inevitable air attack. The guns, hidden in bamboo groves, could fire at targets in Hongkou across the river for only ten minutes before having to hastily move to new positions. In practice, this meant they could be fired only once a day, at dusk, since it was easier to transport the guns under the cover of darkness.[54] Secrecy was the artillery's only real defense and, therefore, it had to be maintained aggressively. This was not what happened one day, some time after Zhang's troops had taken up their positions, when one of his battalion commanders invited a journalist to his position. He even had his picture taken, in a heroic pose in front of an artillery piece. The following day the photo was in the local newspaper. Zhang was alerted and immediately ordered the battery to change its positions. He was only just in time. The Japanese also read the newspapers, and their planes bombed the area shortly afterwards. Zhang ordered the arrest of the careless battalion commander.[55]

Among Zhang Fakui's targets were the marine headquarters and the Japanese Consulate across the Huangpu River. The soldiers under his command also carried out mock cross-river attacks against the Japanese. They would board motor boats or sampans and head for the other side, yelling "Charge! Charge!" as artillery shelled the Hongkou riverbank, only to turn back at the last moment. Actual assaults across the river were never seriously considered, as the Japanese defenses remained too formidable.[56]

The main prize, however, was the *Izumo*, and it was one Zhang Fakui pursued with the same zeal as Captain Ahab hunting the white whale. He had no success, as it constantly shifted anchorage. This was noticed by a senior British official in the Shanghai Customs who contacted the Chinese military offering to smuggle a Chinese artillery observer to the Customs building across the Huangpu, closer to the Japanese cruiser. In the following days, the observer, dressed in civilian clothes, reported on the changing positions of the vessel along hastily laid telephone wires.[57] Even this failed to put an end to the old cruiser's string of lucky escapes. All told, the *Izumo* was not hit even once. The big white whale remained afloat.[58]

For some foreigners, the war raging around them was still a source of detached amusement. "Guests at the swank Park Hotel," wrote American correspondent Edgar Snow, "could gaze out through the spatial glass façade of its top-story dining room, while contentedly sipping their demitasse, and check up on the marksmanship of the Japanese batteries."[59] Even so, the central belief—that the war had nothing to do with Shanghai's western residents and would never really affect them—was getting harder to maintain as shells kept falling indiscriminately and killed and maimed everyone unlucky to stand close enough to the blasts, regardless of nationality. "I was terrified by the artillery fire from Zhabei," wrote Liliane Willens, the nine-year-old daughter of the Russian Jewish émigrés, "but nevertheless took the elevator to the roof of our apartment building and saw in the distance dark gray smoke floating skywards."[60]

The shock of "Black Saturday" was still working its way through the community when tragedy again struck in Shanghai. At noon on Monday, August 23, while rumors were circulating around the city about Japanese landings downriver, a shell crashed through the side of Sincere Department Store, an exclusive multi-storey building on Nanjing Road in the city's busiest shopping district. The explosion gutted the lower three floors and hurled shrapnel and debris through the air with such force that the Wing On Department Store across the street was also severely damaged.[61]

It was a scene of carnage that had become drearily familiar. Dead customers were everywhere in Sincere Department Store—huddled in aisles, sprawled across stairs and buried under piles of merchandise. Some had died at the instant they had reached for their purses to pay. One elevator was crowded with people, and not a single one of them was alive. On the second floor, a water main had broken and sent a steady stream of water splashing to the sidewalk, where it mixed with growing pools of blood and perfume from a shattered window display. The stench was unbearable in its sickening intensity.

A Sikh police officer conducting traffic from a post elevated above the street was killed immediately and hung over the side of his booth, his turban still wrapped tightly around his head. A rickshaw puller was also hit and almost pushed into the passenger seat, his open-mouthed expression making him seem as if he were only taking a nap. A Chinese boy was wandering around in a daze, blood spurting from the side of his head where his ear should have been. The shock wave had sent pedestrians flying across the street to the sidewalk outside the Wing On Department Store. There the bodies lay mingled with wrecked toys. A ghostly sheet of white dust was covering the entire spectacle.

Disasters like this far exceeded anything the city's fire and ambulance workers had encountered during peacetime, but since the events on "Black Saturday," they had established new routines with amazing haste, helped also by civic groups. Red Swastika, the local equivalent of the Red Cross, flew its flag over the scene, as its members mingled with Chinese boy scouts with broad-brimmed felt hats to help the injured. The street was cleared and hosed down, and the wrecked shops were boarded up against looters, within just four hours.[62]

Death continued to rain down from the sky. Three days after the bombing of the department store, the British ambassador to China, Sir Hughe Knatchbull-Hugessen, was attacked by a low-flying airplane as he was traveling from Nanjing to Shanghai in a car carrying a large Union Jack on its radiator, with about 50 miles left of the journey. The ambassador was hit in the stomach during the first run of the Japanese aircraft. The occupants of the car got out and hid in a ditch when the plane made another run dropping two bombs, which did no damage apart from showering them with dirt and debris. Once the plane had left, the other passengers swiftly transported the ambassador to a hospital in Shanghai. The following day doctors said his condition was satisfactory.[63]

Japanese officers did not rule out that one of their planes might have been the culprit, but at the same time they were of the view that anyone traveling through a war zone must have known that he was exposing himself to considerable danger. This cavalier attitude manifested itself again only two days later. At 2:00 p.m. on August 28, five Japanese planes attacked the area around the South Railway Station as hundreds of civilians were standing on the platform. They had been waiting for the 1:30 p.m. train which was to have taken them to the safety of the countryside. The train was late, which sealed their fate.[64]

This attack was followed the day after by a similar raid on the North Railway Station. A small group of Japanese seaplanes dropped a total of 12 bombs. Some of them started fires that kept burning until late in the day.[65] In both cases the Japanese justified the attack by claiming that the Chinese Army was using the train stations continuously to pour in more troops. Little more than two weeks after the start of the battle, the bombing of civilians had become a matter of course. Most of it was accidental, but in cases where it was deliberate, it was explained away as the unfortunate, but necessary, byproduct of war.

––––––––––

August 29 was a day of triumph for Chinese diplomacy. Chiang Kai-shek's government announced a non-aggression treaty with the Soviet Union, which had in fact been signed eight days earlier in Nanjing. Non-aggression treaties would later get a bad reputation because of their uselessness when inked by ruthless dictators in the mold of Hitler. In the 1930s, they were comprehensive agreements marking strategic cooperation between two nations. The pact between Nanjing and Moscow prepared the ground politically and diplomatically for Soviet military aid to China, while at the same time ensuring that the Soviet Union would not reach an agreement with Japan as long as hostilities were still going on.[66]

China hoped that the conclusion of the pact was only a beginning, and that it might have "far-reaching and beneficial possibilities," according to the Chinese ambassador to Moscow, Jiang Tingfu, a level-headed diplomat normally known to hold pessimistic views about the likelihood of Soviet aid.[67] Chiang Kai-shek had initially been suspicious of Soviet intentions, writing in his diary on August 1, when diplomats on the two sides were preparing the treaty, that he feared the Kremlin would use the agreement to pressurize Japan into a similar treaty with Moscow.[68] However, once the treaty was signed, skepticism gave way to optimism. Three days after the announcement of the treaty, Chiang predicted in a bullish speech that the Soviet Union would eventually enter the war against Japan.[69]

China had entertained hopes of Soviet help in case of war with Japan since at least late 1936,[70] and in the months leading up to the actual outbreak of hostilities in the summer of 1937, the Soviet ambassador to China, Dmitry Bogomolov, had done everything in his power to keep those hopes alive. "If [China] would undertake to offer armed resistance to Japan," Bogomolov was paraphrased as saying, "it could confidently expect the armed support of the Soviet Union."[71] The Soviet dictator Joseph Stalin had a straightforward reason to want to spur China into a full-blown war with Japan. It would keep Russia's back free while he concentrated on the strategic challenges in a Europe dominated by Hitler. A war with China might bleed the Japanese foe dry, so he would not have to worry about a threat from Asia even in the long term. Exasperated British diplomats tried at least once to alert Chiang Kai-shek to the Soviet ruse, with a warning that the Russians "only have their own interests in mind,"[72] but this did not seriously shake the Chinese leader's belief in Soviet willingness to help.

At a deep cognitive level, there was a reason why Chiang Kai-shek and others around him wanted to believe that not just Soviet aid, but also direct Soviet participation in the hostilities was imminent. This was how they expected a war with Japan to pan out. The Chinese General Staff's War Plan A, drafted in 1937, was based on the premise that a conflict with Japan would soon set off a larger conflict between Japan and either the Soviet Union or the United States. Therefore, the key aim for China was to hold out against the superior Japanese until it could be relieved by the arrival of a much more powerful ally, whether Russian or American.[73] This plan was not as naïve as it might seem, but was based on the calculation that neither Moscow nor Washington would want to see Japanese power grow too strong on the Asian mainland.

Some of Chiang's commanders believed that it was partly in order to hasten outside intervention that the Chinese leader decided to make Shanghai a battlefield. It was true that Shanghai offered tactical advantages that the north Chinese plain did not, an argument that had been decisive in getting Chiang's own generals to accept opening a new front there. However, these advantages would seem to be a small reward considering the risk involved in luring the enemy to occupy China's most prosperous region. Much more crucially perhaps, Shanghai was an international city and a key asset for the world's most powerful economies, who would not allow it to become Japanese territory, or so he believed.[74] According to Li Zongren, one of China's top generals, Chiang expanded the war to Shanghai because the importance of the city might lead to "mediation on the part of the European powers and the United States or even to their armed intervention."[75]

Despite their success in taking Luodian and Yinhang, the Japanese units still faced an uphill struggle. Their hold on the Shanghai region remained extremely tenuous, and was based on control of two isolated pockets north of Shanghai as well as a beleaguered garrison inside the city. Given their numerical inferiority, they were under heavy pressure from the Chinese. The landings at Wusong and Chuanshakou had initially boosted the manpower available in the Shanghai area by fewer than 8,000 troops, and even though reinforcements were gradually arriving, the pace was slow. Matsui Iwane felt a more radical increase in troop levels was needed to bring about a decisive outcome.

At the end of August, he sent a cable to Tokyo arguing that in order to finish the job he would need a total of five divisions. At a minimum, he requested the dispatch of one more division from the homeland along with the release of the 11th Division's Amaya Detachment, the regiment-sized outfit posted in northeast China, so it could be reunited with the division at Chuanshakou. The Japanese imperial staff and navy command responded mostly favorably, agreeing to the redirection of the detachment to Shanghai along with several units of the elite marines.[76]

While he was waiting for reinforcements, Matsui had to solve his problems on the battleground with the resources he had. One week after the landing, the Wusong fort remained a severe problem for the 3rd "Lucky" Japanese Division and the navy, which was charged with supplying the division. The Chinese artillery made anchoring near the landing zone a risky undertaking, and several naval officers who found themselves in the wrong place at the wrong time were blown to pieces. On occasion, the shelling had been so severe that the vessels had to interrupt their work and withdraw to a berth in the middle of the Huangpu, with only part of the supplies unloaded. The 3rd Division had been disappointingly slow in coming up with a plan for taking out the fort, and it seemed not to have enough manpower to carry out the operation on its own.[77]

Instead, Matsui's staff settled on an alternative plan that also let the 11th Division play a role. While the 3rd Division would launch a frontal attack against Wusong, the 11th was to move the Asama Detachment,[78] a regiment-sized unit, southeast along the Yangtze bank and attack Wusong from the other side. On the way, it was to take the fortress at Shizilin, a town on the Yangtze River. Officers on Matsui's staff suggested simply handing over the entire task of taking Wusong to the 11th Division, which seemed overall to be a more efficient fighting force, but the general turned down the idea. Even if it made sense militarily, it would deal too much of a blow to the reputation of the venerable 3rd Division. The 11th Division was to remain in a support role, dispatching only one regiment.[79]

The attack began at 10:00 a.m. on August 31. After intensive naval and air bombardment involving 30 planes, a regiment of the 3rd Division embarked on landing craft, sailed down the Huangpu and made a landing on the riverbank north of Wusong.[80] All through the afternoon until dark, the soldiers fought scattered Chinese units in front of Wusong, in preparation for final entry into the city. At the same time, the 11th Division's Asama Detachment kicked off its part of the offensive, marching down the bank of the Yangtze towards Shizilin.[81]

The Japanese tightened the noose from the morning of the following day, September 1. The 3rd Division's regiment took possession of a hamlet west of Wusong and prepared a push against the town. The Chinese forces defending it put up strong resistance, and it was late in the afternoon before the Japanese were able to make any advance, aided by ship artillery.[82] The attack was costly. Among those killed on the Japanese side was Major Shimosaka Masao, who was held to be one of his country's foremost experts on amphibious warfare.[83] The Asama Detachment had somewhat more success on that day, managing to take the fort at Shizilin in the afternoon.[84]

The Japanese launched their final push against Wusong at dawn on September 2. The fort fell with surprising ease. Transport ships that had been berthed in the Huangpu River, waiting for the guns of Wusong to be wiped out, could now anchor just below the fort. By 10:00 a.m., Matsui spotted the banner of the Rising Sun hoisted over Wusong. "I felt boundless gratification," he wrote in his diary.[85] Half the Chinese regiment holding Wusong had become casualties.[86] This was a significant loss, not just in manpower but also strategically, and the search for a scapegoat soon began. It was found in the form of the 9th Army Group's 61st Infantry Division, which had been assigned to the defense of Wusong, but was said not to be sufficiently prepared for the attack. Chiang Kai-shek dismissed the commander of the division for this mistake.[87]

With the fall of Wusong, the town of Baoshan had become the last major obstacle to continuous Japanese control of the entire riverbank all the way from Chuanshakou to the outskirts of Shanghai. The town's fort was also a major threat to Japanese naval activity, due to its location near the confluence of the Yangtze and the Huangpu. Chiang Kai-shek perfectly understood the value of Baoshan, and he ordered the unit manning the defenses—a battalion of the 98th Infantry Division commanded by 28-year-old Lieutenant Colonel Yao Ziqing—to hold the town at any price. Baoshan had one significant advantage. Like many Chinese towns of a certain age, it was surrounded by a thick ancient city wall that in imperial times had helped defend against invaders and still served that purpose well.

The Japanese also understood that Baoshan favored defense, and that even a small unit might be able to hold out for a prolonged period of time. To avoid what was likely to be considerable bloodshed, the 3rd Division, which had been given the responsibility of taking the town, initially attempted to get the Chinese to abandon it without a fight by dropping leaflets from airplanes seeking to persuade them to surrender. Matsui considered this an exercise in futility that only added to his frustration with what he saw as the 3rd Division's timid command. The stoicism that he had initially admired in the division's commander had turned out to be more akin to lethargy.[88]

September 4 saw no change in the 3rd Division's slow-moving approach towards Baoshan. When the division suggested around mid-afternoon that a planned direct assault on the town should be postponed until the following day, Matsui lost his temper and insisted that the attack be carried out immediately. He also temporarily put an artillery unit that had just disembarked at the division's disposal, so that its guns could assist by punching holes in the thick city wall. Despite this support, Japanese soldiers sent in waves to scale the wall sustained significant losses and were not able to penetrate the defenses by nightfall.[89]

At noon on September 5, Japanese bombers raided Baoshan while naval artillery rained shells indiscriminately over its gray roofs. The land attack began an hour later when Japanese tanks pushed towards the town gates. This time they succeeded in getting through. Chinese commander Yao Ziqing sent two messages to the 98th Infantry Division. One was a request for reinforcements—impossible because Japanese airplanes strafed and bombed any Chinese units attempting to approach—and the other was a pledge to fight to the death. The young lieutenant colonel, whose round glasses gave him the air of an effeminate intellectual, proved to be fully up to the task, which was, essentially, to kill as many Japanese as possible before the inevitable annihilation of his entire battalion, himself included.

The Japanese pushed the Chinese defenders into a shrinking perimeter. By sunset, Yao Ziqing had only 100 soldiers left. The night passed without incident, because the Japanese did not want to fight without support from the air, but they all knew that dawn would bring the end. The sun had just risen over the horizon when the attack resumed. By the time the city was about to fall, Yao Ziqing ordered a soldier to escape to the outside to pass a report on the situation in the town to his superiors. Unseen by the Japanese, the soldier managed to scale a wall and run into the surrounding countryside. He was the only soldier to survive the battle. With him he brought a message from the battalion: "We are determined to stay at our posts and to continue fighting the enemy until each and every one of us is killed."[90]

The fall of Baoshan enabled the 3rd Division to finally move westwards and link up with the 11th Division.[91] This success came at the same time as other good news for the Japanese. On September 6, the Tida Detachment, part of the 3rd Infantry Division, made a landing at the Japanese Golf Club, now renamed Gongda airfield, and secured its use. Then the Second Combined Air Group moved in.[92] It was an important addition to the air base on Chongming, the large island in the Yangtze estuary, that had been in use since early September,[93] as in time, it would help further reinforce Japanese air superiority in the Shanghai area and improve the conditions for close tactical support of the ground units.[94] Also, and even more importantly, Tokyo decided in favor of a major increase in available manpower in the Shanghai area. On September 7, it ordered the dispatch to the city of the 9th, 13th, and 101st Infantry Divisions as well as the Shigeto Detachment, which consisting of units based in the Japanese colony of Taiwan.[95] The same day, 10 Japanese infantry battalions were ordered to move from the northeast of China to the Shanghai area.[96]

The situation looked bleak to the Chinese. Not only were the Chinese frontline units losing the battle, but they were suffering extraordinarily heavy losses in the process. Yao Ziqing's 98th Infantry Division had casualties reaching 4,960 by early September. These included one regimental commander killed and another wounded. Various units of the division received reinforcements up to four times during the entire battle for Shanghai. At the moment the reinforcements arrived, they would be given a weapon and sent straight to the frontline. "Some were injured immediately upon arrival," said Fang Jing, one of the division's two brigade commanders. "When they got to the hospital, they would have no idea about which unit they belonged to."[97]

The series of defeats and setbacks had a palpable impact on morale in the Chinese Army, mainly at the top. While the rank and file showed general willingness to carry on the fight, senior officers continued to demonstrate weakened determination. "All my soldiers have been sacrificed. There's nobody left," Xia Chuzhong, the commander of the 79th Division, announced in a telephone call to Luo Zhuoying, head of the 18th Army, part of the 15th Army Group. Luo Zhuoying replied: "Aren't you a body? Stay where you are and fight."[98]

––––––––––––

Albert Newiger was frustrated. The 48-year-old East Prussian lieutenant colonel had attempted for weeks to get his modern tactical views through to the people he was meant to advise, but to no avail. He was posted up the Yangtze from Shanghai, at a city called Jiangyin, where river obstacles were being prepared. The problem was that the Chinese commander he was supposed to act as assistant for was typically old-school—undeniably brave but nerve-wrackingly stubborn. During a Japanese air raid that had lasted several hours, the Chinese officer had managed to keep his composure, triggering Newiger's grudging admiration. However, all this mattered little when set against the commander's unwillingness to accept any change, especially not change suggested by a foreigner.[99]

The Chinese commander was an example of just one of the things that were wrong with the Chinese officer class, in Newiger's view. A system of advancement based on kinship and personal connections had produced some grotesque results. In one city on the Yangtze River, Newiger had come across a Chinese commander who had studied at the University of Technology in Hanover and was an engineer by profession, but understood virtually nothing about military matters. "I have no idea how he had become a general," Newiger wrote in his memoirs after returning to Germany. "When one encountered cases such as this, it was impossible to bring about any useful cooperation."[100]

Newiger had arrived in China in 1935 along with Falkenhausen. It had become a temporary home for his family. His son was even born in the country. During the first years, he had been a strategy teacher at the Central Military Academy in Nanjing.[101] Many of his students were actually men well advanced in their military careers who had been ordered back to the classroom to learn from the German lecturers. Some were even his seniors in age and grade, but a traditional Chinese reverence for teachers nevertheless meant that he had been able to form personal relationships that would help him do his job during the battle of Shanghai.[102]

In fact, he had benefited from this personal network even before the war broke out. He had been assigned to the Nanjing area and had been in charge of advising the Chinese officers there on the preparation of defensive positions. It turned out that the head of the operations office in the Nanjing command was a former student of his and was instrumental in bringing about an efficient relationship with the Nanjing command. As a result, the German and Chinese officers were able to do a reasonable job, in spite of having only limited time and resources at their disposal.[103]

The Yangtze fortress at Jiangying was a different matter. There, Newiger was up against intense suspicions, and at times even badly concealed hostility. Some Chinese based their enmity on principle. "All along I . . . felt that Germany was a nation based on militarist principles and that it was in collusion with Japan," one of them reminisced later.[104] Others, such as the commander at Jiangyin, seemed to simply dislike the disturbance to their complacent belief that they knew how to do their jobs. Often the Chinese officers tried to disguise their reluctance to cooperate with the foreigners under a thin veil of "Asian politeness and idioms," Newiger wrote in his memoirs. "Others could not even be bothered to do so."[105]

Newiger's fellow advisor Robert Borchardt, a 25-year-old second lieutenant, was also weighed down by frustrations, but for entirely different reasons. He had attended prestigious military academies in Munich and Dresden,[106] and had a perfect pedigree. Two ancestors had fought in the German wars of liberation against Napoleon from 1813 to 1815. Two other relatives had been in the 1870–1871 war against France. Three uncles had fought in the Great War. One of them had been killed in action and another had died from his wounds shortly after the armistice in 1918. The third uncle, Rudolf Borchardt, had been a poet, the most German of professions, and had served in the trenches "with pride as an East Prussian." Borchardt came from a family that was German to the bone, and felt it. However, there was one problem. He was half Jewish.[107]

Robert Borchardt himself had entered the German Army of the pre-Nazi years, the *Reichswehr*, but was discharged in 1934, a year after Hitler came to power, because of his Jewish descent. Unemployed, he ended up as an advisor working for Chiang Kai-shek. It is possible that he benefited from a decision by Seeckt, the first German chief advisor, to help non-Aryan soldiers to get assignments in China. This has been linked to the fact that Seeckt's own wife had been adopted by Jewish parents and might have been Jewish herself.[108] No matter what the circumstances were, Borchardt faced a dilemma even worse than Falkenhausen, whose younger brother had been killed by the Nazis.

His father, Philipp Borchardt, had been born with a deformed left leg and had not fought in the trenches. He could not even benefit from the modicum of protection Germany afforded its Jewish war veterans. Like Germany's other Jews, Philipp Borchardt was subject to increasing discrimination—discrimination that would eventually see him sent to the notorious concentration camp Dachau.[109] Meanwhile, his son was thousands of miles away, defending his nation's honor against a Japanese Empire that, so many said, was in fact Germany's natural ally in challenging the existing international order. In a world preparing for war, strange allegiances abounded.

―――――――――――

Lu Chuanyong, 26, was in the 11th Class of the Central Military Academy in Nanjing and was about to graduate when war broke out with Japan in the summer of 1937. The school's students had been spread across the countryside surrounding the capital to avoid aerial attack by the Japanese. Everyone knew that they would be sent straight to the frontline upon graduation, and for most it was a tough wait. They could not go fast enough. Graduation was on August 27 and it seemed there would be a minimum of ceremony, in view of the circumstances. The soldiers were given food and ordered to go to sleep in their uniforms, ready to get up and get going with minutes' notice.[110]

At 10:00 p.m. they were rushed out of bed and sent on a forced march through the night for about one hour, until they saw the dark looming outline of a Buddhist temple. In the courtyard was a banner announcing "Graduation Ceremony." At 1:30 a.m. there was a commotion. Someone important had arrived. It was Chiang Kai-shek himself. He delivered an impassioned speech. "The Japanese invaders," he said, "have now attacked Shanghai. They are approaching Nanjing. They want to destroy our China. We cannot stand it any longer. We cannot sit idly by."

Upon graduation, Lu Chanyong was assigned to the 87th Infantry Division, which had moved from the downtown area of Shanghai to the countryside north of the city to resist the Japanese landing forces. "When I reached the battlefield, I realized how difficult the fighting was," he told an interviewer later. "It was not at all what I had expected. Once you were in the frontline, in the daytime basically you couldn't move . . . The Japanese planes circled above our heads, and the instant someone moved and made himself a target, they would swerve down and start bombing."

It was only after dark that the real battle started. As a result, Lu did not get a good night's sleep for two weeks. He taught himself how to march and doze off at the same time. With supply lines interrupted by Japanese air attacks, he learned like others before him to appreciate food—any kind of food—as a rare luxury. "We basically had nothing to eat and were constantly hungry. We would just grab a handful of dry uncooked rice from our pocket and munch it down, or scoop a bit of water from the ditch. We all got rather skinny in the end," he said.

Soon his platoon of more than 40 men had been reduced to little more than 20. It was close to breaking-point, and it would have made sense to withdraw to the rear for replenishment. Regardless, the high command ordered the men to stay where they were. It said an international meeting was coming up, and if they withdrew, Japan would be at an advantage.[111] Therefore, instead of reorganizing in the hinterland, the unit received reinforcements straight at the frontline.

The replacements came from all over the country. Often the young soldiers had been forced to make their way to the Shanghai front as best they could, which frequently meant by foot. When they arrived, they were exhausted and emaciated. Lu's unit would cook porridge for them and help them regain strength as fast as possible. Still, there was only so much even a full stomach could accomplish. Even for a well-nourished infantryman life at the front would have offered a steep learning curve. "The new ones had no experience whatsoever. To think that they were to fight the well-equipped Japanese—it was unilateral slaughter," said Lu.

———————

Chiang Kai-shek would not give up Luodian. He personally called senior commanders to the Third War Zone's headquarters in Suzhou stating that no matter what, it must be retaken. The commanders, in turn, threw entire divisions into the battle for the town.[112] In one of a series of Chinese assaults, Qiu Weida, a regimental commander of the 51st Infantry Division, led a night attack against the southern part of Luodian. Moving quietly and stealthily through the dark, the Chinese force, which had the strength of about two companies, approached a Japanese camp, which was mostly at sleep.[113]

The Chinese launched a speedy attack. They gave the Japanese no chances, shooting and bayoneting them while they were still lying down. The Chinese took over the camp and waited for the Japanese to launch a counterattack. When they did, they began a fighting retreat. This was in fact a ruse, meant to lure the Japanese into an open area in front of a line of well-armed soldiers lying in ambush. Once the Japanese were close enough, Qiu Weida released a signal flare. It was a pre-arranged sign to open fire. Infantry weapons with a range of calibers joined in. As dawn broke, Qiu raised his binoculars to view the scene in front of him. It was covered in a dense tangle of dead and dying bodies.

In a similar engagement near Luodian, Japanese private Toshihara Tokaji had the bad fortune of being wounded and left behind in no-man's-land after his unit withdrew. Together with three other stragglers, two unharmed and one lightly injured, he hid in the thick foliage of a swamp, and started waiting. At night they could hear Chinese voices, and they had to keep quiet and refrain from moving if they wanted to survive. Toshihara jotted down his thoughts in his diary. They mostly evolved around one thing: agonizing thirst. [114]

"Seventh day," read one of his entries. "I want water, water, water! I am so thirsty." He crawled to a nearby creek and found it filled with bloated corpses, but nevertheless filled his flask. This provided some relief, but only for a few days. "I think of my wound to forget my thirst," he wrote later. "Then I think of water to forget the pain in my wound." On the ninth day, the four Japanese spotted a group of Chinese soldiers approaching, and quietly got ready for a fight. The Chinese, however, simply cleared the creek of the corpses, left them in a jumbled pile on the bank, and then disappeared. This gave the Japanese an opportunity to fish food from the pockets of the dead bodies—two cans of meat and raw rice.

On day 13, the thirst again overwhelmed Toshihara. He fell into a delirious sleep and dreamt about a beer hall, until the sound of battle awakened him. "We talked about my dream to forget our thirst," he wrote. In the days that followed, the battle moved nearer, but Toshihara and the other stragglers were so confused about directions that they did not know who was advancing, and who was retreating. Finally, on the 19th day, the front rolled over their swamp. Chinese troops passed within feet of their hiding place—and then they were found by advancing Japanese. "We thought we would all be dead by this time, but the God protected us," Toshihara wrote. "I will never forget this day."

CHAPTER

5

· ·

"Rivers of Blood"

SEPTEMBER 11–30

THIS COULD BE THE WESTERN FRONT, veteran war correspondent Hubert Hessell Tiltman thought as he hunkered down in the dark trench, hoping it was robust enough to offer protection against the Japanese shells that were pouring down on the Chinese positions. The trained ear could easily discern the various forms of artillery, much the same way that a lover of classical music could pick out the individual instruments in a symphony orchestra. There were six-inch grenades, and there were "whizz-bangs," military slang for high-velocity shells that traveled faster than the speed of sound, meaning that the men huddled in their dugouts heard the "whizz" of the shell flying through the air before the "bang" of the field gun that had fired it. The uninterrupted barrage played its deadly tune up and down the Chinese lines and also pummeled the rear areas in search of targets. This, Tiltman reminded himself, was officially described as "a quiet night."[1]

When exploding shells lit up the countryside it was possible to clearly make out the Japanese trenches about one mile away. The Japanese had withdrawn to that position after a massive, but ultimately futile, attack the preceding day. The Japanese were feared in battle, but their adversaries were fierce warriors too. Tiltman was impressed with the Chinese soldiers he had seen in the trenches. They were in excellent shape, they were well-equipped, and there were many of them. On the way to the frontline, he had observed large numbers of reserves of equal quality waiting to be deployed. It was understandable why the Chinese command would allocate forces of such strength to this section of the frontline, straddling the road from Baoshan to Liuhang, as it was of great importance to them. If the Japanese managed to punch through the Chinese lines and take Yanghang, the village right behind the line, they would be significantly closer to achieving the goal of cutting off the Chinese troops fighting in Shanghai proper.

In the first days of September, an intense sense of resignation had set in among the senior Chinese commanders after the Japanese troops had taken stronghold after stronghold along the riverbank—first Shizilin, then Wusong and finally Baoshan. However, the rank and file remained determined to defend every inch of Chinese soil. Fighting along Wusong Creek, stretching west from Wusong, became extraordinarily bloody. "There were huge numbers of deaths on both sides, and the water of the creek turned red," Chinese official Wang Jieshi wrote in his diary. "The saying about 'rivers of blood' turned into actual reality."[2]

Just days after Tiltman's visit to the front, the Japanese commanders launched what they hoped would be the decisive blow allowing a breakout from the Baoshan perimeter. Elements of the 3rd Division were to move down the road towards Liuhang and occupy Yanghang. In the same assault, the 11th Division's Amaya Detachment,[3] which had arrived at Wusong on September 2, was to take Yuepu, a village on the other strategic road leading west from Baoshan that blocked access to Luodian and a link-up with the units under the 11th Division fighting in that area. It was an attempt to finally achieve the elbow room needed to seize Shanghai, and the Japanese threw everything they could spare into the effort.

The artillery barrage began before dawn on September 11, with Japanese guns of all calibers taking part. As well as the usual whistle of shells from naval guns in the river, there were also attacks from land-based artillery, the sound of which had become much more familiar to the Chinese defenders in recent days, as the Japanese had been able to disembark materiel at the landing sites along the Yangtze and Huangpu Rivers for more than a fortnight. After daybreak there were air raids of unusual intensity. The Japanese were deploying all their available aircraft in this narrow part of the front, or so it seemed to the Chinese. Eventually, it was the Japanese infantry's turn to attack.[4]

While this was just the latest in a series of Japanese assaults, the sheer tenacity on display signaled to the Chinese that this time was different. Still, an entire day of fighting led to precious little territorial gain. The defenders had fought with determination bordering on fanaticism, despite a near-complete lack of air and artillery support, and had made good use of the obstacles provided by the canals cutting through the heavily culti-vated area. By sunset, the Japanese had been able to advance no further than the eastern end of Yuepu, although the village had been completely destroyed by artillery fire. Yanghang remained entirely in Chinese hands. In the countryside between the two western roads leading from Baoshan, Japanese units had only been able to occupy land where their artillery and aircraft had literally obliterated the defenders.[5]

From an outsider's point of view, it would look as if the Chinese could breathe a sigh of relief. From the Chinese commanders' own perspective, the situation was entirely different. Their biggest worry was the Japanese superiority in artillery. The contested area north of Shanghai mainly con-sisted of low-lying rice and cotton fields with relatively few trees, offering insufficient camouflage for any but the smallest units. This made it possible for the Japanese naval gunners on the elevated water of the Yangtze and Huangpu to sometimes directly observe the Chinese troops. Even when there was no direct line of sight from the ships in the rivers, they were helped by the directions of observers patrolling in aircraft or hovering in balloons over the horizon.[6]

The Chinese had already known for some time that exposing their units to continuous attack from the naval guns simply played into the Japanese hands and that they would have to move away from the riverbank and the lethal fire from the Imperial Navy. The decision to withdraw would have come sooner or later, but it was hastened by the continuous Japanese pressure on the two roads from Baoshan, since their loss would cause a breach between Zhang Zhizhong's 9th Army Group in the Shanghai area and Chen Cheng's 15th Army Group on his left.[7] General Gu Zhutong, a member of Chiang Kai-shek's inner circle who recently had been appointed deputy commander of the Third War Zone, had witnessed how some of the best divisions were being chopped to pieces in the defense of Yuepu and Yanghang and was in favor of abandoning those two villages. Zhang Zhizhong, meanwhile, was pushing for a withdrawal of troops in Yangshupu, which risked being transformed into a dangerously exposed salient if the breach were to become a reality.[8]

The growing apprehension among the frontline commanders gradually crept up the ranks, all the way back to Nanjing. A tone of exasperation had started to appear in Chiang Kai-shek's diary. "In recent days, the military situation has turned for the worse, and morale is starting to waver," he wrote following setbacks around Luodian. After Japanese troops had taken possession of Baoshan he added: "Our troops have been forced into a passive role."[9] There were other indications that Chiang Kai-shek was preparing for more defensive tactics in the Shanghai area, including the issue, on September 6, of a set of broad operational guidelines. The guidelines called for the elimination of all enemy troops that had landed, but failing that, the Chinese forces were to make use of the terrain in conducting a vigorous defense. This was a signal that withdrawal, and a gradual shift towards trading land for time, had become an acceptable option.[10]

The Third War Zone's order for the two Chinese army groups to withdraw came late on September 11.[11] Under the cover of darkness, the bulk of the divisions pulled back to positions that had been reinforced by reserves in the preceding days. As thousands of soldiers moved several miles to the rear, the Japanese were unaware that anything unusual was going on, and the entire movement took place free from enemy harassment. Only skeleton crews were left in the original Chinese positions. On the morning of September 12, the new frontline stretched from the North Railway Station to the eastern edge of Jiangwan, bent west of Yanghang and Luodian and stretched north to the banks of the Yangtze. Without knowing it, the Japanese had become masters of heavily contested areas from Yangshupu in the south to Yuepu in the north.

The Chinese military leadership tried to explain to the public that it had no choice, and that it had never had any serious expectations that it might be able to throw the Japanese back into the Yangtze, given the hundreds of naval guns at the disposal of the Japanese. "The objective of the Chinese command was to delay and harass the landing," a Chinese military spokesman said in a statement. "It was not hoped permanently to repel the landing."[12] The Chinese proclaimed confidence in the new positions they had withdrawn to. Some even compared them to the Maginot Line along the French border with Germany, which at the time was still considered impregnable. Dutch spy de Fremery, however, was not overwhelmed. When he toured an entire 10-mile section of the front, he came across just one concrete pillbox. The trenches, he said, were secured by "the most primitive, if not entirely inadequate" barbed wire barricades.[13]

By contrast, the advantages that the Japanese enjoyed after the Chinese withdrawal were considerable. They now controlled all the left bank of the Huangpu from Yangshupu to the mouth of the Yangtze. They were in possession of several good roads, some of them interconnected, which could act as supply lines for future attacks. Finally, they were also free to exploit a large number of modern Chinese wharfs and docks, setting the stage for an unimpeded flow of reinforcements. "In this way, the Japanese command had obtained the room for maneuver needed for the successful continuation of the entire Shanghai operation," one of the German advisors later ruminated regretfully in his account of the battle.[14]

Matsui Iwane woke up at his headquarters, set up at the Shanghai Fisheries College near Wusong, at 6:00 a.m. on September 12. It was his first night of sleep on land since departing from Japan. He washed, brushed his teeth, and bowed respectfully to the rising sun. Then he sat down in a pavilion in the middle of the campus and started meditating. He noticed how a flowerbed nearby had been left untended and had slowly withered away. Nevertheless, fresh wild plants were protruding from among the shriveled leaves. Matsui felt it as if the blooming oleander was smiling at him. It set off all kinds of associations. Deep in thought, the ageing general composed a poem:[15]

South of the Yangtze, a magnificent view:
Coquettish flowers come back to life.
The righteous knight has gained victory,
And is greeted by the bloom of the oleander.

Matsui had good reason for being pensive. The preceding days had seen a string of local victories for the Japanese forces, but overall the advance from the landing zones had not been smooth at all. Attempts at taking Yuepu and Yanghang had proceeded at a snail's pace. "The advance on Yanghang is not going well," Matsui had written the day before in his diary. "It's a great pity."[16]

The general's worries were to disappear on that September day. Some time after he had completed the morning's meditation, Matsui received word from the Amaya Detachment that it had finally taken Yuepu. Having driven the Chinese out of the village, the detachment had established a defensive perimeter in a semicircle 500 yards around the western edge of the village. Nearly simultaneously, the Ueno Detachment, a unit attached to the 3rd Division, reported that it had occupied Yanghang and had pursued the enemy to a position about two miles west of the village. In both instances it seemed that the enemy had abandoned his positions under the cover of night.

Matsui of course welcome news that the villages were finally his. However, a precious opportunity to pursue the retreating enemy while he was on the run had been lost. In his frustration, Matsui made up a simple limerick, much earthier than the lines he had composed earlier in the day:

With Yanghang 'n Yuepu up for grabs,
Amaya and Ueno took daylong naps.

Perhaps the lack of offensive spirit was the result of the alien climate, he speculated. Then he resignedly thought to himself that it was no good worrying about lost opportunities in the past. What mattered now was how to proceed.[17]

Above all, Matsui needed more men. In the three weeks leading to September 11, the Japanese had managed to land 40,000 soldiers and establish a bridgehead measuring roughly 25 miles in length and more than five miles in depth. Together with the troops already present in Shanghai, this meant that Japan had about 50,000 troops in the area. It was a significant force, but it was still not enough to ensure the conquest of Shanghai, especially not given the rapid attrition that it was subject to. As of September 9, the 3rd Division's losses amounted to 589 killed and 1,539 injured, while the numbers for the 11th Division were 616 dead and 1,336 wounded.[18]

Matsui's requests for reinforcements had not triggered an immediate response from Tokyo. The main obstacle was posed by his direct superiors. The Japanese Army's top brass saw Shanghai and central China in general as a sideshow to the north Chinese theater, which they considered more important given its proximity to the Soviet threat. This perception was only reinforced by the signing of the Sino-Soviet agreement in late August. On a more practical, tactical level, the Japanese Army was reluctant to deploy troops in Shanghai because of its difficult terrain, which favored defense, and because the large number of Chinese troops crammed into the area made the task of achieving victory seem hardly within reach. The army's preferences were reflected in the distribution of its troops. While there were so far only two Japanese divisions in the Shanghai area, in the north the army had deployed no fewer than six.[19]

The main advocate of the army point of view was Ishiwara Kanji, head of the General Staff Operations Division. Opposed to the war in China from the outset and favoring a policy of non-expansion instead, he advised that troops be spared for what he and many others believed was an inevitable showdown with the Soviet Union. Concentrating on China and ignoring the Soviet menace was, in his eyes, like "chasing the dogs away from the front door while forgetting the wolves approaching the back door."[20]

However, Ishiwara's reluctance to send more troops to Shanghai was overruled. On September 4, a meeting of officers in Tokyo led to the conclusion that the battle in the Shanghai area should be completed by late October or early November and to that end, sufficient troops should be deployed.[21] Three days later, Emperor Hirohito approved the reinforcement of the Shanghai front and the dispatch of three extra infantry divisions from the home islands, along with units from the garrison forces in the colony of Taiwan.[22] Ishiwara was so upset with the decision that he handed in his resignation. He was later appointed to the army in the northeast of China.[23]

There was little doubt in Japanese minds that the deployment of the reinforcements marked a serious escalation in the war. The situation was different from anything Japan had ever experienced before. Army Minister Sugiyama Hajime said in a statement to his commanders: "This war has become total war."[24] Adding to the conflict's special character, for the first time in modern history Japan was facing an enemy literally prepared to fight to the death. "The enemy resistance is undeniably strong," a Japanese officer inspecting the Shanghai front wrote in his report upon his return to Tokyo. The determination of the Chinese defenders, he warned, was not to be underestimated. "Whether they are bombed out or surrounded, they do not retreat."[25]

When 28-year-old Wu Yafu arrived near Luodian with China's 58th Infantry Division in early September, neither he nor anyone else in his battalion wasted any time. Their first priority was to dig trenches, fast. They knew that this was the only effective defense against the Japanese artillery. They had only dug down a few feet before they hit water, which was not surprising since they were digging in low-lying land that in some places was even below the Yangtze a few miles to the east. Soon they were standing in ankle-deep mud, but they kept digging. They knew they had no choice if they wanted to stay alive. The local farmers, poor as they were, came out of their small huts to help them. They tore down parts of their own homes for timber to improve the soldiers' positions. They also helped camouflage the dugouts so they were not so easily detected from the air.[26]

After they were finished, Wu Yafu and his comrades sat down to wait. More than a week passed, and still the Japanese had not attacked. But they would come sooner or later, everyone knew that. The farmers, too, were aware that the war was about to reach their homes, and they disappeared a few at a time, joining the growing army of refugees roaming the countryside around Shanghai. Meanwhile, a continuous heavy downpour made life in the trench even more uncomfortable than before. Wu Yafu and the other soldiers of his battalion rarely had any real rest. The Japanese guns saw to that. Every now and then Wu and his comrades would hear the shrill scream of an incoming shell, and for a few tense seconds they would be waiting and praying, heaving a sigh of relief when they heard the explosion somewhere else.

Then on September 14, the Japanese assault finally came. As always, the attackers were preceded by a heavy artillery barrage. However, luckily for Wu Yafu's battalion, the downpour had turned the dirt roads near their positions into sticky quagmires and made it impossible for the enemy to use tanks, so they only had to deal with the infantry. From behind their defenses, Wu's unit beat back the Japanese, inflicting heavy losses. Over the next three days, the Japanese changed their tactics and subjected the Chinese positions to repeated air attack. This had some effect. Five men from Wu's battalion were killed, and ten injured. Even so, they still held their position.[27]

Luodian had stayed under Japanese control since late August, but the surrounding countryside remained largely Chinese territory. Even though the Japanese stepped up the pressure after the Chinese withdrawal south on September 12, they advanced only slowly and haltingly. Taken aback by the sudden gain of Yuepu and Yanghang, and demonstrating their usual tardy response to unforeseen events, it had taken them several days to even send out patrols for probing attacks against the new Chinese defenses. This gave the Chinese commanders extra time to reinforce their positions near Luodian, especially on both sides of the road from Yuepu, which they assumed, correctly, was to be the main route taken by the Japanese attackers.[28]

Chinese preparations were merely one of the reasons why Japan's mid-September assault was only a moderate success. The Japanese, like the Chinese, had yet to develop much skill in coordinating infantry and armor operations. The road connecting Yuepu and Luodian, unlike the area defended by Wu Yafu and his fellow soldiers, was of relatively good quality and allowed the Japanese to deploy a force of about 25 tanks to act as the spearhead of the thrust. The armored vehicles quickly eliminated the Chinese positions closest to the road and rolled at great speed all the way to Luodian. However, the accompanying infantry, men from the Amaya Detachment, was unable to follow suit. The Japanese only commanded a few yards of countryside on either side of the road. Beyond that narrow belt, the area was teeming with Chinese soldiers for whom the Japanese soldiers marching down the elevated road were easy targets. The Japanese infantrymen were bogged down, and it was only after dark, when Chinese defenders north of the road decided to withdraw west, that they had a chance to reach Luodian.[29]

To be sure, the debacle on the road to Luodian was not only a question of flawed training in the Japanese ranks. The area around Shanghai, a latticework of small farm plots divided by creeks and canals, was not at all suited to tank warfare. This terrain had been a main argument used by the

Japanese Army against large-scale deployments there. Even so, once the decision was made in Tokyo to send enough troops to win the battle for the city, the generals had to think of ways to overcome the difficulties posed by the terrain. One solution was to deploy amphibious tanks. But the tactics adopted called for the use of the tanks in a supportive role, rather than in the vanguard of attacks across waterways. If a creek needed to be crossed, the Japanese commanders would initially order a small infantry unit to wade or swim to the other side and, under the cover of darkness, prepare the opposite bank to make it possible for the tanks to make a landing. While it was still dark, the tanks would cross and be able to support the infantry by daybreak.

It was a cumbersome procedure, almost putting the cart before the horse, and the Japanese did it exactly by the book time and again. This allowed the Chinese opponents to acquaint themselves with Japanese doctrine to the extent that they could usually predict what the Japanese would do next. This could have proven immensely valuable, but once again the German advisors were frustrated by a Chinese reluctance to use expensive equipment, even when faced with the promise of maximum effect. Fear of losing the equipment dictated a policy of keeping it too far in the rear. "Here as in all other cases where the Japanese used tanks at Shanghai," the German armor specialist Robert Borchardt wrote upon returning home, "the Chinese anti-tank guns could have had good results if they had been used in a purposeful manner and above all close enough to the frontline."[30]

While flawed tactics prevented either side from shaking the Luodian front out of its stalemate, they both kept pouring in reinforcements. The Shigeto Detachment arrived from Taiwan and was attached to the 11th Division on September 14, the same day that the Amaya Detachment made its way up the road from Yuepu and returned to the division's direct command. By the middle of the month, the division had become a sizeable fighting force. The problem was that the enemy it faced around Luodian also grew stronger by the day, and would pose a significant threat to the division's right flank if it were to rush south towards Dachang and link up with the 3rd Division there. Therefore, on September 18, the Shanghai commanders ordered the division to initially focus on wiping out the Chinese troops amassed around Luodian.[31]

By that time, heavy rain had already fallen on the region around Shanghai for three days, gradually causing the fighting to slow down. The Japanese disliked the rain because it turned the roads into muddy rivers making transportation difficult, if not impossible, while also grounding most of their aircraft. By contrast, the Chinese welcomed the lull, as it gave them an opportunity to improve their positions. The challenge of punching through the Chinese positions was only getting harder as time passed.[32]

The Chinese Army's performance during the initial stage of the fighting in Shanghai changed the world's perception of the nation's military capabilities. China, which had lost every war for the past century, invariably to nations much smaller than itself, had suddenly taken a stand. "There is most emphatically no resemblance whatever discernable between the Chinese army of yesterday and the confident, well-disciplined men whom I saw," wrote Hubert Hessell Tiltman, after his visit to the Chinese frontline. "They are facing incredible hardships with a courage which deserves the most flattering tribute that a pen can write."[33]

At Shanghai, the Chinese Army had seen more bitter fighting than anyone could have anticipated, and it had lost manpower that had taken years to build up. However, it had won prestige and respect, even among its Japanese adversaries. "The era of timid and despicable Chinese is gone," a Japanese soldier told his compatriots back home. "Some of them are quite courageous."[34] Even the withdrawal on September 12 was greeted with sympathy and admiration in capitals around the world. The feeling was that the Chinese Army had distinguished itself with its "magnificent . . . resistance against the overwhelming weight of Japanese metal," Reuters reported from London.[35]

The Chinese Army was a riddle to many of the foreigners who saw it in action. Its soldiers often did not live up at all to western ideas about what hardened veterans ought to be like. "They looked as though a high wind would blow them away," wrote a foreign correspondent after seeing members of the elite 88th Division from up close. "A few carried oiled-paper umbrellas. One actually carried a canary in a cage. Many walked hand in hand. It seemed preposterous that these thin, tattered boys . . . were heroes of the Chinese Republic!"[36] Nevertheless, these boys with their paper umbrellas were able to carry out amazing feats in battle.

Perhaps it was their stoicism and ability to endure hardship that made the difference. American correspondent Edgar Snow recalled touring the battlefield outside Shanghai with U.S. naval attaché Evans Carlson and meeting a young Chinese soldier, probably aged no more than 16, who greeted the two westerners cheerfully. He was still smiling as he explained to Snow that he was the sole survivor of a group of 18 soldiers who had been in a dugout that had taken a direct hit in an artillery barrage the night before. Snow was amazed by his coolness and self-possession.[37] "An absence of nerves, and a sense of fatalism when once exposed to death, are assets in Chinese troops which it is doubtful if any Western race possesses," Snow wrote in his memoirs.[38]

"My admiration for the Chinese soldier has risen fifty percent," Snow's co-traveler to the battlefield, Carlson, wrote to Franklin D. Roosevelt, the pro-Chinese U.S. president who had asked for regular letters about what the American officer saw and heard in China. "With the use of a good spade, a few machine guns and a lot of courage and determination he has made his adversary pay dearly for the few miles he has advanced in the last three months. He sticks to his position through innumerable air bombings and artillery bombardments, and when the Japanese infantry attempt to rush his position he is on the business end of a machine gun to stem the attack. The Chinese soldier has the utmost contempt for the Japanese infantryman. He claims that the latter will not come close in and fight man to man."[39]

Every journalist who was in Shanghai in the fall of 1937 had a story to tell about the remarkable Chinese soldier. The American journalist Carroll Alcott spent many hour in dugouts in Zhabei. While Japanese shells pelted down over their heads, the Chinese soldiers sat unfazed in their self-made caves, cooking rice, vegetables and sometimes a small bit of pork over a charcoal brazier. They would dispel the inevitable boredom with games of checkers and mahjong, and write letters home to their families. There was safety and a primitive kind of comfort in the Chinese trenches. Hygiene was lacking, however. Alcott reported having to be deloused every time he returned from Zhabei.[40]

The Chinese themselves had more ambivalent views of their own armed forces, although traditional attitudes were gradually changing because of the national crisis they found themselves in. "Good iron is not made into nails; a good man does not enlist as a soldier," according to an ancient Chinese proverb. In imperial times, soldiers had usually been mercenaries, and interaction between the military and surrounding society had been extremely limited. After the republic was established the men in uniform were often little better than hooligans serving local warlords, who themselves were hard to distinguish from powerful mobsters.[41]

Even after the outbreak of the war in 1937, some Chinese felt estranged from the military. It was not unusual to encounter the view that soldiering was a profession like any other, albeit one best suited for unruly and adventurous youngsters who could not fit into more stable occupations. "Fighting is what soldiers do. We have chosen other careers," was a typical response even among patriotic Chinese when asked why they themselves were not in uniform. Middle-class merchants in Shanghai could even be heard complaining that the soldiers should show more professional pride in a job well done. "Why are the soldiers so lazy?" they asked, shaking their heads. "They get paid so well now, and it's unbelievable that they still haven't thrown out the Japanese."[42]

That view was by no means universal, and the outline of a generation gap was forming in Chinese society. For the first time ever, the most accomplished of the young generation wanted to join the military. This left older Chinese dumbfounded, as they could not fathom why promising men in their prime of youth would rush to volunteer.[43] However, the trend was undeniable. Literacy, a feat made harder by the need to memorize thousands of characters, was generally more widespread inside army ranks than outside. "Sure they read; in fact, there are less illiterates in the army than in the civilian population in China," a western journalist commented.[44]

The cultural change that the higher educational level brought about in the armed forces is likely to have contributed to a more positive opinion in the public. "In this critical period most foreigners testify to the courtesy and kindness of Chinese soldiers with whom they have come into contact," the *China Weekly Review* wrote. "Millions of Chinese are rallied together in enthusiastic support of their soldiers; upper-class men contribute funds, women prepare clothing and comforts for the soldiers, boys and girls give strenuous service as 'scouts' or collect money for the men at the front. It is 'our army' of which Chinese now speak; it is 'our soldiers' and 'our heroes'."[45]

It was already dark when Lieutenant Gong Yeti took off in his Curtis Hawk III from the airfield near Nanjing at 7:40 p.m. on September 18. The target: Shanghai. Daylight raids had long been out of the question because of enemy's air superiority, and even night sorties were becoming riskier as the Japanese built up their anti-aircraft assets on the ground in and around the city. Despite the dangers, there was no doubt in anyone's mind that this night's raid was needed. It was to mark the anniversary of the incident in 1931 that had triggered Japan's invasion of Manchuria. The Chinese pilots wanted to pay back just a little for all the suffering that had been brought on their people during the six long intervening years.[46]

The planes were to attack in four waves of six aircraft each, spaced out with one hour between them. Gong Yeti was in the first wave. Along the entire route they could see scattered fires lighting up the dark countryside 5,000 feet beneath them, and when they approached Shanghai they could clearly distinguish the objective, Hongkou district, hemmed in between the Huangpu River, Suzhou Creek and the massive waterworks building. The tracer rounds fired from the anti-aircraft guns cut thin white lines through the sky, while shells exploded around them, opening up like fiery flowers. The lead airplanes went into a dive, and Gong Yeti followed shortly afterwards. He aimed for the area where the first aircraft had already dropped their loads. As he saw the explosions from the bombs he had released, he felt intense satisfaction.

The moment he ascended from his dive, the Japanese on the ground switched on a dozen searchlights, momentarily causing him to lose his bearings. While the other planes turned east towards Pudong, he veered west and suddenly found himself alone over pitch-black countryside. On his right, he saw a village ablaze, probably Luodian, and he smiled to himself when a Japanese warship anchored in the Yangtze tried to fire at him from an impossible distance. However, just few minutes later, the lights disappeared behind him, and he suddenly had no idea if he was flying over water or land. He looked up and saw tiny lights. Those must be the other planes heading back to the base in Nanjing, he thought to himself. Seconds later, his heart sank. He had been looking at the stars, which had seemed to be moving against the canopy of clouds. He looked down and was almost certain that he had spotted the lights of the other planes. However, once more he was disappointed. Again, it was the stars, or rather, their reflection in the rice paddies below. He felt a small pang of panic.

Finally, he noticed real light below. He flashed his own signal light three times, as arranged beforehand. Someone below replied, flashing a light three times. He really was on the way home. Minutes later he landed on his airfield, the first to return from the raid. One after the other, the rest of the pilots touched down, assembling in the mess hall and eagerly sharing their stories from the mission that had just ended. But one pilot, Li Yougan, was missing. After a long wait, the telephone rang. The call was from Shanghai. One of the Chinese aircraft had been shot down. Li Yougan had been killed. Of course, the other pilots felt sad. On the other hand, losing comrades was becoming routine, just as U.S. ace Eddie Ricken-backer had explained in his book. Anyway, they told each other, he had been given the rare honor of dying for China on this special day, exactly six years after the Japanese aggression had begun.

According to the *North China Daily News*, the series of attacks Gong Yeti participated in were "the worst air raids in [the city's] history." The incendiary bombs sent flames and sparks high up into the night sky in the style of "Roman candles," the paper's journalists reported, and shrapnel from the Japanese anti-aircraft guns caused numerous casualties in the International Settlement and the French Concession. Several businesses, ranging from the Shanghai Cotton Mill to the China Soap Co., were damaged.[47] A firefighter told the paper about his experiences after he entered the blazing area in a fire engine. "We were about to turn tail for the station when an incendiary bomb burst about 60 yards away. In a flash our men were cringing against walls or diving under the engine. It was a most terrifying sight, as though the earth had opened up and squirted fire far and wide. It landed in the rear of some Chinese buildings; had it struck the road none of us could possibly have survived."[48]

It was the largest Chinese air raid of the entire campaign, and it was the last one. The Second Combined Air Group of the Imperial Navy had been based at Gongda Airfield in Shanghai since it had become operational on September 10, and it was preparing to strike back. Initially, the facilities at the airfield had been poor, and the weather had turned the runway into a quagmire. Even though ground crew had worked day and night, 11 fighters had been damaged while taking off or landing during the first nine days. This had been a crucial period, and a more determined Chinese effort to prevent the airfield from becoming of any use could have had a major impact on the battle, Japanese officers said after the war. However, Chinese aircraft had attacked only at dusk or during the night, and no damage was done to the airfield. Artillery attacks also had been used to only limited effect.[49]

The result was that once the airfield was ready for use, the Japanese were free to prepare for a decisive blow against the Chinese fighters stationed at Nanjing. The plan was simple. Carrier bombers and sea reconnaissance planes were to approach the Chinese capital at a height of 10,000 feet, in full view of the enemy. The bombers were to release their load over Nanjing, but should not worry about accuracy. It didn't matter what they hit, since their main role was as bait. A large number of fighters were to accompany them, but remain unseen, at 13,000 feet, ready to move into action once the Chinese fighters had been lured out by the ruse. The aim was to annihilate the Chinese fighter arm once and for all. "I wish that every member of the fighter plane units will go forth to battle, convinced of victory, and will destroy every enemy plane in sight, and display the glory of our navy to the rest of the world," said the commander of the Second Combined Air Group when he explained the plan to his officers on September 17.[50]

The carefully prepared raid commenced on the morning of September 19, just hours after the Chinese air attack on Shanghai. The first Japanese wave, numbering 45 aircraft, approached Jurong Airfield near Nanjing at 9:50 a.m. As predicted, Chinese fighters were scrambled. The aircraft, 12 Curtiss Hawk IIIs and six Boeing 281s, went straight for the slow-flying bombers, and only discovered the nimble Japanese Type 96 fighters hovering above when it was too late. In the furious dogfight that followed, several of the Chinese planes were shot down. Ten minutes later, the Japanese planes were over the center of Nanjing, where more than 20 other Chinese planes were waiting for them. The Japanese fighters, joined by the reconnaissance planes, engaged them individually. Only a handful of the Chinese pilots survived the encounter and disappeared from the attackers' view. The bombers took advantage of the absence of any enemy planes to drop their load on a military airfield nearby, destroying even more fighters. The raid was a complete success, a success that was repeated the same afternoon with another raid on Nanjing.[51]

Shanghai's famous waterfront The Bund seen from the south. The Huangpu River is to the right. The WWI memorial is in the foreground. *From the American Geographical Society Library, University of Wisconsin-Milwaukee Libraries*

Above: Two soldiers in a position on the outskirts of Shanghai. They both wear the German M35 helmet, with the Nationalist Chinese symbol, a white star on a dark blue background. *From the American Geographical Society Library, University of Wisconsin-Milwaukee Libraries*

Left: A Chinese soldier wearing a typical uniform from the elite 87th and 88th Infantry Divisions deployed in the Shanghai area from the first days of the battle. He is carrying his two stick grenades in pouches hanging from his shoulders. *From the American Geographical Society Library, University of Wisconsin-Milwaukee Libraries*

Above: Chinese infantry manning defenses outside Shanghai. The soldier in the foreground is aiming a Belgian-made Fabrique Nationale M1930 light machine gun, based on the American M1918 BAR. He has not inserted a magazine into the weapon, making it likely that the group is engaged in mock battle for the benefit of the photographer. *From the American Geographical Society Library, University of Wisconsin-Milwaukee Libraries*

Right: Chinese soldiers in action. Both men closest to the camera fire Hanyang 88 rifles, modeled on the German Gewehr 88. It had been produced in China's Hanyang Arsenals since 1895 and was so successful that it even was used by Chinese forces in the Korean War. The soldier in the middle has an umbrella slung across his back. *From the American Geographical Society Library, University of Wisconsin-Milwaukee Libraries*

Above: A camouflaged Chinese tank captured by the Japanese. It is a Vickers-Armstrongs light tank Mark E Type B. Having rolled off the assembly line at the Elswick Works in Newcastle upon Tyne in October 1934, it was one of about 20 Mark E tanks purchased by the Chinese Nationalists in 1935 and 1936 as part of a military modernization drive. The Mark E was one of the most popular tanks in the 1930s. The Type B left room for two crew members in the single turret, providing it with significant firepower. *From the American Geographical Society Library, University of Wisconsin-Milwaukee Libraries*

Right: Chinese infantry manning a hastily built barricade in Zhabei. They are wearing the British Mk1 steel helmet, or its American counterpart, standard issue for the US and British forces in the Great War. *From the American Geographical Society Library, University of Wisconsin-Milwaukee Libraries*

Right: A Chinese soldier during the Shanghai battle, exhibiting the eclectic mix of the uniforms worn by Chiang Kai-shek's troops. *From the American Geographical Society Library, University of Wisconsin-Milwaukee Libraries*

Battlefield bravado shown by one Chinese soldier. The broadsword, often featured in Chinese propaganda, was of some use in close combat, Chinese veterans of the battle would later state. *From the American Geographical Society Library, University of Wisconsin-Milwaukee Libraries*

Top: Chinese soldiers on the move near Shanghai. The soldiers' headwear was modeled on the German ski cap, and became an iconic uniform item for the Nationalist army in the 1930s and 1940s, made famous not least by Chiang Kai-shek himself. *From the American Geographical Society Library, University of Wisconsin-Milwaukee Libraries*

Bottom right: A Chinese squad deployed outside Shanghai. Gas masks were standard issue, at least among the best Chinese units, and there were several reports of the use of gas on either side during the campaign, although it has proven a challenge to separate reality from propaganda. *Author's collection*

Bottom left: The Chinese military benefited from the help of German advisors, professional officers often with extensive experience from the Great War. Here some of them pose for a photo in Nanjing in 1936. Their leader, General Alexander von Falkenhausen, is in the middle of front row. Their assistance in Shanghai was so crucial that some of their Japanese adversaries later called it "the German war." *Courtesy Bundesarchiv (German Federal Archives), Photo 146-1978-007-13/Photographer unknown*

Top right: Chinese soldiers in commandeered office pose uneasily for a foreign photographer. *From the American Geographical Society Library, University of Wisconsin-Milwaukee Libraries*

Bottom right: Injured Chinese soldiers at a crowded makeshift hospital. Shanghai had better and more numerous hospitals than any other Chinese city, but as the 1937 battle wore on, even they became filled beyond capacity, and new facilities, such as dance-halls emptied by war, had to be commandeered. *From the American Geographical Society Library, University of Wisconsin-Milwaukee Libraries*

Below: A member of China's elite 88th Division, as indicated by his T-shirt, in a rare moment of rest. *From the American Geographical Society Library, University of Wisconsin-Milwaukee Libraries*

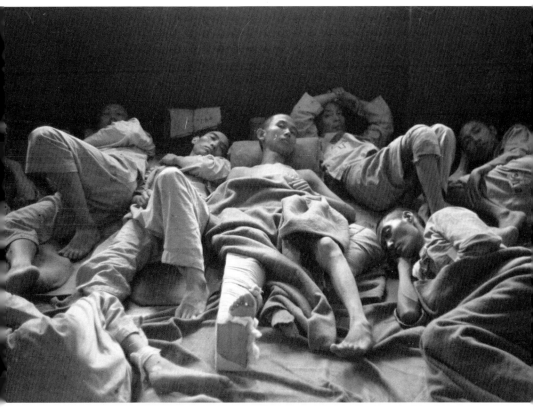

Top right: An exhausted Chinese soldier has collapsed into deep sleep next to his rifle. Mosquito repellent is burning between him and the next soldier. Insects were a nuisance described by soldiers in the early stages of the battle. *From the American Geographical Society Library, University of Wisconsin-Milwaukee Libraries*

Bottom right: Dead bodies floating in one of Shanghai's streams. The two men have their hands tied behind their backs. *From the American Geographical Society Library, University of Wisconsin-Milwaukee Libraries*

Below: A doctor inspects an injured Chinese soldier at a Shanghai hospital, while other wounded servicemen look on curiously. After the war moved inland, away from the big-city facilities, the medical services, and the chances of survival, deteriorated for ordinary Chinese soldiers. *From the American Geographical Society Library, University of Wisconsin-Milwaukee Libraries*

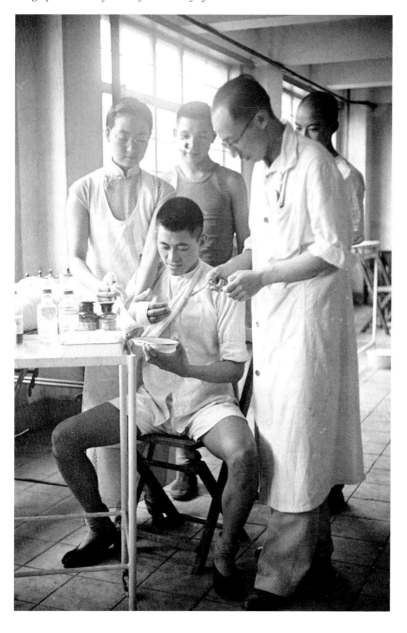

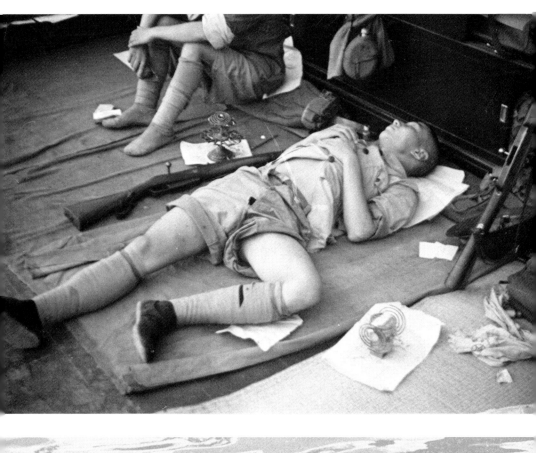

Top left: Shanghai residents rushed to buy the flags of other nations in the autumn months of 1937, hoping that they could provide a measure of safety from aerial attack against their homes or businesses. *From the American Geographical Society Library, University of Wisconsin-Milwaukee Libraries*

Top right: A Chinese mob leads away a half-naked man accused of being a spy for the Japanese, after he has been denounced by the woman walking in front. Dozens if not hundreds of real and imagined agents and saboteurs were lynched by angry crowds during the three months of battle. *From the American Geographical Society Library, University of Wisconsin-Milwaukee Libraries*

Bottom left: Refugees flee from the district of Zhabei across Suzhou Creek in the direction of the International Settlement. In the background the Union Church, built by British missionaries in 1885. *From the American Geographical Society Library, University of Wisconsin-Milwaukee Libraries*

Top right: Japanese inspect a vehicle at a roadblock on Garden Bridge across Suzhou Creek. The vehicle is equipped with a Union Jack in front to mark it as a neutral. *From the American Geographical Society Library, University of Wisconsin-Milwaukee Libraries*

Bottom right: Chinese police and foreign military on the border of the International Settlement. *From the American Geographical Society Library, University of Wisconsin-Milwaukee Libraries*

Bottom left: Chinese refugees are loaded onto boats, assisted by members of the Red Swastika, the local equivalent of the Red Cross, picking as its emblem an ancient Buddhist symbol, which also happened to be favored by the Nazis. The Red Swastika proved of great service, for example in rescue efforts after bombings of civilian areas in Shanghai. *From the American Geographical Society Library, University of Wisconsin-Milwaukee Libraries*

Above: Foreign military forces load refugees from the war zone onto a truck. The fighting created a massive refugee problem which was only resolved in November, with the establishment of a special safety zone. *From the American Geographical Society Library, University of Wisconsin-Milwaukee Libraries*

Left: Western soldier carries a Chinese child through gate to safety in International Settlement. *From the American Geographical Society Library, University of Wisconsin-Milwaukee Libraries*

Gong Yeti had watched the entire battle from the ground, as he did not get a chance to join in the fight himself. By the time he had finished his duty the previous night, he had been in a state of continuous activity for 24 hours. He had gone back to his quarters and fallen into a deep sleep. He had woken up to the sound of planes, which was not unusual, but when he stepped out of his building, he noticed the flaming red sun on the wings of the aircraft overhead and immediately realized what was going on. He watched in dazed disbelief as the more maneuverable Japanese fighters shot down one Chinese aircraft after the other. With deep dismay, he noticed that not a single Japanese plane was downed.[52]

The young lieutenant would not fly again during the battle for Shanghai. That day he was grounded, and the same happened the next day, when yet another major Japanese raid took place. There was no point in taking off to be shot down immediately by a much stronger foe. The Japanese air superiority in the entire Yangtze Delta region had become unassailable. There was nothing more for Gong to do. He was evacuated west along with other surviving pilots. On the morning of September 21, they boarded a steamboat heading up the Yangtze. They stood on the deck, watching the Nanjing docks disappear in the mist. "We felt dejected, thinking about the calamity awaiting the capital," Gong wrote in his diary.[53]

"You're from Hunan. You don't fear death!" Chiang Kai-shek's spy master Dai Li had used simple logic when ordering Shen Zui, one of his young field agents, to enter into the lion's den in Hongkou. Dai Li had uttered the words around the time of the outbreak of hostilities in Shanghai while on a visit to the French Concession, hoping to set up an intelligence network behind Japanese lines. Shen Zui was not sure he agreed with the stereotype that every single person from his home province of Hunan in southern China, man, woman and child, was fearless and death-defying, but he wasn't exactly in a position to contradict his superior. Dai Li was one of China's most feared men, and for a good reason.[54] He had allies in the Green Gang and did not shy away from kidnapping and torture in the interest of obtaining useful intelligence. Later in the war, foreigners would even refer to him as "China's Himmler."[55]

Shen Zui's task was to set up a functioning espionage operation inside

Hongkou at a time when hostilities were already getting underway. He was to monitor Japanese troop movements and report back by wireless. He had to recruit people he could trust, and find credible cover identities for them. He had to scout for locations from where he and his agents could observe the enemy while being reasonably sure that they would not be detected themselves. He had to find safe apartments to spend the night, and other locations where he could store his radio. It was the kind of activity that took months to set up, and it would have been complicated even in peacetime. In the middle of a war, and under orders to deliver actionable intelligence instantly, it was a nearly impossible task.

Simply finding people to spy for him was hard. Few who had heard of the Japanese secret police, the Kempeitai, and its methods were tempted to embark on this type of adventure. Shen Zui had been forced to truly scrape the bottom of the barrel. He eventually managed to come up with the eight group members that Dai Li had requested, but only after hiring complete novices, including a peripheral acquaintance who happened to be in Shanghai to visit Shen Zui's brother.

Shen Zui was paying for Chiang Kai-shek's year-long obsession with the Communist threat—an obsession that had led to intelligence work against the Japanese menace being all but ignored. In fact, even after the battle of Shanghai had broken out, while the Japanese Army was moving in to conquer the city, Dai Li's agents continued to arrest suspected Communists in the downtown districts, although they were slightly more discreet about it than previously, as a concession to the official propaganda declaring a united front against the Japanese aggressor.

After about a month in Hongkou, Shen Zui's network was compromised, and Japanese counterintelligence moved in to arrest everyone. It was time to leave. Shen Zui salvaged his radio, while one of his agents supplied a pram and a one-year-old child. Hiding the radio under the baby, they managed to roll it out under the noses of the Japanese guards. He was greeted in the International Settlement by one of his superiors, who thanked him for a job well done and asked him when he would be ready to go back in again. Not now and not for a long time, Shen Zui answered. He had had enough excitement to last him for quite a while.[56]

Chiang Kai-shek had decided as early as September 15 that change was needed at the top of the command of the Third War Zone.[57] What that meant became clear six days later when Chiang sent two separate cables to the zone's senior officers. In the first cable he himself took over command of the Third War Zone from Feng Yuxiang, the Christian General, and dispatched him to the Sixth War Zone further north.[58] It was a sideways move rather than a direct demotion, but it undeniably removed Feng Yuxiang from the single most important theater at the time. Even so, the decision seemed logical to most senior officers in Suzhou. Feng Yuxiang had never managed to do much while in overall command of the Third War Zone. None of his direct subordinates had ever really considered him to be in charge, and instead they had continued to treat Chiang as their actual commander.[59]

Feng Yuxiang's hands-off style certainly did not help him get a firmer grasp of his role as commander, but the main reason for his lack of efficiency was that he had been put in a position at Shanghai where he had to deal mostly with officers closely connected to Nanjing. These were people with whom he had none of the intimate personal ties that were vital in order to achieve anything in the Chinese Army. Equally important, Chiang Kai-shek never completely gained confidence in Feng Yuxiang and consistently undermined his old rival's authority by interfering directly in the campaign in Shanghai. Feng Yuxiang later described how at one point he had been contacted by Zhang Fakui, the commander of the Pudong troops. Zhang had tried to locate an artillery unit which he believed was under his command, but it was nowhere to be found. Feng looked into the matter and discovered that Chiang Kai-shek had withdrawn the unit single-handedly, ignoring the chain of command and telling no one.[60]

In the second cable of the day, Chiang Kai-shek went one step further and relieved Zhang Zhizhong of his duties as commander of the 9th Army Group. He replaced him with a general much more to his liking, Zhu Shaoliang, a staunch ally who was, if possible, an even bigger enemy of communism than he himself. For Zhang Zhizhong, the decision came as no major surprise. He had faced Chiang Kai-shek's constant reproaches right from the early days of the battle. Chiang may initially have picked Zhang because of his close connections to the divisional commanders that he led. However, he grew increasingly disenchanted with Zhang's style of command—much talk and little action—and vented his irritation both in front of his staff and in private. The day Wusong fell, Chiang again blamed Zhang. "This is because of his lacking ability," he wrote in his diary.[61]

It was an awkward time for a major shake-up. The Chinese forces were under growing pressure along the entire front, and they needed firm command more than ever. It was, therefore, unfortunate that when the generals retired they took their entire staffs with them, leaving a hiatus of one to two weeks before their successors and their staffs were up to speed.[62] Still, Chiang Kai-shek was convinced that the change had to be made. There may have been an additional reason for this. Disagreements in the top echelons of the Third War Zone had threatened to bring about paralysis. Zhang Zhizhong had not got along well with Chen Cheng, the commander of the neighboring 15th Army Group. "Chen Cheng isn't capable enough," Zhang Zhizhong had told those who would listen. Chen Cheng had retorted: "Zhang Zhizhong loves to show off." It had been a management nightmare for Chiang Kai-shek, and Feng Yuxiang, whose formal position as Third War Zone commander should have made it his responsibility to mediate, simply did not have the personal clout to make any difference.[63]

It had been in order to solve this complicated situation that Chiang Kai-shek had sent Gu Zhutong, a person better qualified to mediate among the explosive tempers, to act as second-in-command in the Third War Zone. Nevertheless, it was a cumbersome arrangement, and Chiang Kai-shek probably hoped to bring about a simplified command structure by weeding out senior officers who weren't performing and placing himself in the central position. That made sense. What made less sense, to some of Chiang's officers at least, was a decision on the same day to divide the Shanghai front into a left, a central and a right wing. The rationale was to partition the ever growing number of troops in the Shanghai area into groups of manageable size. While that had some logic to it, the move also inserted a new level of command in between the war zone and the army groups and further increased the potential for confusion and dissent, just at the time when the Chinese needed to act in unison against an enemy attack that was quickly picking up momentum.[64]

Zhang Zhizhong was not surprised to be let go. He had seen it coming for some time. Nevertheless, he was depressed, and perhaps even a broken man, after his dismissal. He had been working day and night, and eating on the run, while trying to keep Shanghai's defenses intact. However, it was not enough. In the last weeks before he was officially fired, Zhang Zhizhong felt increasingly sidelined.[65] It did nothing to improve his fragile health. More than a month of intense mental pressure had taken an immense toll. Always of slim build, he now came across as downright emaciated. When in late September he returned to his ancestral home in the eastern province of Anhui, his family barely recognized him. He would stay awake long after his family had gone to bed, preferring to sit in his study reading his favorite Chinese classics. He never spoke to his family abut the war. He hardly ever spoke at all, and when he did speak, he had the air of someone who had lost all his strength.[66]

The foreign residents of Shanghai pretended that there was no war on. Shanghai Football Association held its annual meeting in September to the distant rumble of artillery fire, and reelected the same president it had had since 1925.[67] Mailmen brought post past Japanese barbed wire near Sichuan North Road.[68] British wharf managers on the Pudong side of the Huangpu River spent their afternoons drinking tea and playing tennis, while Chinese positions were being bombed a mere 500 yards away.[69]

Shooting and shelling did not change the fact that business was the business of Shanghai. The city was eager to return to its beloved pastime of making money, second in popularity only to the pastime of spending it. The Cathay and Palace Hotels, shut down after the tragedy of "Black Saturday," opened again in mid-September following extensive repairs. Two movie theaters, the Grand and the Cathay, also showed the latest blockbusters, and nightclubs welcomed customers, although they closed at 11:00 p.m. to allow the patrons 30 minutes to return home before curfew. Shops opened with signs saying "Business (behind sandbags) as usual."[70] The stiff upper lip was being put to the test.

Despite determined attempts at creating an atmosphere of normalcy, there was no denying that the city was going through its biggest crisis ever and that the future was uncertain. These were not ordinary times after all, and with the hostilities occasionally spilling over the borders into the International Settlement, an inceasing number of people felt it advisable to make the necessary precautions to stay safe. Defying the gregarious mood that usually characterized the expatriates of Shanghai, many now preferred the safety of their homes. When the Municipal Orchestra organized an evening of classical music at the Nanjing Theater, only two thirds of the seats were filled.[71]

As if to emphasize the precarious situation, several of the foreign garrisons received large reinforcements, many of them the elite of their respective armies. About 800 Italian Grenadiers of Savoy arrived on September 14, "fresh from conquest in Abyssinia," as local media put it, with pith helmets adorned with large sun goggles.[72] They were followed less than a week later by 1,435 U.S. marines, their flat British-style helmets and campaign hats a reminder of the Corps' exploits two decades earlier on the battlefields of Europe.[73]

In the Chinese part of the city, no one even tried to pretend that times were anything but unusual. Military experts said Zhabei received the heaviest bombing ever showered over any piece of land of a similar size.[74] Some residents in no-man's-land in the Hongkou and Yangshupu areas were too frightened by the constant fighting to venture out, and some eventually starved to death in their own homes.[75]

The Mid-Autumn Festival, one of China's three major traditional holidays, was on September 19, but all celebrations were canceled due to the war situation.[76] Weddings were made simpler by the circumstances. The "ceremony" would often consist of a notice in the local paper announcing that a couple had tied the knot. At the end might be an apology for not informing acquaintances directly: "As addresses of friends and relatives have been changed during the trouble, it is regretted that announcements cannot be individually sent."[77]

Refugees were quickly emerging as the single most serious problem for Shanghai's municipal authorities, foreign as well as Chinese. By September, tens of thousands of people uprooted from their homes in the war-torn countryside north of Suzhou Creek had flooded into the International Settlement.[78] The leaders of the expatriate community felt that urgent action was needed to care for the growing flood of homeless, both out of genuine humanitarian concern and for fear that foreign property could be damaged.

Jacquinot, the one-armed Jesuit, was actively involved in seeking ways to mitigate the plight of the refugees, and an idea was gradually forming in his head. He had followed a public debate that had been ongoing since the late 1920s, on the possibility of creating safe zones for civilians in wartime. He believed that possibly such a zone could be formed in Shanghai. He made the proposal in a meeting with Hasegawa Kiyoshi, the commander of the Japanese Third Fleet, in late September. Hasegawa was noncommittal, but Jacquinot was determined to move ahead with the plan no matter what.[79]

The strain that Shanghai was under also had an economic side to it. Although it had been a bumper year for both rice and cotton, the two most popular crops in the area,[80] many farmers were unable to harvest because of continued heavy fighting around the city.[81] Labor disputes simmered and occasionally broke out into the open. On September 14, a group of workers hired on short-term contracts by the Fou Foong Flour Mill in the western part of the International Settlement locked themselves inside and refused to leave until a demand of 10 months' salary was met. Police and members of the Reserve Unit, a special anti-riot outfit, attacked the premises with tear gas and managed to dispel the protesters. Later, ambulances had to drive 25 injured males to various hospitals from the mill.[82]

As if the city was not already suffering enough hardship, a cholera epidemic had broken out and was taking its toll as well, especially among the poorest inhabitants. As of September 13, it had lasted for a month, with 119 confirmed cases and nine deaths.[83] Less than a fortnight later, it had infected 646 and killed 97. Once the outbreak had peaked by early October, it had claimed a total of 355 lives.[84] These statistics merely marked the tip of the iceberg, as they counted only the patients at hospitals in the International Settlement, leaving out the probably much larger numbers in the Chinese part of the city.[85] In a way, they were collateral damage. A doctor who worked with the patients stated with a great degree of certainty that the disease had probably been brought to Shanghai with troops from the south.[86]

––––––––––

"The white house," was the Japanese soldiers' name for the large villa hovering over the flat countryside south of Luodian. The former owner, who had obviously been a man of great riches, had called it "Villa of the Lucky

Plants." This name was written over the elaborate gateway along with characters extolling the former owner's ancestors.[87] The entire compound was surrounded by a tall white wall, as if to shield the inhabitants' wealth from the poverty in the countryside all around it. It had become pockmarked and blackened showing signs of intense and prolonged fighting. The Chinese had held the villa for four weeks, refusing to budge. Entrenched outside, the Japanese Army's 44th Regiment, also known as the Kochi Regiment, was being steadily worn down as attempts at storming the stronghold had all failed. Regimental commander Wachi Takaji, the sword-wielding colonel who had reaped much honor when leading the capture of Luodian the month before, had been forced into uncharacteristic passivity.[88]

Over the time that had passed since arriving at Luodian, the regiment had tried repeatedly to take the building, but with no success. Artillery support was limited because difficulties transporting supplies to the frontline meant that each artillery piece was down to only one fifth of its normal daily allowance of ammunition. The Chinese defenders by contrast were well-equipped, and showed off their impressive firepower every time Wachi threw his troops across the 70 yards separating the Japanese trenches from the white walls, cutting down row after row of Japanese soldiers. This situation had lasted for 27 long days. "This concerns the reputation of the Kochi Regiment," said Wachi. Another solution had to be found.

On September 19, engineers began digging a tunnel from the trenches towards "the white house." Four days later, they had dug exactly 35 yards, halving the distance the infantry would have to run across open land before reaching the wall. A new attack was launched on September 23, the second day of the Festival of the Autumnal Equinox. On this day in the lunar calendar, the emperor, a living god to most Japanese, would worship at the shrine of his ancestors, confirming the link between the Japan of the present age and the proud Japan of history. It was a reminder to all Japanese of what made them special and set them apart from the rest of mankind. On such a day, the attack could not be allowed to go wrong.

In the early afternoon, the Japanese kicked off the assault in their usual way. First came the artillery bombardment, then air raids. Finally, the tanks rolled up and moved towards the walls, as small clusters of soldiers followed in their tracks. In addition, the attack had one surprise in store for the Chinese. Just as the assault got underway, the mouth of the tunnel suddenly opened up, and soldiers leaped out in single file, so close to the wall that the Chinese machine gunners had no time to swing their barrels towards them. They rushed forward, carrying heavy satchels of explosives. Pressing against the walls, they lit the fuses then hastily sought cover. Loud explosions followed, and as the dust settled, the Japanese poured through the new gaping holes in the walls, fanning out inside the compound. After a fierce, two-and-a-half hour fight, the building was taken over by the Japanese. The regiment's honor, and Colonel Wachi's, had been saved.

The capture of "the white house" was part of a major offensive launched by the 11th Division in the Luodian area. It had originally been planned for September 20, but was delayed for several days because preparations took longer than expected, as was usually the case in the difficult countryside around Shanghai. The division attacked south of the town, opting for a narrow front in order to assemble enough troops to achieve a powerful, concentrated punch through Chinese positions. The Japanese used massed armor in the attack, deploying aircraft to take out any anti-tank weapons that appeared. Their tactics worked. The Chinese were pushed back in several sections of the front.[89] In order to muster enough forces for the attack, the division had put the Shigeto Detachment in charge of covering its right flank north and west of Luodian. However, the newly arrived detachment, which was still brimming with morale, did more than that, attacking vigorously and trying to push back the Chinese in its assigned sector. The detachment achieved relatively little of any significance, and lost a large number of soldiers. "The detachment has already had 200 casualties," Matsui wrote. "They can't go on attacking blindly like this."[90]

Further south the 3rd Japanese Division also launched attacks against Chinese positions, mainly in the area in front of Liuhang. The fighting in the area once again showed Japan's material superiority to be so pronounced that the Chinese feared to use heavy weaponry, even when it was available. All anti-aircraft guns in the area had been positioned near artillery batteries, but counterproductively, they hardly dared release any fire, lest they gave away the artillery's position. The result was that the Chinese Army enjoyed effectively no air defense whatsoever.[91]

Generally, the local Chinese reserves were unable to throw back the

Japanese, and the see-saw battle that had characterized the front since early September gave way to a several-day period when the Japanese held on to the positions even after dark. Under the circumstances, the Chinese commanders decided to carry out yet another major retreat along the entire front north of Shanghai. They used a lull in the Japanese attacks on September 25 to pull back to a line roughly one mile to the rear. As before, they implemented the withdrawal with perfect discipline, and it was two more days before the Japanese completely understood that their enemy had melted away.[92]

Following hard on the heels of these Japanese successes, major changes started to happen. The three divisions that the Japanese high command had ordered dispatched to the Shanghai area early in September gradually started arriving. First to land in the area south of Wusong was the 101st Division, which began disembarkation on September 22, and was ordered to deploy on the left flank of the 3rd Division. The 9th Division arrived in the same area on September 27, followed by the 13th Division on October 1.[93] Japan now had five divisions in Shanghai, against more than 25 divisions fielded by the Chinese.

Even if no one could doubt China's numerical superiority, the disparity was not as drastic as would seem. A typical Japanese division had 15,000 men, and combined with the marines and infantrymen defending Hongkou, the Japanese had roughly 90,000 soldiers at its disposal in and around the city. Chinese divisions, by comparison, frequently had as few as 5,000 men, and therefore it is unlikely that China deployed more than 200,000 soldiers in Shanghai at the time. Besides, the Japanese more than compensated for their numerical inferiority with their large superiority in materiel and airplanes, as well as with their naval artillery, which was still able to reach important parts of the Chinese front.[94]

All in all, the three new divisions marked a massive boost to the Japanese forces, and Matsui and his staff immediately started preparations for what they hoped would be the final blow to the Chinese defenders. Their plan was simple. They would launch a single powerful thrust across Wusong Creek and move from there to Suzhou Creek. Their aim was to surround and annihilate the main Chinese force in a maneuver that they had intended to carry out ever since they landed in China. After all, encirclement was the fundamental operation favored above any other in Japanese military doctrine. The only reason they hadn't already staged such an attack long before was a lack of resources. Encirclement with just two divisions, the 3rd and the 11th, would have caused the flanks to be too thinly manned and exposed to Chinese counterattack.[95] Now Matsui finally had the strength needed to launch the operation that would trap the Chinese in the city they were supposed to defend.

Nothing could go seriously wrong if you were in a mortar unit. Most of the time you would be located 500 yards behind the frontline, offering support for the infantry at the sharp end. At least, that was what the soldiers in Maebara Hisashi's unit told themselves when they shipped off to China. Maebara himself was a 30-year-old reservist, and had unexpectedly been torn out of his civilian routine in late August when he received the order to mobilize. It was inconvenient, but he, too, had left Japan with quiet confidence in victory.[96] After it had arrived in the Shanghai area, Maebara's unit was deployed for several weeks without casualties. However, in the end, they ran out of luck.

During a skirmish, the company's mortars received three direct hits from Chinese artillery. The shrapnel chewed through the crews, and the shockwave sent bodies and body parts flying through the air, shattering them against the walls of buildings nearby. A lump of red-hot metal had hit one of the soldiers in the chest. His blood poured out in a thick, dense stream, and he died almost instantaneously. Next to him, a piece of shrapnel had sliced open a soldier's stomach. His intestines had spilled out all at once like a bag of slippery eels. Medics arrived, stuffed the innards back in and hastily unraveled the injured soldier's puttees in order to use the strips of mud-covered cloth to dress the gaping wound. "This is screwed up," the injured soldier said in a voice marked by both pain and anger. "Do I really have to die in this hole?" Gradually, his loud swearing transformed into quiet whimpers, then complete silence. He was one of 18 Japanese killed in the attack.

After the shooting along the front died down, Maebara's unit received orders to cremate those killed and prepare the ashes for the return to Japan. The problem was, they were in the middle of a barren battlefield, and they did not have enough wood for suddenly disposing of 18 corpses. Someone had an idea: let's get the Chinese to provide the fuel, he suggested. Full of resentment, the soldiers walked to a farm building nearby, tore it down and carried away the beams. As Maebara watched the flames of the pyres rise towards the night sky, two separate thoughts kept recurring in his mind. "If this goes on, I won't live for very long. I better start bracing myself for the fact that death can occur any moment," was his first thought. His second thought: "You Chinese made our brothers die in this terrible way. We'll make you pay! It's because of you that we've come here to fight and suffer. You wanted this war. It's your fault!" For the first time, Maebara was consumed by actual hatred of the enemy.

He soon found out that he was not the only one who felt this way. A mood of poorly repressed fury spread through the company. Revenge was in the air. The next day guards grabbed three ordinary Chinese who happened to pass by their bivouac. There was no way they could be mistaken for soldiers. They were men in their early 30s, wearing tattered peasant clothes. Their unruly hair and undisciplined demeanor showed they had never worn a uniform. However, they would do. Yelling at the captives while punching and kicking them mercilessly, the Japanese soldiers tied their hands behind their backs and made them kneel in the mud. The Chinese appeared to know something terrible was going to happen to them. All three shut their eyes tight.

A group of soldiers grabbed one of the Chinese and dragged him to the side. They unbuttoned the top of his shirt and forced him to stretch out his neck for a cleaner cut. It didn't work. The soldier who had taken on the role of executioner was clearly doing it for the first time. He swung his sword ineptly, and brought it down with too little force, managing to make only a gash at the back of the Chinese man's neck. He swung the sword a second time, and a third. It took four clumsy attempts to finally sever the head from the body. He did not have much more luck with the other two men. When he was done, he was splattered from top to toe in his victims' blood. "We did poorly today," the Japanese soldiers complained to each other later that day. "Not a single head came off with just one strike. We'll have to do a better job next time."

CHAPTER

6

· ·

Verdun of the East

OCTOBER 1–23

"WE'RE BEING SHOT AT BY OUR OWN," WAS OGISHIMA SHIZUO'S FIRST thought when he heard the sound of rifles from the rear and saw bullets hit to the left and right of his position. It was before dawn on the south bank of Wusong Creek, and Ogishima, a 27-year-old reservist in the Japanese Army's 101st Division, had just been through his first night at the front. Soldiers around him in the trench got up, some from an uneasy slumber, shouting at the top of their lungs and waving their hands to make the firing stop, but it didn't. Someone near Ogishima held up the flag of the Rising Sun. That actually seemed to attract the bullets.[1]

Ogishima ventured a quick look over the edge of the trench. It was still dark and difficult to distinguish much of what was going on, but he thought he caught a quick glimpse of a helmet in a foxhole close to the edge of the creek. It was not a Japanese helment. It then occurred to him that the gunfire was not in error. "It's the enemy! The enemy!" he shouted. Other started yelling too. "The enemy! They're behind us! Turn around!" Under the cover of darkness, a Chinese unit had managed to sneak around the Japanese lines to attack them from behind. Aggressive shooting started. A Japanese heavy machine gun also chimed in. However, most bullets were fired at random into the darkness.

As it grew lighter, it was easier to get an idea about the size of the Chi-

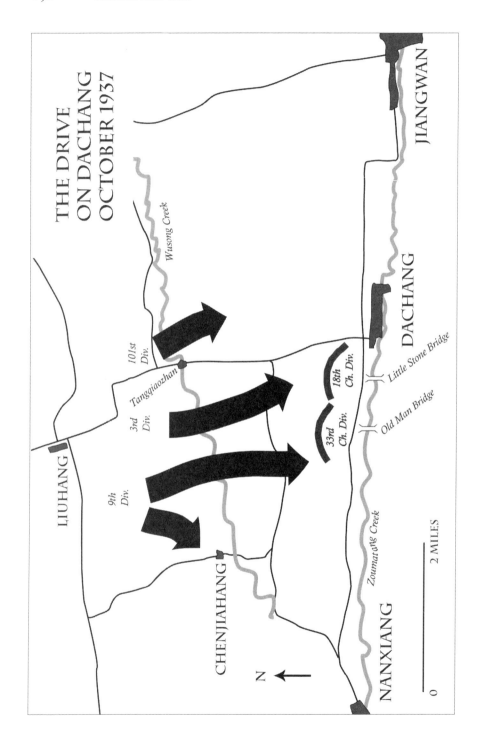

THE DRIVE ON DACHANG OCTOBER 1937

nese unit. It turned out that the intruders comprised a force of about 50 soldiers. The Japanese officers gave the orders to storm their positions. The infantrymen leapt over the edge of their trench, conditioned through years of drills to obey any command, even if it meant imminent death. Ogishima was not among the ones picked for the assault, but watched it with apprehension from his trench. The Chinese waited until the Japanese soldiers were just yards away and then let loose a ferocious barrage of fire. The first row of Japanese soldiers was mowed down.

Undeterred, the officers ordered a new attack. This time Ogishima was in it. Yelling like madmen, they stormed across the open land towards the Chinese position, lobbing hand grenades once they were close enough. They jumped into the foxholes occupied by the Chinese, and a fierce hand-to-hand struggle followed. Ogishima thrust his bayonet into the belly of a Chinese soldier. It was his first kill. He felt no emotion, only slight curiosity over the fact that the stab wound forced the other man to kneel down.

It was all over in a matter of minutes. The Chinese had been on a suicide mission. Not a single one of them survived. However, the battle had also been costly for the Japanese. Ogishima looked around. Familiar faces were everywhere among the dead. They were faces that only half an hour earlier had been full of life. Now they were set in the expressions they had when they died. One corpse was still clutching his combat knife. With the danger over, medics came running up, and quietly talked to each other in horror about the terrible carnage they were witnessing.

It was the morning of October 7 and Ogishima found it hard to believe that it was little more than a month since he had received his mobilization orders, two weeks since he had arrived in China, and just a day since he had first tasted battle. The 101st Division had crossed Wusong Creek from the north in the early hours of October 6—or more precisely, half of the division had made the crossing. The other half remained on the other side, unable to get their boats past the 300 feet of water guarded by invisible Chinese machine guns and mortar crews who would open fire at the smallest sign of movement on the north bank. Dozens of corpses were floating in the brown water as a testimony to the slaughter of the past 24 hours.

————————

Ogishima, like tens of thousands of other soldiers on both sides, was entering the most grueling part of the Shanghai campaign. Ahead lay weeks of combat that would rival the battlefields of the Great War in their pointless waste of human life. Twenty years after the carnage of the Western Front, tactics and technology still remained heavily in favor of defensive strategies. Both sides had armor at Shanghai, but neither had the quantity or quality of tanks to allow them to be deployed in a way that could bring about a breakthrough in the way armor would a few years later in Europe. It could be seen as ironic that the bloody melee that would ensue south of Wusong Creek was caused by Matsui Iwane's vision for a quick end to the battle of Shanghai. On the other hand, even with the benefit of hindsight, it is difficult to see how he could have done anything differently.

Matsui outlined his plans in an order issued on September 29. The attack was to be carried out by, from west to east, the 9th, 3rd and 101st Infantry Divisions. The 11th Infantry Division was to follow behind the 9th Division and secure the right flank against Chinese counterattacks from the west. The 13th Infantry Division formed the reserve. The attack force was to take Dachang, an old town surrounded by a medieval-looking wall, and then move on as fast as possible to cut through the Chinese lines north of Suzhou Creek.[2] Matsui had prepared an unusual concentration of manpower. The three divisions were lined up on a front that measured just three miles across, meaning each division was given less than half the length of frontline that the Japanese field manual prescribed.[3] The decision to squeeze the divisions into a narrow front was partly to make up for the weakness in artillery that continued to hamper the Japanese offensive.[4]

The Japanese attackers faced a formidable and well-prepared foe. After lengthy debates, the Chinese commanders had finally agreed they had no choice but to shorten their front line. The defense of Liuhang, a town on the road from Luodian to Dachang, had become too costly with no chance of eventual victory. Chen Cheng, the commander of the Chinese left wing, had frequently visited Liuhang and knew how hopeless the situation was. He had repeatedly called for the unwinnable fight to be given up and for valuable troops to be moved back to stronger positions. However, his arguments had initially fallen on deaf ears. Chiang Kai-shek was mainly guided by the notion that war was about winning or keeping real estate, and he had insisted on holding on to Liuhang at any price.[5]

Only after the Chinese front north of Wusong Creek had been penetrated in several places in late September did Chiang relent, and the commanders made hasty preparations to pull back the forces in order to preserve their strength and ensure their ability to wage a long-term campaign aimed at bleeding the enemy to death. The Chinese started a fighting retreat during the evening of October 1 and had completed the operation by dawn of October 3. It was yet another of the disciplined withdrawals at which the Chinese defenders had become experts.

The new line stretched a little more than a mile west of the road from Luodian to Dachang, offering the Chinese defenders excellent opportunities to harass the Japanese Army with flanking fire for several miles during its advance south.[6] At Wusong Creek, the Chinese line bent east and followed the southern bank for several miles. The creek offered the Chinese defenders a devastating advantage. Despite its name, it would be more precise to call it a river. It had a width of up to 300 feet across, and in several places the southern bank was a steep six-foot wall. Anyone managing to scale this obstacle under heavy mortar bombardment would be met at the top by rows of barbed wire and heavy machine gun fire. For an entire mile south of the creek, the Chinese had spent weeks building a dense network of defenses, turning farm buildings into impenetrable fortifications connected by deep trenches. The Chinese had learned a lesson from their German masters, veterans of Somme and Verdun, and they had learned it well.[7]

––––––––––

Matsui only had vague notions of the strong enemy forces awaiting his men south of Wusong Creek, and for him the main question was when to launch the crossing. By early October, he felt a compelling sense of momentum. As his troops advanced closer to the creek, assisted by tanks and artillery, the Chinese put up a determined defense as usual, but even so, they retreated from one strongpoint after another. On October 3, Matsui's soldiers took Liuhang and managed to hold on to their prize, even though the Chinese immediately launched counterattacks in a bid to take back the town.[8] Japanese reconnaissance flights behind enemy lines revealed significant troop movements, leading Matsui to suspect that a general withdrawal was under way. "Along the entire front, signs are emerging that the enemy is wavering," he wrote in his diary.[9]

The following day, October 4, also went smoothly for the Japanese attackers. Even the middle-aged reservists in the 101st Division were able to beat an enemy force and take 300 prisoners. Matsui felt the time was right for a decisive blow. The only slight reason for doubt was the weather. It had changed from bright sunshine the day before to a somber dark sky and it was only a question of time before it would start raining. This was bad news for Matsui's soldiers, dressed in thin summer uniforms. Even so, he made up his mind. He issued his order for the 9th, 3rd and 101st Divisions to implement the planned crossing of Wusong Creek and move to a line about half a mile south of the creek.[10]

Beginning on October 5, the three Japanese divisions attempted crossings at several points along Wusong Creek. They managed to carve out a narrow bridgehead on the south bank, but all along the front they were met with staunch resistance. The Chinese commanders were fully aware that everything must be done to prevent a Japanese breakthrough as after Wusong Creek, the only major remaining natural obstacle to a Japanese offensive cutting off all of Shanghai was Suzhou Creek.

Two miles west of the strategic road from Luodian to Dachang, battalion commander Yan Yinggao of the Chinese Army's 78th Division's 467th Regiment was waiting in tense anticipation for the Japanese attack. The regiment had set up positions in three fortified villages facing the creek. In their sturdiness, they were similar to dozens of other strongholds prepared by the Chinese in the the preceding weeks. The buildings had been reinforced with sandbags and barbed wire, trees had been cut down to ensure clear fields of fire, and deep trenches enabled troops to quickly and securely move from one sector to the other. The regiment's 1st Battalion had occupied the westernmost village, while the 3rd Battalion held the two others. Yan Yinggao's 2nd Battalion was kept in reserve.

The first Japanese attack was preceded by a ferocious artillery barrage. The Japanese infantry that followed shortly afterwards took heavy casualties at all three villages and had to withdraw. They returned in the afternoon, and this time the preparatory artillery fire was even more intense. The 1st Battalion took a series of hits that killed a large number of men, including the commander. The unit disintegrated, and it yielded the village to the Japanese. Yan Yinggao, who had watched the struggle from the rear, sent a company as reinforcement, but it was completely wiped out within less than ten minutes.

At the same time, the eastern village has also fallen into Japanese hands, leaving the 3rd Battalion in the central village, Tangbeizhai, nearly surrounded. At this point, Yan received orders from the regiment to move up with his troops and relieve the beleaguered battalion. As he marched towards Tangbeizhai, he noticed a Japanese column of about 50 or 60 soldiers approaching his destination from the opposite direction. Suddenly, a series of shots were fired from the smoking rubble of the bombed-out village. The Japanese column panicked, dispersed and withdrew to the rear. One of the few surviving 3rd Battalion soldiers in Tangbeizhai had decided to make a last stand. He had expected to be overrun by the attacking Japanese, but in the end succeeded in holding the village just long enough for the 2nd Battalion to arrive and take over the defense.[11] It was a small triumph, but a temporary one. Like numerous other strongholds in the war-torn landscape south of Wusong Creek, Tangbeizhai would eventually be crushed by the Japanese juggernaut.

The Chinese commanders were desperate to keep the front intact for as long as possible, and any fresh forces that turned up in the Shanghai area were likely to be sent to the frontline immediately. Some were of good quality. Among them were units from the Tax Police Division. Despite its name,[12] the division had developed into a fully equipped military formation with a highly motivated and trained corps. Consisting of six regiments, it was a force of more than 25,000 well-armed soldiers, with a backbone of tough and experienced officers who had previously served under the northern warlord Zhang Xueliang.[13]

In all haste, Tax Police units were ordered to Tangqiaozhan, where the road from Luodian to Dachang bridged Wusong Creek. It was the key position in the entire operation, and the longer the Chinese could keep the bridge, the greater their hope of stalling the Japanese advance. The Tax Police, who set up strong positions at the northern end of the bridge, found themselves surrounded on three sides. The opposing forces engaged in fierce fighting, at times meeting in hand-to-hand combat. On the second day after they arrived, casualties has grown so large that the Tax Police units were pushed south across the bridge, which was lost to the advancing Japanese.[14]

A crisis atmosphere reigned when the staff of Third War Zone held its meeting, chaired by Chiang Kai-shek, in Suzhou on October 11. There was general agreement that the attempts made so far to stop the Japanese advance south across Wusong Creek had not worked. Each time troops had been hurled into battle, they had merely bounced off the Japanese front, without regaining any major ground. A more ambitious undertaking was needed. Chen Cheng, the commander of the left wing, suggested an attack in his sector targeting the area around Luodian. However, the majority view in the meeting was that an operation of this kind would not have any immediate impact on the Japanese advance near Wusong Creek, and it was dismissed.[15]

Instead, the meeting heard a rival suggestion by Bai Chongxi, a south Chinese general with the serene demeanour of a Buddhist cleric.[16] Bai, who was attached to the Third War Zone in an informal advisory role, called for a simultaneous attack along both banks of Wusong Creek into the right flank of the advancing Japanese. It would be a major operation and would require a large number of troops if it were to have any chance of succeeding. Bai knew exactly where he was going to get the necessary manpower—four divisions from south China's Guangxi province, who were already in transit, were due to arrive in Shanghai within few days. Chiang Kai-shek liked the idea of a single, devastating blow aganst the Japanese. The meeting approved Bai's proposal.[17]

The enthusiasm was not shared by the German advisors. As the battle evolved, they watched with growing apprehension as the Chinese decision making got bogged down in endless talk. One example was a lengthy debate about whether the Jiangwan salient should be abandoned in order to shorten the front and avoid spreading the troops too thinly. Only after long hours of discussion did the Chinese commanders decide to give up the idea as it would cause a dangerous shrinkage of the link between Shanghai and the Chinese interior.[18]

The Germans believed that much talk that in the end produced few decisions was a consequence of the way the Chinese command was structured. Gu Zhutong, Chiang's deputy in Suzhou, was served by not just a chief of staff but also two advisors. There were also individual generals attached informally to Gu's headquarters. In German eyes, Bai Chongxi was a prime example. With no formal command, he was supposed to provide his views on operational issues. To the Germans, used to clear military hierarchies, this was an arrangement bound to create inefficient solutions. "The responsibilities of the actual chief of staff had been watered down and the scene was set for endless and fruitless councils," wrote Albert Newiger, one of the advisors, after his return to Germany.[19]

One area where the arrogant Germans had to concede that their Chinese apprentices had improved was artillery. For the first time in the entire Shanghai campaign, during the battles around Wusong Creek the Chinese command decided to concentrate nearly all the artillery at its disposal. A total of six artillery battalions were moved to positions in the vicinity of Nanxiang and placed under the unified command of the head of the Tangshan Artillery School near Nanjing. From there, they carried out coordinated barrages for the duration of the fight for the crucial area south of Wusong Creek.

The Chinese commanders had been reluctant to carry out this measure, due to their well-founded fear that any gathering of artillery would immediately attract enemy air attack. To defend the positions, they deployed several batteries of 2cm anti-aircraft guns and one battery of 3.7cm anti-aircraft guns, which were positioned on both sides on Nanxiang. It turned out that these guns, which were not particularly numerous and of small caliber, were sufficient to intimidate the Japanese aircraft, so that they either avoided attacking the artillery altogether or did so from such an altitude that the effect was negligible.

"We caught a spy!" someone shouted. Sone Kazuo rushed towards the voice. Since the 22-year-old Japanese squad leader had landed at Wusong with the 3rd Division, he had not seen a single Chinese up close, and he was curious about what they looked like. The "spy" was a woman of about 60. With lowered voice she kept mumbling away in her own language. More soldiers started crowding around, and they began discussing what to do with her. Suddenly, a voice cut through the chatter: "I'll kill her." The voice belonged to a young soldier with a cultured appearance that betrayed a wealthy family background. He had a combat knife in his hand. Without hesitation, he walked up to the old woman, shouting: "Hey, you!" As she turned around, he stabbed her in the chest. The woman cried out briefly. She was dead before she hit the ground.[20]

Sone Kazuo had been brought up by his grandmother, a devotee of the Buddhist faith, who had taught him that the greatest possible offense was to kill a living being. As a boy he had taken this seriously and felt sorry even when he happened to step on ants on the way to school. However, that was all in the distant past and he had decapitated his first prisoner not long after disembarking at Shanghai. His unit had found three enemy soldiers while overrunning a Chinese position. Initially, they wanted to shoot them, but an older soldier, who had been fighting previously in northeast China, had a better idea. "Why don't we cut off their heads," he said. He turned towards Sone. "It's really rare you get to chop someone's head off. It's an experience you can take back home. Sir, you should try it."

Being a squad commander and standing in front of his troops, Sone did not dare show weakness. He agreed, and the old soldier eagerly took the initiative, ordering a group of privates standing nearby to escort the three prisoners to a riverbank, where they were forced to their knees. Sone stepped behind the first prisoner and raised his sword. He suddenly felt slightly panicky, but he could not back down. "Kill!" he shouted at the top of his lungs. He struck with such force that the the sword cut clean through the man's neck and burrowed its edge into the soil in front of his boots. The severed head rolled down the embankment like a football and fell into the river with a small, innocuous plop. Sone turned around and looked at the decapitated body. A thick stream of blood poured out. Then it became a trickle. It had all taken a few seconds, but for Sone it had been like a slow-moving dream.[21]

The war between China and Japan was one where no quarter was given. The Japanese claimed in public that all prisoners were being treated well,[22] but the reality was very different. Matsui Iwane mentioned in his diary how a unit fighting a successful engagement near Wusong ended up with 500 prisoners. The defiant attitude of the captives caused the Japanese to worry that they might pose a security threat. "So they were all shot," Matsui wrote.[23] The Dutch spy de Fremery mentioned what he described as "an improbably low" number of prisoners of war. The Japanese claimed to have seized several hundred, but de Fremery wondered "if they ever did exist, which may be heavily subject to sincere doubt."[24]

There were very few desertions from the Chinese Army. The soldiers had nowhere to run. Few were from Shanghai and would not be able to get by in the alien environment, where the dialect was entirely different from their own. However, more importantly, they exposed themselves to the risk of running into the Japanese Army, and rumors had been circulating from early on of their brutal handling of prisoners.[25] Anyone ending up in Japanese hands was considered as good as dead. Captives, including civilians suspected of spying, were interrogated and once they had no more information to offer, they were disposed of. The likely fate awaiting Chinese prisoners was also well understood within the Japanese ranks. When a Buddhist priest serving as military clergy handed over a Chinese soldier he had personally overpowered, he begged the Japanese soldiers to preserve his life, knowing full well that this was far from a foregone conclusion.[26]

Typically executions were in the traditional manner of decapitation. Shanghai residents got used to the sight of headless bodies, frozen in the kneeling position they had assumed at the moment of death, floating down Suzhou Creek.[27] Those were the lucky ones. There were reports that injured Chinese prisoners were tied together, face down, doused with gasoline and burned. "Their corpses had the sheen of black lacquer and their limbs were all contorted," read an account of such an instance shortly after the battle of Shanghai. "Crawling on the ground they looked like turtles."[28] It is not unlikely that the prospect of mind-boggling cruelty at Japanese hands contributed to the Chinese determination, exhibited from early on in the battle, to fight to the last man.

The maltreatment of prisoners was mutual. Accounts of Japanese prisoners being kept for long by the Chinese were virtually non-existent. Frequently, this was due to circumstances at the front, whether in the urban areas or the surrounding countryside. Under confusing and dangerous battlefield conditions, there was simply nowhere to place captives. Officers saved themselves endless trouble by simply ordering prisoners killed. However, even when facilities were available, nothing was done to accommodate enemy POWs. Dutchman de Fremery never saw or heard about a single instance of any Japanese troops being among the 20,000 injured soldiers being treated at Chinese hospitals in the Shanghai area.[29]

Especially at the start of the Sino-Japanese war, the treatment of Japanese prisoners at the hands of the Chinese "beggared belief" and marked a

throw-back to a less-civilized past, according to the German war correspondent Lily Abegg. Often civilians took part in the maltreatment of captured Japanese. Abegg mentioned an example of two Japanese pilots who
were shot down during a raid of Nanjing. They were "torn to pieces" by a
furious mob, and when military police arrived they could not find a single
trace of them remaining on the scene.[30]

The killing of Japanese prisoners, often in a horrific fashion, was a
source of concern for the Chinese command. It wanted to be able to show
off well-treated prisoners for propaganda purposes, and doubtless, it also
wanted to exploit the captives for their intelligence value. In the end, it
offered a money prize for any Chinese, soldier or civilian, who was able to
hand over a living Japanese prisoner to the authorities. However, this had
little effect. "The soldier's hatred toward the Japanese," a Chinese general
said a little later in the war, "is enormous. It's impossible to have a prisoner
delivered to headquarters although we pay from 50 to 100 yuan upon deliv-
ery, and there are severe punishments for not doing so. The soldiers say
that the prisoners die along the way."[31]

The scene reminded Sun Liren of the situation when a group of tourists
step off a train and are mobbed by staff from competing hotels all scrambling to offer rooms. The only difference was that when he got off the train
with his soldiers in the pitch black at Nanxiang Railway Station on October
7, the people grabbing at his sleeves begging him to come with them were
ranking officers from depleted divisions along the front, desperate for reinforcements. At age 36, Sun was commanding one of China's best units,
the 4th Regiment of the Tax Police, a coveted asset. The upshot of the confused scene at the train station was that he was assigned to the 88th Division, which had suffered heavily in the battles since late August in the
northwestern part of Shanghai.[32]

By noon the next day, almost all of Sun's regiment had been cannibal-
ized and sent to reinforce worn-out units all along the 88th Division's frontline. All that was left was Sun himself and a group of about 20 orderlies
and clerks. By 2:00 p.m. he got a call from the division. It needed more
reinforcements, as the front was about to collapse near a small bridge north
of Zhabei. Sun replied that he had no more soldiers available, but the offi-

cer at the other end insisted: "It's an order. If you disobey, you'll be court-martialed."

Sun had no choice but to hastily organize the two dozen soldiers over whom he maintained direct command and march to the bridge in pouring rain. When they arrived, he saw Chinese soldiers withdrawing across the bridge in large numbers. He asked what they were running away from, and the answer was prompt. "The officers have all left," one of the soldiers said. "We also don't want to die." Sun told them he was an officer, in fact the commander of an entire regiment, and that he would stay and fight with them.

The Japanese, who were in close pursuit, were astonished to see the Chinese abruptly turn around and make a stand. Sun watched with satisfaction as the enemy troops immediately lost momentum, and started moving back to their original positions. They must have thought, he said to himself, that the Chinese defenders had received strong reinforcements, rather than just a small group of 20 bespectacled staff aides. The Japanese advance in the sector had been halted. Wet to the bone and freezing, Sun went back to report to the divisional commander. The general was sitting in his headquarters, shielded from the rain and cold and the bullets of the enemy, together with two of his regimental commanders. Sun wondered what they were doing there, so far behind the frontline and his glee turned to dismay.[33] Sun would continue to fight bravely on the Shanghai front for the next month, but he had become aware that officers and men were not sharing the hardship in equal measure.

In the first days of October, while the battle of Shanghai was being decided in the fields west of the city, the municipal area and the immediate suburbs continued to see heavy fighting. The Japanese also launched several attacks against the semi-rural Jiangwan sector on October 2 and 3, mostly in an attempt to divert the attention of the Chinese artillery, which at the time was posing a significant danger to the Japanese column preparing to attack across Wusong Creek. All the assaults were beaten back, at high cost to the attackers, due to a combination of Japanese arrogance and Chinese professionalism.

The Japanese had underestimated the Chinese and had prepared the operation with a minimum of secrecy, allowing the divisions about to be attacked, the 87th and 36th, to gather detailed intelligence about their plans. Equally devastating to the Japanese, they had assembled the attack force too close to the frontline, without preparing a robust defensive perimeter, giving the Chinese the opportunity to launch preemptive strikes against them. To the German advisors on the scene, the successful intelligence work was testimony to the fact that Nanjing divisions, which they themselves had trained, remained superior to almost any other units in the Chinese Army.[34]

In Zhabei district, a more urbanized area, visiting foreigners were astonished to witness the thoroughness of the Chinese fortifications. "Every street was a defense line and every house a pocket fort," wrote an impressed correspondent after visiting the area. "Thousands of holes had been knocked through walls, linking the labyrinth of lanes into a vast system of defense in depth. Every intersection had been made into a miniature fortress of steel and concrete. Even the stubs of bomb-battered walls had been slotted at ground level for machine guns and rifles." The city looked deserted at first sight, but sentries were posted at all important locations, ready to rouse the troops resting fully equipped inside the larger ruins. "No wonder the Japanese Army was months behind its boasts," the foreign correspondent commented.[35]

The artillery on the east side of the Huangpu River remained active in October, but it was constrained by the certainty that any attack it launched would be met almost immediately by a strong Japanese response. Under these limitations, Sun Shengzhi, the commander of an artillery regiment in Pudong, was ordered to launch a barrage across the river on the Gongda airfield, which was becoming increasingly active and provided close air support for troops fighting in the Shanghai area. For the attack to have any effect, careful preparation was called for, and Sun Shengzhi carried out reconnaissance and planning in cooperation with Gustav Boegel, a German lieutenant attached to the Pudong artillery as an advisor.

On the eve of the attack, Chinese soldiers rolled a battery of eight Bofors guns to a predetermined position 300 yards from the riverbank. They were all in position by midnight. Hours of waiting followed until shortly before dawn, when the airfield turned on its lights. From then until the first plane took off, there was a window of about 50 minutes, reconnaissance had shown. It took a couple of shells to register the target, and then all eight guns fired in rapid succession, using up their shell supply within just minutes. Their mission accomplished, the crews hastily packed up and retreated before the rising sun would expose them to a lethal barrage from the naval guns in the middle of the river. Later intelligence reports suggested that five Japanese planes had been destroyed and seven damaged in the attack.[36]

Another, even more successful, attack followed. By mid-October, the German-trained 88th Infantry Division took advantage of a lull in the fighting to prepare for one of the most ambitious attacks in municipal Shanghai since late August. It was a strike meant to cut off Sichuan North Road, a major supply line from the Japanese-controlled docks to the Japanese units in the north of the city. The assault would again use the tactics developed by the German *Stosstruppen* in the latter years of the Great War. For *Stosstruppen*, the main means of weakening the enemy line was infiltration rather than massive frontal attack, and mobility was prioritized over firepower.

The attack took place on October 18. After a brief bombardment by artillery and mortars, the lightly equipped Chinese soldiers moved at great speed down streets near the North Railway Station and managed to take the dazed Japanese defenders by complete surprise, occupying a segment of Sichuan North Road. As a result, the supply chain using the road was interrupted for several days afterwards. The German advisors saw the attack as a fresh departure from a Chinese way of war that was too heavily dependent on large-unit operations and unimaginative wrestling over strongholds. In the international press it was seen in conjunction with the attacks carried out by the Pudong batteries and erroneously interpreted as a precursor of a major Chinese offensive.[37]

———————

In the fall of 1937, Shanghai was on the front pages of the world's newspapers. The battle was the most dramatic manifestation yet of Japan's aggressive imperialist ambitions and the public wanted to know more. At the same time, convenience entered the picture. This was not a distant battlefield, reached by aventurous reporters at overwhelming personal hazard, but one of the great cities of the world. Foreign correspondents were already present in great numbers, or could easily sail in from places like Tokyo and Manila. They could report on the progress of the war at the same time as they enjoyed the relative luxury of Shanghai's five-star hotels, which continued to operate as before despite the war on their doorsteps.

Journalists and photographers enjoyed an unprecedented freedom of movement. In the early stages of the battle, when fighting was confined to the municipal area, they could easily cover both sides of the story within a single day. First thing in the morning they could visit the Japanese positions, take a detour and then arrive at the Chinese side of the front. Once they had what they needed they could return to the neutral territory of the International Settlement and file their stories without having to worry about being censored by anyone.[38]

Later, as the war moved to the outskirts of Shanghai, the Japanese restricted coverage by foreign journalists, but access was as uninhibited as ever on the Chinese side. The services of a modern transportation system made the urban battlefront even more accessible to inquisitive correspondents. When the battle was reaching its climax, Erik Nystrom, a Swedish correspondent, used a press conference to ask the Shanghai mayor where the front was. "The end of our line is just west of the railway, beyond Jessfield Park," the mayor said. "Umm, I tank I yust take the Yessfield buss out to the front tomorrow," the Swede said, seeing no reason to waste money on expensive transportation.[39]

The Chinese and, despite the restrictions they imposed, the Japanese both understood the value of propaganda and tried their best to project their respective views to the world public. They both held daily press conferences, helpfully spaced out so correspondents who were covering the story on their own did not have to miss out on anything. Even so, most foreign journalists had a clear preference for the Chinese. This partly came down to the fact that they were mostly members of China's foreign press corps, and, as is often the case with correspondents, had gradually come to sympathize or even identify with the country they were reporting from. At a more fundamental human level, it was also a reflection of the pity they felt for the young Chinese republic as it was being victimized by naked Japanese aggression.

This made for a tense atmosphere at the daily news conferences carried out by the Japanese military, despite a generous offering of drinks ranging from coffee and tea to beer and whiskey. One army representative, and one from the navy, would deliver the day's briefing in Japanese, with the translator "Bob" Horiguchi providing a perfect rendering in idiomatic American English. After that it would be time for questions at which time the anglophone correspondents and especially the Americans, perhaps emboldened by the free flow of liquor, would delight in asking impossible questions, setting off a to and fro of scathing remarks.[40]

As the novelty of the battle rubbed off, reporters working for local media found that their audience in the International Settlement lost some of their interest in the fighting over hamlets in the countryside near Shanghai and wanted to be entertained with the usual journalism fare of true crime and celebrity scandals. This required a certain degree of versatility. Carroll Alcott, an American journalist with years of experience in Asia, remembered witnessing a major battle between Chinese and Japanese soldiers, followed by a walk through streets littered with gore after an air attack. He ended the day covering a court case against a gang of jewelry thieves led by a dubious character known as Hatchet-Face Rosie.[41]

However, for the vast majority of reporters present in Shanghai, it was the epic battle that mattered. Journalistic careers were founded in the rubble of the city and the trenches of the suburbs. Eyewitness accounts straight from the frontline were at a premium. Descriptions of how a journalist himself had narrowly escaped death to bring his story to the readers were likely to reach a wider audience. Yet, despite the stiff competition for scoops, the journalists seemed to live charmed lives. No one from the neutral media lost his or her life while reporting from the frontline for the entire first three months of battle. This was a remarkable record that was to stay unchanged until the very last day of hostilities in the city.[42]

Kuse Hisao's company, part of the Japanese Army's 9th Infantry Division, was roused before dawn and started the march to the frontline at 6:00 a.m. on October 13. The mood was dejected as the column trudged down muddy paths, softened by days of incessant rain. The soldiers passed a spot where, so they muttered to each other, an entire Japanese battalion had been wiped out in a night attack. Their own mission could end up equally as deadly. There were to take part in yet another attack on the town of Chenjiahang, located just north of Wusong Creek. It was an important and heavily defended stronghold that obstructed the southward advance of the Japanese Army. The Chinese would hold onto the village fanatically, like they did any other fortified village. It would become bloody.[43]

When Kuse Hisao's unit had almost reached the front, the soldiers were told to rest. Chenjiahang was somewhere in the distance, behind tall cotton fields. The order to attack came at 1:00 p.m. The Japanese artillery started exactly at the arranged minute. The Chinese artillery answered in kind, but with much greater force. It was an unpleasant surprise for the Japanese to be so heavily outgunned, but the assault went ahead nonetheless. Wave after wave of attackers marched off obediently, disappearing into the cotton fields. The plants offered some cover, but not enough. The Chinese defenders fired from invisible positions, especially aiming at the machine gunners, who were always the first to be targeted because of their firepower. One was shot through the thigh, while another received a wound to the face.

The Chinese fire grew so dense that it was almost impossible for the Japanese to move. Kuse Hisao's platoon slowly crawled forward across the field, through the sticky mud created by the downpour of the recent days. Over the noise of weapons being fired, the wailing of the injured could be heard, but it gradually became weaker. Kuse Hisao was relieved when he reached a small creek, rolling down the slope in the hope of gaining cover from the fire there. However, his relief turned to horror when he discovered the water was filled with Japanese and Chinese corpses in various stages of decomposition.

The attack on Chenjiahang had bogged down, and Kuse Hisao and his platoon spent the night in the dreary company of the dead soldiers. The following day the order arrived for two neighboring platoons to renew the attack. Kuse Hisao's platoon was kept in reserve, but the day's battle was no more successful than the previous day's, and when it was almost dark, they too were ordered to advance. Like the previous day, they moved by crawling across the field. They passed the bodies of several soldiers from the two other platoons, who had been killed and lay in pools of blood. Eventually, they reached another creek. Barbed wire was rolled out along the bank, and engineers were busy removing it, keeping as low as they could. On the other side, behind a bamboo grove, they were told, was Chenjiahang.

The sun had already set, and Kuse Hisao was crouching in the dark, waiting for orders about what to do next. Suddenly, a huge white flame lit up the night. The engineers had brought a flamethrower, the most dreaded weapon of the Japanese Army, and had crossed the creek. The bamboo grove on the other side was ablaze. "Attack!" someone shouted. They jumped into the waist-deep water, waded across, and grabbed branches of bamboo trees to haul themselves onto the other bank. Quickly scaling the slope, they found themselves in a maze of Chinese trenches, which were apparently deserted. They took a quick break, triumphant and relieved at the same time. They had occupied a corner of Chenjiahang, without even firing a shot.

It was a brief pause, interrupted when Kuse Hisao heard lowered voices. They were not speaking Japanese. A split second later, a German-style stick hand grenade was lobbed into his trench. The next thing Kuse Hisao remembered was gradually emerging from a daze, with a humming sound in his ears. He felt a sharp pain in his eyes, and he was unable to open them. He was grateful to be alive but he expected the trench to be overrun and that he would be killed any moment. However, the Chinese attack did not come. Kuse Hisao spent the night, helpless and blinded, until dawn finally broke and friendly hands carried him back to the rear.[44]

Few would have been able to place Chenjiahang on a map before the war, but for several weeks, beginning in early October, the Chinese and the Japanese fought bitterly over its increasingly devastated streets. Along with Yanghang, Chenjiahang was considered one of the two key points that the Japanese absolutely needed to control in order to be able to move south towards Dachang. They would do anything to take Chenjiahang, and the Chinese would do anything to keep it. The see-saw battle over the town continued even long after Japanese troops had managed to break through the Wusong Creek barrier elsewhere along the front.[45]

The Chinese commanders hurled a large number of their available troops into the Chenjiahang sector to prevent a collapse. These troops included units newly arrived from the Chinese provinces. In the early part of October, they deployed two divisions from the southwestern province of Sichuan. These divisions did not command much respect among the German advisors who deemed that insufficient training and equipment rendered them incapable of carrying out divisional-level operations in the field and concluded that they were best deployed in a regimental fashion to relieve burnt-out troops.[46]

The Sichuan troops were pulled out again when in the middle of the month four fresh divisions arrived from Guangxi, a province in southern China. The Chinese field commanders were eager to use the new troops, easily recognizable in their light brown uniforms and their British-style "tin hat" helmets, and they sent one of the four, the 173rd Guangxi Division, straight to Chenjiahang. Ordered to march on the evening of October 15, the division arrived before dawn the following day, to take over positions held by another division that had suffered severe attrition and needed to withdraw to the rear.[47]

While the handover of the positions was still taking place, the Japanese, who had detected the movement along the Chinese front, launched an intense air and artillery attack, causing serious casualties in the 173rd Division's ranks before it had even properly deployed. Later the same day, when one of the division's regiments was sent to engage the Japanese, it was slaughtered on the spot. By nightfall, two thirds of its soldiers had become casualties. The battle went on for the next four days, and gradually the three other Guangxi divisions also moved to the front. There was no breakthrough on either side, only desperate fighting over the same few inches of soil. "I had heard the expression 'storm of steel' before, but never really understood what it meant," said a Guangxi officer. "Now I do."[48]

By mid-October, Matsui's initial optimism about his push south had shifted to weariness. The rain had already lasted for more than a week and had become a particular concern. It slowed down operations at all levels. The supplies took longer to reach the front, and the troops were unable to advance fast enough, if they were able to advance at all. He had received unconfirmed intelligence that senior Chinese commanders had moved from Suzhou to Nanxiang or even Shanghai proper. He had no idea if the reports were true, but they gave him food for thought. If the Chinese commanders were moving closer to the front, it meant that they were not about to abandon Shanghai. "It's obvious that earlier views that the Chinese front was shaken had been premature," he wrote in his diary. "Now is definitely not the time to rashly push the offensive."[49]

The poor weather caused Matsui to repeatedly postpone a major shock attack to punch a hole through the Chinese defenses, which had been planned for some time. However, the rain also had its benefits. The pause in the fighting was a relief for exhausted soldiers on both sides. The Chinese got rest, but so did the Japanese, and in addition the Japanese were given precious time to gradually dig their way closer to the Chinese lines. The next time they charged across no-man's-land, the stretch of open field where they would be exposed to murderous Chinese fire would be a little shorter. The Japanese artillery had also finally reached the front in significant numbers, after being delayed for days on roads transformed into mud pools by the pouring rain. Nevertheless, the batteries were still using their shells sparingly, saving their ammunition for later. Their plan was to pulverize the Chinese strongholds one after the other, once the time had come.[50]

It was getting colder, and a parcel of warm clothes that Matsui had arranged to be sent to him from Tokyo the month before still had not reached him. At least winter uniforms had arrived for the 3rd and 11th Divisions. They needed all the encouragement they could get. The soldiers in the frontline had seen heavy attrition in recent weeks, and reinforcements had not been able to fully make up for that. The 3rd Division, for example, had taken more than 6,000 casualties, many of whom were from the division's backbone of experienced officers and NCOs. Therefore, even though the division had received 6,500 new men as replacements, and thus on paper looked like it had been more than replenished, this was not really the case. Matsui estimated that its combat strength had decreased to about one sixth of the original level.[51]

Adversity was unavoidable in battle, and Matsui had great affection for the common soldiers who tried to keep a cheerful attitude despite all their trials. This made the unnecessary hardships caused by incompetence at the senior levels difficult for him to stomach. Matsui was dissatisfied with the work the officers had done before the advance south. Supply was a huge problem, mainly because they had not taken into account the possibilities for transportation by boat offered by the extensive creek and canal system. This was how the Chinese had moved goods around for centuries, if not millennia. The Japanese could do the same. In fact they had been doing the same since September further north bringing supplies from the Yangtze River to the troops fighting near Luodian. A little extra forethought, Matsui thought, and a significant amount of trouble could have been avoided.[52]

On October 19, Matsui received the first reports that soldiers from

Guangxi had arrived in the Shanghai area and were deployed around Wusong Creek. Despite all the reinforcements that he himself had received in recent weeks, there was no denying that Matsui faced a formidable foe, capable of pouring new troops into this theater more or less indefinitely. Deception was necessary to make up for the imbalance. To relieve pressure on the front, the Japanese Navy sent a mock invasion force up the Yangtze on a major three-day diversionary mission. The fleet, consisting of eight destroyers and more than 20 transport vessels carrying smaller landing craft, anchored ten miles upriver from Chuanshakou. They then subjected the surrounding area to intensive bombardment as if in preparation for a landing. There had been other maneuvers like this, but this was the first to also entail actual live fire against targets inland. "It's sure to have a visible effect," Matsui wrote in his diary.[53]

Politics was never far below the surface during the battle of Shanghai. Much of what happened in and around the city was really meant for an international audience. The intelligence about the Guangxi troops arrived at Matsui's headquarters along with other information suggesting that the Chinese were strengthening their defenses further south. This indicated they were preparing to keep fighting for Shanghai even if the lines at Wusong Creek were breached. It followed a military logic, but diplomatic motives probably weighed just as heavily. An international conference on the war was approaching, scheduled to take place in Brussels. Chiang Kai-shek needed to keep his presence in the only Chinese city most foreigners were likely to have ever heard about.[54]

The battle for world public opinion was waged on several fronts. One topic bound to have a particular impact was poisonous gas. Less than two decades after the end of the Great War, it stood as the ultimate horror of modern warfare. Anyone caught using it would immediately be typecast in the role of the villain in the newspapers' narratives. On October 14, China filed a complaint at the League of Nations accusing Japan of using gas on the Shanghai front. It said a total of 45 Chinese soldiers had fallen victim in two separate attacks that same month.[55]

Whether the Japanese actually did use gas in the Shanghai area was a matter of debate, and remained so in the years after the battle. Zhang Fakui, the Chinese commander in Pudong, was not aware of any instances of Japanese deployment of the weapon.[56] In some cases, the extreme awareness of the risks posed by gas warfare caused soldiers to suspect gas attacks even when something much less sinister was actually taking place. During an attack against Japanese positions south of Wusong Creek, Chinese soldiers mistook a Japanese smoke grenade for a shell containing poison gas.[57] It is also possible that the Japanese used non-lethal gas to temporarily incapacitate their enemies leaving them vulnerable to attack. Not that it really mattered if the gas was of the lethal sort or not, since the end result would be the same: death to the Chinese.[58]

According to the Japanese, the Chinese also resorted to gas on several occasions during the course of the battle for Shanghai. One of the times they accused them of utilizing it was during the bitter struggle over Chenjiahang, and they published photos meant to sway the public at home and abroad in their favor.[59] Earlier in the campaign they had also claimed that China had been using sneezing gas, a chemical adopted by belligerents in the Great War. Shanghai's mayor Yu Hongjun, a favorite among reporters for his quotable one-liners, replied promptly: 'The Japanese sneeze because they've got cold feet."[60]

De Fremery, the Dutch spy, believed neither side, basing his argument on considerable experience gathered through his own career in the artillery. "It seems to me highly unlikely the warring parties have used any form whatsoever of poisonous gases," he wrote in a report. "I am well aware that at least until 1935 the Chinese were heavily opposed to this weapon of war and had not made any preparations for their use, not even for protecting themselves against such as weapon."[61]

———————

Ogishima Shizuo, the 27-year-old reservist of the 101st Japanese Division who had crossed Wusong Creek early on, was convinced he would not survive the battle for Shanghai, and he started making preparations for his own death. The rotting bodies everywhere on the south bank of the creek told him what needed to be done. If he were killed, it was far from certain that anyone would have the time to have him cremated and send his ashes back to his mother. Instead, he packed a few belongings that he did not need at the front and arranged to have them shipped back home. That way, at least, his family would have some concrete objects to comfort them in their memory of him.[62]

After the first confusing days following the crossing, the frontline had stabilized somewhat. The two enemy armies stared at each other across 150 yards of no-man's-land. Every now and then, the Japanese officers would order charges against the Chinese lines. The attacks invariably ended the same way. Rows of soldiers were cut down by the enemy's heavy machine guns, and the survivors hastily retreated to their own lines. The unfortunates who were left between the frontlines with injuries so severe that they could not move were condemned to slow deaths, beyond rescue. Even though their screams were almost unbearable, no one dared to venture out and bring back their wounded comrades. The Chinese snipers never slept.

Incessant rain had turned the trenches into a knee-deep bog where cooking was impossible. Instead, meals consisted of handfuls of sticky rice. Weapons frequently malfunctioned. At one point, all the heavy machine guns in Ogishima's company were sent back for repairs, forcing the soldiers in their dugouts to rely on their rifles and their bayonets, not much different from generations of infantrymen before them. Also like earlier generations of infantrymen, much of their talk revolved around how much worse off they were compared to the artillery and the transportation troops enjoying relatively comfortable lives far behind the front.

The officers grew paranoid that the mounting casualties and the abject conditions overall would cause dereliction in the ranks. The soldiers were regularly lined up so that their health status could be checked. Anyone trying to fake a disease ran the risk of being branded a deserter, and deserters were shot. The officers' suspicions were not entirely baseless. "The soldiers in the frontline only have one thought on their minds," Ogishima wrote in his diary. "They want to escape to the rear. Everyone envies those who, with light injuries, are evacuated. The ones who unexpectedly get a ticket back in this way find it hard to conceal their joy. As for those left in the frontline, they have no idea if their death warrant has already been signed, and how much longer they have to live."

Like on the battlefields of Flanders a generation earlier, lives were expended on a massive scale in return for little or no territorial gain. Also like Flanders, the terrain favored defense. Nohara Teishin, a soldier from the 9th Division, lived through a terrible fight against an entrenched and partly invisible enemy who fired at the advancing Japanese through holes in the walls of abandoned farm buildings. The officers urged on the privates, who charged across open fields. They would run for a short stretch, fall on their stomachs, catch their breath and resume the attack. Out of 200 men, only about ten were still fit to fight after the battle. "All my friends died there," he later said. "You can't begin to describe the wretchedness and misery of war."[63]

Watanabe Wushichi, an officer who also served with the Japanese 9th Division, faced a special challenge. He was responsible for securing water supplies to soldiers in the frontline. It would seem to be a simple task in countryside filled with large and small streams, but not much of the water was potable. Ponds and creeks throughout the area were filled with the fly-covered corpses of men and horses emitting a horrible stench. For many soldiers, the thirst gradually became unbearable, and the moment someone stumbled over a new unpolluted well, the soldiers would crowd around it and, with surprising speed, turn it into a mud pool. To prevent that from happening, the officers posted soldiers with rifles and fixed bayonets at each newly discovered water source.[64]

Like most other Japanese, Watanabe had been surprised by the tenacity of the Chinese defenders, and the sheer number of those willing to die for their cause. On the occasions when he had the chance to inspect conquered Chinese pillboxes, he was awestruck by the sight of dead defenders literally lying in layers. Childlike features showed that many of them couldn't even have reached the age of 20. Some of the Chinese corpses were still clutching their rifles, and the Japanese often found it impossible to prise them from their hands. It was, they said, as if their ghosts had returned to offer resistance.[65]

––––––––––

The battle might not have been going China's way, but its diplomatic behavior in mid-autumn showed continued confidence. World public opinion, at least in the democratic nations, was largely on China's side, and calls were growing for Japan to pay for its aggressive behavior. On October 5, U.S. President Franklin D. Roosevelt delivered a speech in Chicago that, albeit in veiled figurative language, called for concrete steps to be taken against Japan. "It would seem to be unfortunately true that the epidemic of world lawlessness is spreading," Roosevelt said. "When an epidemic of physical disease starts to spread the community approves and joins in a quarantine of the patients in order to protect the community against the spread of the disease."[66]

Coinciding almost exactly with Roosevelt's speech, Chiang Kai-shek instructed his foreign ministry to push for international sanctions against Japan with the aim of depriving the resource-starved island nation of oil, iron and steel—raw materials necessary for waging war. The League of Nations had proven an inefficient tool for rallying support for concrete measures against Japan. The Chinese diplomats also had few hopes of any tangible results coming out of the conference in Brussels. However, they felt some confidence that a conciliatory Chinese tone at the conference could help win sympathy. That way, Japan would appear to be the inflexible party, and the road to sanctions would be cleared.[67]

Optimistic that deft diplomacy could come to China's rescue, Chiang Kai-shek was not in a mood to settle for peace at any price. On October 21, Japanese Foreign Minister Hirota Koki approached the German ambassador in Tokyo, Herbert von Dirksen, with an inquiry about China's willingness to negotiate. Germany declared it was prepared to act as mediator, and in response the Japanese government laid out its demands. These included, among other things, important Chinese concessions in the north of the country as well as an expanded demilitarized zone around Shanghai. Even so, the German go-betweens considered the requests rather moderate, and Oskar Trautmann, Berlin's ambassador in Nanjing, conveyed them to Chiang Kai-shek.

Initially, Chiang did not reveal his views, but instead asked the German envoy about his. Trautmann said he considered the Japanese demands a basis for further talks, and used the example of Germany in the Great War as a warning. The sorry end that Imperial Germany met showed that it was unwise to postpone negotiations until complete military exhaustion had set in. Once that point had been reached, participation in any talks would take place from a disadvantaged position. Chiang was not convinced. He replied that he could only accept negotiations with the Japanese if they were willing first to restore the situation to its pre-hostilities state. There was little room for compromise.[68]

Once the long-expected Guangxi troops had all arrived at the front by the middle of October, the southern general Bai Chongxi's plan for the coun-terattack into the Japanese right flank picked up speed. Participants at a meeting of the National Military Council agreed on the need to act fast. "By seizing the opportunity to strike at the enemy at his moment of fa-tigue," they said, "it will be possible to break through the troops that have already advanced across Wusong Creek."[69] The attack was set for October 21. It would begin in the evening, so the Chinese could take advantage of their natural ally, darkness, in the initial period of the operations.

In the days that remained, the Chinese prepared their assault force. It was built around a core consisting of the four Guangxi divisions, which were extricated from the battle around Chenjiahang. This created an accu-mulation of troops behind the Chinese front that the Japanese reconnais-sance planes could not help but notice. "The enemy will launch a coun-terattack along the entire front tonight. It seems the planned attack is mainly targeted at the area south of Wusong Creek," Matsui wrote in his diary on October 21, just hours before the Chinese moved. He actually welcomed the prospect. "It will give us an opportunity to catch the enemy outside of his prepared defenses, and kill him there."[70]

At 7:00 p.m., the Chinese artillery barrage began. One hour later, the troops started moving east. The left wing of the Chinese attack, north of Wusong Creek, was led by the 176th Guangxi Division. At first, it made rapid progress, but soon it ran into the same obstacles that caused any attacker in this area, whether Chinese or Japanese, to lose speed—creeks and canals cutting through the country everywhere, at all angles. The van-guard feared that if it moved too fast, the supply train would not be able to keep up, and as dawn approached, it gave up much of the ground it had gained, hoping to take it back the following night.[71]

The attack south of Wusong Creek, led by the 174th Guangxi Divi-sion, did not fare any better. It ran into unexpectedly strong enemy resist-ance, and was unable to force its way across the canals it encountered, as bridge-building material had not been prepared in sufficient quantities. Before dawn, fearing artillery and air attack, that division, too, decided to withdraw back behind the start line, abandoning all the territory it had won at the cost of much blood during the night. On both sides of the creek, the Chinese divisions dug in, hoping to be able to stand their ground during the dangerous daylight hours when the Japanese could enjoy the full advantage of their superiority in the air.

As expected, the counterattack came after sunrise on October 22. In the 176th Guangxi Division's sector north of the creek, the Japanese had surrounded an entire battalion before noon. A few hours later, they had wiped it out completely, every man from the battalion commander down. The main success that day was scored by a Guangxi unit subjected to an attack by Japanese infantry supported by five tanks. Their front initially was close to collapsing, but a hastily arranged defense succeeded in beating back the Japanese. Of the tanks, one was destroyed, two were stuck in a canal, and two retreated—testimony to the near-impossibility of tank warfare in the river country around Shanghai.[72]

The night between October 22 and 23 saw the Chinese move under the cover of darkness to take back some of the positions they had lost during the daytime. Then dawn broke over the last and crucial day of the Chinese attack. This time the Japanese were mobilizing all available resources to stop the advance, as the commanders of the Guangxi troops commented later in the after-action report. "The Japanese enemy's army and air force employed every kind of weapon, from artillery to tanks and poison gas," it said. "It hit the Chinese front like a hurricane, and resulted in the most horrific losses yet for the army group since it entered the battle."[73]

From the moment the sun rose, the Japanese airplanes were in the air. At 9:00 a.m., they descended on the soldiers of the already severely battered 174th Guangxi Division south of Wusong Creek. A Guangxi general who survived the attack described what happened: "The troops were either blown to pieces or buried in their dugouts. The 174th disintegrated into a state of chaos." Other units were chopped up in similar fashion. By the end of October 23, the Chinese operation had cost a huge number of casualties including two brigade commanders, six regimental commanders, dozens of battalion and company commanders and 2,000 soldiers. Three out of every five Chinese soldiers in the first wave had been either killed or injured. The assault had to be halted.[74]

The entire counterattack had been a fiasco. Some Guangxi veterans would hold grudges for years against the officers who sent them into a hopeless battle. First of all, they had chosen to attack the enemy in the wrong place, hitting him exactly where he was at his strongest. Despite the recent reinforcements, the Japanese remained undermanned in the Shanghai area, and to gain a critical mass in a frontal attack like the one across Wusong Creek, they had to stretch their troops thin everywhere else. A powerful Chinese counterattack further north would have had a much better chance of succeeding. "But Bai Chongxi wanted to punch through the center of the enemy forces to show the fighting ability of the Chinese Army to the world," Lan Xiangshan, a Guangxi officer, wrote later in his memoirs.[75]

With hindsight, it was obvious that it had been an impossible mission, and it had been launched with a minimum of preparation. According to a possibly apocryphal claim made by Lan Xiangshan, when Bai Chongxi outlined the attack on a map, he did not pay any attention to the scale, resulting in far too large a front for the two divisions leading the charge. There was also little reconnaissance undertaken, and not enough engineering materiel to overcome the numerous waterways that the troops encountered. Most seriously, the commanders had picked troops entirely unsuited for an undertaking of this difficulty. Many of the Guangxi troops had been absorbed from local militia-type units with very little actual combat experience. Ignorant and incompetent leadership "had forced the Guangxi troops to make extreme sacrifices," Lan Xiangshan wrote. "And it had all been for nothing."[76]

To the German advisors, the Chinese practice of sending new troops straight to the frontline, and often to the most critical sectors, was also a cause of dismay. In the desperate situation faced by the Chinese generals, with a front that could buckle at any time, it was perhaps understandable, but in light of the need to preserve forces for a protracted war, it did not make sense in the long term. Freshly arrived in the Shanghai area, reinforcements from elsewhere in China invariably faced a situation that was completely alien to them, and without proper preparation for warfare in the special terrain offered in an unfamiliar part of the country, they were at a severe disadvantage. As a result they suffered enormous losses.[77]

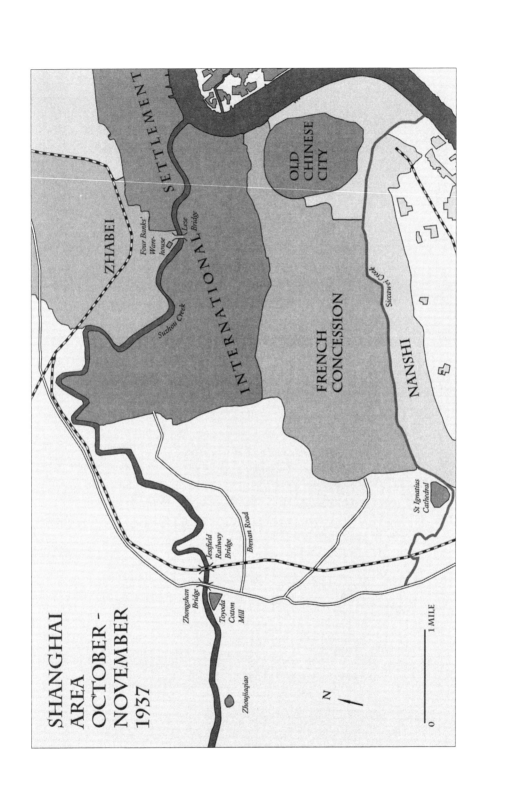

SHANGHAI
AREA
OCTOBER -
NOVEMBER
1937

ZHABEI

SETTLEMENT

INTERNATIONAL

Four Banks'
Ware-
house

Lese
Bridge

Suchou Creek

OLD
CHINESE
CITY

FRENCH
CONCESSION

Siccawei Creek

NANSHI

St Ignatius
Cathedral

Zhongshan
Bridge

Jessfield
Railway
Bridge

Brenan Road

Toyoda
Cotton
Mill

Zhoujiaqiao

N

0   1 MILE

CHAPTER

7

....

The "Lost Battalion"

OCTOBER 24–NOVEMBER 4

THE FRONT WAS COLLAPSING. THAT MUCH WAS CLEAR TO ZHANG Boting as he rode in his staff car west out of Shanghai on his way to his high-level rendezvous. Stragglers and small groups of injured soldiers staggered along the road, which ran parallel with the railway to Nanjing, away from the city and away from danger. It was a chaotic scene. Discipline among the scattered groups of military men was breaking down. That made them easier targets. Enemy aircraft were constantly circling in the sky, scouting for prey on the ground below. Whenever the pilots spotted a cluster of Chinese soldiers, they swept down, nearly touching the treetops, and strafed them mercilessly. Zhang's own driver had to stop the vehicle repeatedly to take cover.[1]

Zhang Boting was the 27-year-old chief of staff of the 88th Infantry Division, the German-trained elite unit that had been fighting in the area around the North Train Station since the start of the battle. On the morning of October 26, the same day as he was traveling to his meeting, the Third War Zone deputy commander Gu Zhutong had called Sun Yuanliang, who had led the division in battle since its arrival in August. Gu Zhutong had surprising news. As everyone had suspected, the Chinese Army was about to withdraw from northern Shanghai. However, the plan was to carve the 88th Division into smaller independent units and have

187

them stay behind in Zhabei to wage guerrilla-style warfare behind enemy lines. Sun Yuanliang thought it would be a pointless waste of the soldiers, but he was unable to explain his thoughts on the matter fully over the telephone. Instead, he dispatched Zhang Boting.

After several miles, which felt longer than they were because of the constant air raids, Zhang's car stopped by a narrow river. He got out and walked for another two miles until he came to a small straw hut. It looked innocuous from the outside, but looks were deceptive and the entire battle of Shanghai was being waged from inside. It was Gu Zhutong's field headquarters. When Zhang Boting entered, Gu Zhutong was studying a map of the deteriorating situation in and around the city. Zhang Boting gave an account of the situation at the front and at the same time described the conditions he had witnessed on the way to the meeting. He urged Gu Zhutong to immediately withdraw his headquarters to a safer place. They then moved on to the main topic.

"Chiang Kai-shek wants your division to stay in Zhabei and fight," Gu Zhutong said. "Every company, every platoon, every squad is to defend key buildings in the city area, and villages in the suburbs. You must fight for every inch of land and make the enemy pay a high price. You should launch guerrilla warfare, to win time and gain sympathy among our friends abroad." The command was more about diplomacy than war-winning tactics. The so-called Nine Power Conference was set to meet in Brussels the following week,[2] and it was important that China kept a presence in Shanghai, as the foreigners would immediately appreciate the importance of the city. If the war had moved on to unknown hamlets in the Chinese countryside by the time the delegates met in Brussels, it would be harder to convince them of the urgency of the matter. It all made sense politically, but not militarily. Zhang Boting asked permission to speak.

"Outside of the streets of Zhabei," he said, "the suburbs consist of flat land with little opportunity for cover. It's not suitable for guerrilla warfare. The idea of defending small key points is also difficult. The 88th Division has so far had reinforcements and replacements six times, and the original core of officers and soldiers now make up only 20 to 30 percent. It's like a cup of tea. If you keep adding water, it becomes thinner and thinner.[3] Some of the new soldiers we receive have never been in a battle, or never even fired a shot. At the moment we rely on the backbone of old soldiers

THE "LOST BATTALION" • 189

to train them while fighting. As long as the command system is in place and we can use the old hands to provide leadership, we'll be able to maintain the division as a fighting force. But if we divide up the unit, the coherence will be lost. Letting every unit fight its own fight will just add to the trouble."

Gu Zhutong nodded, but asked what alternatives were available. "Chiang Kai-shek's instruction is aimed at strategic objectives," said Zhang Boting. "He wants to direct attention towards Japan's aggressive behavior, and since Shanghai is an international city which has the eyes and ears of the global community, he wants to bring the realities of the combat in Shanghai to the (Brussels) meeting . . . Leaving troops in Zhabei for a final battle will be tantamount to sacrificing them, whether it's a large force or a small one. Whether we stay and fight for a large number of strongholds or just one or two strongholds, it has the same meaning: We stay and fight. The most important thing is to pick a unit that is just right for doing this job."

"Sun Yuanliang made similar comments on the phone this morning," Gu Zhutong said, "but he didn't specifically say how many troops we should leave behind. He also didn't say which strongholds they should defend." Zhang Boting replied that an elite formation of no more than regimental size would be enough to hold on to one or two high-profile positions in the Zhabei area. Gu Zhutong thought it over quickly, and then made up his mind. "Time is short," he told Zhang Boting. "I want you to immediately return to Sun Yuanliang and order him to proceed according to this plan. If you have carried out the necessary arrangements by evening, I will be able to report back to Chiang Kai-shek."

Zhang Boting rushed back east towards Shanghai, but the road had become even more clogged and disorganized than before. Near a major bridge, he encountered a huge traffic jam caused by vehicles of all sizes seeking to escape the advancing Japanese. An old friend of his, an officer of the 87th Infantry Division, came up to him. His left hand was bandaged and he was waving a submachine gun with his right. It was impossible to continue this way, he told Zhang. The Japanese had already broken through the line to the north, and an enemy tank column was heading in their direction.

Zhang Boting decided to make a detour and told his driver to take the car to the International Settlement. From there he hitched a ride across Suzhou Creek on board a small wooden boat. When he returned to the 88th Infantry Division's headquarters, inside the Four Banks' Warehouse right next to the creek, he found Sun Yuanliang pacing up and down the floor, as was his habit when he was pondering a tough issue. He had already talked to Gu Zhutong by telephone, and knew that his proposal to keep a small force in Shanghai had been adopted. What remained was to pick the unit that was to stay behind and in all likelihood fight to the last man.

Suddenly, Sun Yuanliang stopped pacing, a sign that he had reached a decision. He wanted the very building they were standing in, the five-storey Four Banks' Warehouse, to be the position where the last stand was to be made. It was a large and easily recognizable structure, and it was within direct sight of the International Settlement, giving it exactly the exposure that was its raison d'etre. However, Sun Yuanliang thought a regiment was too big a unit for the job. It would be hard to supply so many men for a prolonged period of battle. More importantly, he was loath to squander so many lives on what was essentially a public relations exercise. Sun Yuan-liang had made his pick. The task of showing to the world that there was still fight left in the Chinese had fallen on the 1st Battalion of the 524th Regiment. It was about to gain global fame as China's "Lost Battalion."

—— ———

By the time Zhang Boting made his trek on October 26, the situation west of Shanghai had changed markedly. The stalemate around Wusong Creek that had characterized most of the month of October had given way to sudden, rapid movement. The 9th Japanese Division's successful defense against the counterattack carried out by the Guangxi troops from October 21 to 23 had shaken the Chinese, as had minor Japanese advances else-where. On the night between October 23 and 24, intelligence reached Matsui Iwane suggesting that the Chinese were reducing their troops on the frontline, possibly in preparation of a withdrawal.[4]

Matsui had been planning for the major drive south aiming for Dachang, and the sudden fluidity of the situation prompted him to speed up these plans. He had originally wanted to call a meeting with the division commanders and explain his intentions, but instead he phoned each of them from 9:00 a.m. on October 24 ordering the attack, stating that more detailed written orders would follow in the afternoon. Within just a few hours both the 3rd and the 9th Divisions managed to reach Zoumatang Creek, which ran from the west to the east two miles south of Wusong Creek. The 9th Division even succeeded in gaining a foothold on the other side.[5]

However, Matsui was not satisfied and felt his troops could have moved in a more aggressive manner in pursuit of the retreating Chinese. He reasoned that they had been hampered by Zoumatang Creek, a natural obstacle, but more importantly he believed the weeks that the soldiers had spent in the trenches had caused them to lose their feel for mobile warfare.[6] In the middle of the afternoon on October 24, he ordered the divisional commanders to meet him at his headquarters. They all seemed to appreciate the need for speed, but they explained that lack of supplies caused them to move slower than they wanted. In particular, the 9th Division was still waiting for new weapons. At present, it only had between 200 and 300 rifles per battalion, and it was not equipped for effective pursuit of the enemy.[7] It is also likely that after heavy attrition and the loss of some of their best troops, the Japanese officers had adopted a more cautious approach to battle. Understandably, they did not spell this out to their commander.[8]

In preparation for the battle, Japanese planes had dropped thousands of leaflets over Chinese positions, urging the soldiers to give up the fight. As an added incentive, the leaflets offered each soldier who laid down his arms five Chinese yuan, or the equivalent of about one and a half U.S. dollars at the exchange rate of the time.[9] The tactic did not appear to have had much of an impact, if for no other reason then because all the Chinese were aware that the Japanese rarely, if ever, took prisoners. Rather, the Japanese advance benefited from a continued Chinese withdrawal on the night between October 24 and 25, which also pulled out of battle the Guangxi troops who had been pushed to near exhaustion by an intense week on the frontline. Most of the retreating troops moved to positions that had already been prepared north and south of Suzhou Creek, the last remaining natural obstacle to a Japanese victory in Shanghai.

As had happened before during the Shanghai campaign, in the first hours after daybreak on October 25, the Japanese did not immediately detect the changes that had taken place in the dark hours, and only gradually realized that the Chinese positions they were facing were occupied by skeleton crews. But once reconnaissance troops had established how weak the enemy in the immediate frontline was, they quickly attacked and wiped out the token resistance left in their path.[10] The Japanese took advantage of their superiority in the air, deploying hundreds of planes. They also carried out "creeping" artillery fire, perhaps for the only time during the entire Shanghai campaign. The procedure, which had been used to considerable effect during the Great War, called for a barrage of artillery shells to gradually move forward, protecting the assault force following immediately behind. However, in this case, the barrage was kept 600 to 700 yards in front of the advancing Japanese and gave the Chinese defenders sufficient time to emerge from cover and re-man the positions they had abandoned while under artillery fire.[11]

Despite the general withdrawal from the positions south of Wusong Creek, several Chinese divisions were charged with mounting a strong defense around Dachang. Two strategic bridges across Zoumatang Creek, in the area west of Dachang, were held by one division each. The defense of the westernmost of the two, Old Man Bridge, was the responsibility of the 33rd Division, which had recently arrived in Shanghai. The 18th Division, another new arrival, was positioned around Little Stone Bridge, closer to Dachang. Neither division was any match for the Japanese steamroller. On October 25, a Japanese column spearheaded by more than 20 tanks swept away the 33rd Division's defenses and took Old Man Bridge. In the ensuing hours, as the Chinese division tried to carry out a fighting retreat towards Dachang, it was nearly annihilated by the superior Japanese firepower. By mid-afternoon only one in ten of its officers and men was fit to fight. Even the division commander had been injured.[12]

The Japanese force moved on to Little Stone Bridge, and after bitter fighting with the 18th Division, which lasted until sunset, that bridge too ended up in Japanese hands. The 18th Division, meanwhile, moved into Dachang. Here the division commander Zhu Yaohua received a message from Gu Zhutong pointing out in terms hard to misunderstand that Dachang must be held at any cost. "Those who disobey this order will be court-martialed," Gu Zhutong stated curtly.[13] Zhu Yaohua feared that giving up Little Stone Bridge might already be enough to put him in the dock and hastily arranged a nightly counterattack to recapture it. It turned out the Japanese had foreseen that eventuality and had prepared strong defenses near the bridge. The Chinese attempt failed miserably.[14]

There was no doubt that on October 26 the Japanese threw every available piece of equipment in that section of the front into an all-out effort to take Dachang. The town had, by that point, been reduced almost entirely to rubble, the ancient wall the only indication that it had ever been home to any significant number of people.[15] Up to 400 airplanes, including heavy day bombers, attacked Chinese troops in and around Dachang, killing both people and large numbers of pack animals. A western correspondent observing from a distance, later called it the "fiercest ever [battle] waged in Asia up to that time." It was a "tempest of steel" released by Japanese planes flying lazily over the Chinese positions, guided to their targets by observation balloons spotting any movement on the ground. "The curtain of fire never lifted for a moment from the Chinese trenches," the correspondent wrote in his memoirs of the Shanghai campaign. "This was no battle among ruins but straight-out positional warfare in open, flat country."[16]

After the aerial attack, more than 40 Japanese tanks appeared west of Dachang. The Chinese had nothing that could stop such a force, as they had already withdrawn their artillery to safer positions further behind the front. Their infantry was left to its own devices in the face of the moving wall of enemy armor, and it was overwhelmed.[17] The defending divisions, including Zhu Yaohua's 18th, never had a chance and were crushed by the materially superior foe. After a short fight, the victorious Japanese could march in and claim the town, which was by then a sea of flames.[18] Matsui felt deep satisfaction at the sight of the banner of the Rising Sun over the burning ruins of Dachang. "After a month of bitter fighting, today we have finally seen the pay-off," he wrote in his diary.[19] Zhu Yaohua, on the other hand, immediately faced reproaches from his superiors and his peers who thought he could have done more.[20] The humiliation was too much to bear. Two days after his defeat at Dachang, he shot himself in the chest, inflicting a mortal wound.[21]

Even before Dachang fell, and despite the threat to court-martial anyone leaving his post, a general withdrawal of all Chinese forces in the Jiangwan salient had been underway. As early as the night between October 24 and 25, the divisions inside the salient had been ordered to move baggage trains and support services back southwest across Suzhou Creek, using the Zhongshan Bridge and Jessfield Railway Bridge. As the fighting raged north of Zhabei in the following days, the stream of soldiers, vehicles and pack animals continued, and on the night between October 26 and 27, the Chinese vacated metropolitan Shanghai north of Suzhou Creek entirely. "The enormous Chinese army simply melted away and at dawn the Japanese found themselves facing empty positions," a foreign journalist wrote. "The two armies were no longer in contact."[22]

As the Chinese retreated from Zhabei, they systematically set fire to thousands of Chinese shops and homes, carrying out a scorched earth policy.[23] At 7:00 a.m. on October 27, eight narrow arrows of smoke pierced the horizon from one end of Zhabei to the other. Two hours later, they had become "huge black pillars stretching towards the azure sky."[24] By afternoon, a four-mile-long massive wall of smoke towered thousands of feet into the air.[25] In the words of a German advisor, it was a fire "of unimaginable extent" which raged out of control for several days and repeatedly threatened to spill over into the International Settlement.[26] Refugees who had left Zhabei weeks or months before and hoped to return now the fighting finally appeared to be over were devastated as they saw their homes devoured by a vast sea of flames.[27]

The Japanese Army, or more precisely the doctrine guiding it in the field, had failed in two respects by letting some of China's best divisions escape the trap that it itself had set for them. First of all, on the evening of October 26, after taking Dachang, the Japanese columns could have moved onwards across Zhabei all the way to the edge of the International Settlement. Instead, they followed orders and halted at the line they had reached at sunset. "The only explanation for this is the lack of independent thinking among junior Japanese commanders and their fear of erring even in the slightest bit from a plan of attack that had been laid right down to the smallest details," German advisor Borchardt wrote after returning home from China.[28] "Since the Japanese concentrated on rallying and reorganizing their forces after the fall of Dachang," Borchardt wrote, "they missed an opportunity for a victory so decisive that the Chinese would have been forced to give up their continued resistance in Shanghai."

If the Japanese committed a first error by leaving a door open that the enemy could escape through, they made themselves guilty of a second error by not even noticing that the enemy was using that door. Although Japanese reconnaissance planes kept a watchful eye on the two main bridges used by the Chinese to escape, and even sent down parachute flares to detect night-time movements, they almost inexplicably failed to spot the Chinese withdrawal.[29] The retreat was carried out exactly according to plan. Even the artillery was pulled out to the last piece. This gave the Chinese a chance to occupy prepared positions south of Suzhou Creek and around Nanxiang, and enabled them to fight another day.[30]

Despite their mistakes, the Japanese initially treated their conquest of Zhabei as a triumph, planting thousands of small Rising Sun flags throughout the ruins of the district. Against this sea of white and red, the only reasonably intact building, the Four Banks' Warehouse, stood out as a stark reminder that the Chinese had maintained a foothold north of Suzhou Creek. Rumors started spreading that the soldiers inside had sworn to fight to death. The Japanese realized that their victory in Zhabei would look flawed, and even appear like a defeat of sorts, as long as the warehouse was in Chinese hands.[31]

No one who had met Xie Jinyuan could be in any doubt that he was the perfect choice to lead the battalion that was to stay behind, holed up inside the Four Banks' Warehouse in a corner of Zhabei, and prove to the public at home and abroad that China remained determined to resist Japanese aggression. The 32-year-old graduate of the elite Central Military Academy, who had been in Shanghai with the 88th Division since the start of the hostilities in August, was a soldier to the core. He stood as straight as a bayonet, and even in a mask he would have been recognized as a military man, said a foreign correspondent who met him. He was, in the correspondent's words, "modern China stripped for action."[32]

The moment Xie Jinyuan received his assignment on the night of October 26, he went straight to the warehouse, and he was pleased with what he saw. It was a virtual fortress. Each of the walls was pockmarked with dozens of rifle slots, so attacking infantry would be met with a wall of rifle fire from the building's well-protected defenders. It was clear that once the

Japanese arrived, they would surround the building on three sides. Still, a link remained to the International Settlement in the south across Lese Bridge. British forward positions were as close as 40 feet away, and with a bit of stealth, and a little luck, it was likely that the injured could be evacuated under the cover of darkness. Tactically, it was an ideal location.[33] However, it could be further improved, and he ordered the soldiers who had already arrived to work through the night to strengthen their positions. They had exactly what they needed just at hand—thousands of large bags filled with wheat and corn, which proved to be excellent substitutes for sandbags.[34]

Xie Jinyuan's first challenge was to rally the soldiers of the 524th Regiment's 1st Battalion, who were to man the positions at the warehouse. It was a complex task, given the short notice, as the companies and platoons were spread all across Zhabei, and some, unaware of the orders their battalion had received, had started moving west along with the rest of the Chinese Army. Throughout the night, Xie and his second-in-command, Yang Ruifu, sent out orderlies through the blazing streets, hoping to locate their men amid the mass of retreating of soldiers. Eventually, they succeeded. By 9:00 a.m. on October 27, the last remaining soldiers of the battalion turned up at the warehouse.[35] By then, Xie Jinyuan's force consisted of slightly over 400 officers and soldiers. It was a tiny number when compared to the might of the Japanese military, and they were put to the test almost immediately.

An advance outpost had sent word back at 7:30 a.m. that it had seen Japanese marines near the North Train Station, and 45 minutes later it reported that the enemy's flag was flying over that building. The Chinese soldiers were ordered to engage the advancing Japanese, and over the following two hours they made a fighting retreat back towards the warehouse. A brief pause ensued, which the Chinese defenders used to get ready, some taking up positions on the different floors of the warehouse, others crouching behind an outer wall surrounding the building. At 1:00 a.m. a Japanese column approached the warehouse, proudly and confidently marching down the middle of the road behind a large Rising Sun banner. It looked more like a victory parade than a tactical maneuver. Once they were close enough, the Chinese officers ordered their men to fire. Five Japanese soldiers went down, while the rest of the column scrambled for cover.[36]

Within an hour, the Japanese had gathered enough troops to attempt to take the warehouse by storm. A sizeable force moved in on the building, and put up so much firepower that the Chinese had to abandon the outer wall and withdraw to the warehouse itself. Despite the solid defenses, the crisis was not over, and the attackers seemed to have gained dangerous momentum. At this point, Yang Ruifu, the second-in-command, ordered a dozen soldiers to run to the roof and lob hand grenades at the Japanese from there. This stopped the attack. As the Japanese withdrew, they left behind seven dead.[37] Much of the fighting was followed by excited Chinese on the other side of the 60-yard Suzhou Creek. Every time word spread that yet another Japanese soldier had been killed, an unpitying cheer rose from the crowd.[38]

Foreign correspondents also witnessed the battle from the safe side of Suzhou Creek. They had a front-row seat to the bitter reality of urban combat. One of them noticed how a small group of Japanese was slowly and carefully approaching the warehouse, picking their way through the broken masonry and twisted metal. Crawling from cover to cover, it took them 50 minutes to cover 50 yards. Apparently the Chinese defenders, watching from hidden vantage points, had been monitoring them all along, and once the Japanese party was close enough, they rained hand grenades on them. After the dust had settled, they used their rifles to finish off those who still moved. Several Japanese who crept up to rescue wounded comrades were killed too. It was a war without mercy.[39]

Even after darkness had fallen over the warehouse, there was no time to sleep. All soldiers were set to work repairing damages and further bolstering their positions. At 7:00 a.m. the following morning, October 28, large numbers of Japanese planes appeared overhead, but they did not drop a single bomb on the warehouse. The defenders told themselves this was because of the machine guns they had placed on top of the building due to a lack of genuine anti-aircraft guns. The proximity of the warehouse to the International Settlement was probably at least as important as it made the Japanese wary of engaging in aerial bombardment, fearing that they could cause a disaster on the scale of "Black Saturday."[40]

Shortly before noon, Xie Jinyuan climbed to the roof with his lieutenant, Yang Ruifu. All around them, Zhabei was burning. Dense black smoke rose from thousands of fires, covering the sun entirely. As the two officers were watching the scene in awe, they noticed a group of Japanese soldiers lingering in the street some distance away. Xie Jinyuan ordered a sentry to hand him his rifle. He lifted the weapon to his cheek, aimed carefully, and squeezed the trigger. As the lone shot echoed across the ruined cityscape, one of the distant silhouettes collapsed to the ground. "Good shot," a smiling Yang Ruifu said to his commander.[41]

At 3:00 p.m., the Japanese attempted a second major attack on the warehouse. This time they pulled up five artillery pieces and also posted machine guns on the roofs of adjacent buildings. The defenders came under even greater pressure than the day before, and only after two hours of intense fighting did they succeed in beating back the enemy. Not long after the shooting had died down, bad news arrived. The Japanese had managed to find the water supply and cut if off. Yang Ruifu ordered strict rationing. Each company was to place its water reserves under guard and collect urine in large barrels for use if fires needed to be extinguished.

The number of wounded had started growing, and there was little that could be done for them in the primitive conditions at the warehouse. Through the last remaining phone link, Yang Ruifu organized their transfer across nearby Lese Bridge, through the International Settlement to hospitals in the Chinese part of Shanghai. As a party of medics prepared to leave with the injured, Yang Ruifu had a last order for them. "If anyone asks how many soldiers are inside the Four Banks' Warehouse, say there are 800," he told them. "Under no circumstances let anyone know how few we really are. That would embolden the Japanese." A legend was born—the legend of the "800 Heroes" of Shanghai.[42]

The battle of Shanghai had arguably always been unwinnable for the Chinese. It was only a matter of time before the Japanese would gain the upper hand by virtue of their material and technological advantage. As the fighting dragged on, and the Japanese gained stronghold after stronghold in the countryside around the city, invariably exacting an immense toll on the defenders, a growing number of Chinese generals started questioning the wisdom of hanging on to a city doomed to fall in the end anyway. They were pushing for a more comprehensive withdrawal, rather than the tactical retreat from Zhabei and Jiangwan that had taken place. Otherwise, thousands more would die in vain. Just as seriously, morale could suffer a dev-astating blow, and China's ability to continue the fight would be compro-mised.

This was a very real concern. The Chinese troops, who had entered the battle in an upbeat and patriotic mood, had gradually lost their fervor as they suffered huge numbers of casualties fighting a hopeless battle. Once a division was down to one third of its original strength, it was sent to the rear for reorganization and replenishment, and then returned to the front-line.[43] Most soldiers saw the odds of survival heavily stacked against them. But in spite of frequent visits to the front, Chiang Kai-shek knew very little about this. Officers who were aware of the real conditions in the trenches also were familiar with the supreme commander's stubborn character and his determination to stick to the defense of Shanghai to the bitter end. Under the circumstances, they found it inadvisable to break the truth to him. It was a charade which could not go on forever. In some units the sit-uation was getting so desperate that it was only a matter of time before the soldiers would simply leave their positions.[44]

With mutiny an increasingly likely scenario, senior commanders sought to convince Chiang Kai-shek that a complete withdrawal of all Chinese troops from the Shanghai area to a fortified line from Suzhou to Jiaxing, a city about 35 miles to the south, was the only option available. In early November, Bai Chongxi told Chiang that the officers at the front could no longer control their men and that a pullback would be a face-saving measure, forestalling open rebellion in the ranks. Nothing they said made any impression on Chiang Kai-shek. Li Zongren, another general who had previously tried to make the case for retreat, knew that it was pointless to argue with the man at the top. "War plans were decided by him personally, and no one else was allowed to say anything," Li said in his memoirs.[45]

Even so, at times Chiang seemed tantalizingly close to actually being swayed by the views of his lieutenants. As early as the first days of October, he appeared to have decided for a withdrawal of the front, but subsequently changed his mind. A similar situation emerged late in the month when Chiang had called a meeting with his frontline commanders in a train car-riage at Songjiang Railway Station southwest of Shanghai. Before Chiang's arrival, the generals discussed the battle and concluded that they could do nothing against the enemy's superior firepower.

Once Chiang had arrived, Zhang Fakui, the commander of the troops in Pudong, suggested moving ten divisions to lines further in the rear, where the positions had been well prepared and defense would be easier than in Shanghai. The majority agreed. At this point, Madame Chiang Kai-shek, as belligerent as ever, made her entry dressed in an expensive-looking fur coat, fresh from a visit to the Shanghai front. "If we can hold Shanghai for ten more days," she declared, "China will win international sympathy." She wasn't any more specific than that, but it appeared to those present that she was referring to the upcoming Brussels conference. That did it for Chiang. "Shanghai must be held at all cost," he declared with firm conviction in his voice, as if that was what he had felt all along.[46]

By the first week of November, Shanghai's refugee problem had become close to unmanageable, and a humanitarian catastrophe of unprecedented scale was in the making. Hundreds of thousands of homeless had crammed into the diminishing parts of the city that remained more or less untouched by war. At the same time the frontline moved closer and threatened to eventually sweep over the entire municipal area, leaving no district un-scathed. If that situation were to become reality, the stage would be set for unimaginable suffering, as civilians squeezed into narrow alleys would be exposed to the modern instruments of war.

Incidents were already accumulating showing that non-combatants could expect no mercy. As the Chinese defenders withdrew from Zhabei, the civilians who still remained north of Suzhou Creek rushed to escape with whatever possessions they could carry before their homes were overrun by the Japanese Army. They took the same route as the troops, pouring over the Zhongshan and Jessfield bridges to the safety of the international zones. Some of them were not fast enough. While they were still making their way across the partly destroyed Jessfield Railway Bridge, a Japanese vanguard caught up with them. A machine gun swept the entire bridge, cutting down men, women and children.[47]

To the south, Brenan Road stretched parallel with the creek and led to the British outposts guarding the entrances to the International Settlement. This, too, was turned into a killing ground by the advancing Japanese. A number of silver-colored Japanese monoplanes were bombing nearby railway carriages when three of them suddenly broke formation and started strafing civilians walking along the road. An eyewitness estimated that 200 were killed or injured. "I saw six ambulance loads taken away," he said. "A large number of others, wounded to various degrees, stumbled into the Settlement or were helped along by others to safety."[48]

Desperate cries could be heard as far away as the north bank of Suzhou Creek, where children and old women were unable to move any further, exhausted after a long trek and nervous about stepping onto the railway bridge, having seen what happened to the others. In the end, British soldiers watching the carnage taking place right on their doorstep decided to intervene. Rolling up their shirtsleeves, they moved out to assist them that final short distance to safety. "Once, twice, endless times they patiently helped the refugees in the same manner as they would have treated their own family members," said a Chinese witness.[49]

As rumors spread that civilians were being machine-gunned at the Jessfield entrance to the International Settlement, the refugee streams soon started moving to other areas, which were already under severe stress after taking in large numbers of people from the war zones. The Catholic settlement around St Ignatius Cathedral on the edge of the French Concession was one such place. By early November, the monks and nuns were taking care of 7,000 civilians. A large number were children or elderly who had been separated from family members they depended on. "Many come to the camp in dying condition and, especially among the small children, resistance to disease is so small that they become easy victims of common ailments," the *North China Herald* reported. "Often are the priests called to the side of a dying child whom the devoted nursing sisters cannot possibly save."[50]

Much worse was in store for the future unless a more comprehensive solution was found. The Jesuit priest Jacquinot, who had been appointed one of the vice chairmen of the recently established Shanghai Red Cross, decided that the time was right to move more decisively on his vision for a safety zone for non-combatants. Three intense days of negotiations with Chinese and Japanese authorities followed. After securing Shanghai Mayor Yu Hongjun's agreement to a zone adjacent to the French Concession, he moved on to the difficult part, dealing with the Japanese. Consul General Okamoto Suemasa was favorably disposed, in principle at least, but he would have to consult his government back home. Everything was now up to Tokyo.[51]

Yang Huimin's curiosity had been getting the better of her as the sound of the late-night fight around the Four Banks' Warehouse was carried across Suzhou Creek into the International Settlement. Hoping to watch the battle from up close, she had followed the creek west until she had been stopped by a British soldier pointing his rifle at her. "Boy scout," the foreigner said, half contemptuously. He had been fooled by the 22-year-old woman's tomboy looks and by her uniform. Since her factory had been closed down due to the hostilities, she had devoted most of her time to the Girl Guides, helping refugees holed up in the International Settlement. The soldier had led her pass, however, and from a British bunker she had been able to follow the combat that raged around the warehouse across the creek until dawn.[52]

After sunrise, she had noticed how all of Zhabei was covered in Japanese flags, while on her side of the creek, over the bunker, the Union Jack was hoisted. "Where was the Chinese flag," she thought to herself. The red banner with the white star on a blue background was missing in all this—and after all, this was Chinese territory. She had gone home, and after some consideration, she had decided what to do. She had wrapped a large Chinese flag around herself under her uniform and returned to the British bunker, and there, on the evening of October 28, she waited for an opportunity to make the dangerous trip across the Lese Bridge to Zhabei.

Taking advantage of a brief moment when the British sentries were not paying attention, she snuck onto the bridge and rushed across to the other side. Once there, she lifted her face to see the warehouse with its empty windows staring down at her like a many-eyed giant. The most dangerous part still remained—crossing the street without being shot by either British or Japanese sentries. While she was waiting for a chance to move, gun fire started all around her. For a few seconds, she thought she had been detected, but anxiety was overtaken by relief when she understood that the shooting was directed at the warehouse. She had ended up in the middle of yet another Japanese attempt at taking the building.

When the fire had died down, she quickly ran over to the warehouse, entered through a hole in the barbed wire surrounding the building, and soon stood face to face with Xie Jinyuan, commander of the "Lost Battalion." Yang Huimin took off her scout's coat and unwrapped the flag, now soaked in her sweat after the exertion and the danger. There was no flagpole anywhere in the building, and instead the soldiers jerry-rigged one from two bamboo poles. They climbed the stairs to the roof and hoisted the flag in a quick and low-key ceremony, performed by a dozen soldiers shortly before dawn. Yang Ruifu, the second-in-command, made a short speech. "Now that our flag is flying over the warehouse," he said, "no one can dispute the fact that Zhabei is sovereign Chinese soil!"[53]

Yang Huimin had noticed a large number of injured lying on the floor of the warehouse and offered to stay in order to help look after them, but Xie Jinyuan declined. As the sun was rising on October 29, he sent her back, urging her to choose a different route for the return trip. "Jump into the creek," he told her. She followed the advice, dashing to the bank and leaping into the foul water. Immediately, she heard Japanese bullets whizz over her head. She was a good swimmer, and did most of the trip under the surface. When she emerged on the other side, a crowd was standing along Suzhou Creek, cheering and clapping. They were not celebrating her, but the Chinese flag, flying over Zhabei again for the first time since the withdrawal.

Inside the warehouse, fatigue was now widespread. The defenders had been fighting for three days, and the nights had been spent improving their positions. Yang Ruifu had been walking from platoon to platoon after dark, kicking everyone who was slumbering. "If we don't do everything we can to prepare the positions, the enemy will kill us," he shouted angrily. "What do you want, to sleep or to live? Anyone caught sleeping from now on will be severely punished!" The privates quietly cursed the officer behind his back, as they got up and set to work on their positions.

Everything indicated that the Japanese wanted October 29 to be the last day in the embarrassing battle for the warehouse. The first warnings started arriving early in the afternoon from across Suzhou Creek, where sympathetic Chinese civilians were secrety spying on enemy troop movements. The battalion was informed by telephone that a major force, consisting of hundreds of soldiers, had been put together and was marching towards the warehouse. Minutes later, it got a similar warning from British soldiers who were guarding the exits from Zhabei and who had no special love for the Japanese military after one of their numbers had been killed in an air raid in late October. Then the attack started. The Japanese had rolled up numerous artillery pieces and shelled the warehouse for more than an hour. However, the defenders crouched behind ten-foot-thick defensive walls, and escaped with only minor injuries. They also succeeded in beating back the following infantry attack. But it was obvious that they could not hold out for much longer.

By this time, the Chinese Alamo-style battle in Zhabei had been a resounding propaganda victory. The "Lost Battalion" had captured the imagination of the world, and for a few days, journalists paid intense attention to its fate. Zhang Boting, the 88th Division's chief of staff, had been sent to Shanghai's foreign districts to keep in touch with Xie Jinyuan and his men. He felt that after four days of fighting, the battalion had made its point and the next step for it was to disengage from the enemy and withdraw. The only escape route was across Lese Bridge to the International Settlement, and hopefully from there to the suburbs and the Chinese positions there. There was one obstacle to this move. It would require the agreement of the western powers.[54]

On October 30, Zhang Boting turned up at the residence of Yang Hu, the Shanghai defense commissioner, and nominally the most senior military figure in the city. Located in one of the most exclusive areas of the French Concession, it was a sumptuous villa nested in a luxurious flower garden, a home worthy of an official widely rumored to be corrupt.[55] Also present were Mayor Yu Hongjun and, more importantly, Alexander Telfer-Smollett, commanding officer of the British forces in Shanghai. Yang Hu got straight down to business. "The supreme commander of the Chinese forces has ordered the Lost Battalion to withdraw from the Four Banks' Warehouse," he said. "But we need to confer with the British army on ways to bring this about, with a view to the possible impact on the International Settlement."

"Do you know about this issue?" Mayor Yu asked the British general. Telfer-Smollet replied in the affirmative. "Our troops have been neighbors with your division across the creek for some time now, and we've become friends," he said. "We'll do our best to assist the withdrawal of the battalion, but how do you plan to bring it about?" Zhang Boting said the only way out was through the International Settlement. "The Japanese have set up a machine gun position and searchlights, covering the exit at Lese Bridge. We need your protection in order to make a withdrawal possible," he said. Telfer-Smollett rose and patted Yang Hu on the back. "Don't worry. Yang Hu and I are friends."[56]

Late that afternoon, the Japanese bombardment of the warehouse had become so intense that British soldiers abandoned patrolling Lese Bridge for the sake of their own safety. The order for the "Lost Battalion" to finally withdraw into the International Settlement came none too early and was received with relief. There was no real plan. They would simply have to run across the bridge as fast as they could, trying to escape before the Japanese understood what was going on. If the Japanese did notice the evacuation and opened fire, they just had to hope that the machine guns wouldn't kill too many of them. The British soldiers would be expecting them on the other side.

As night settled over ruined Zhabei, the Japanese moved their artillery even closer to the warehouse. This time the plan was to keep shelling the building until its defenders were dead or gone. Observers across the creek, watching the batteries serve up miniature barrages so close to the target, noted that the sound of the gun firing and the sound of the shell bursting merged into one prolonged "cra-ack!" After each barrage, a Japanese searchlight would move around the wall to inspect the damage. A Chinese soldier tried to destroy the searchlight by throwing a hand grenade from a window, but it fell short.[57]

Amid the continued barrage, the battalion began the evacuation. They moved in a gradual manner to keep the Japanese in the dark for as long as possible. Every now and then, a lone shadow, or a cluster of shadows, would dash across the bridge. Each time, a Japanese machine gun posted near the north end of the bridge would open fire. Because of the darkness and the extreme confusion near the warehouse only a few were hit before reaching the British lines and laying down their arms. Yang Ruifu was able to run almost to the other side before being shot through the leg. In spite of the pain, he hurriedly hopped the last short distance to safety on his uninjured foot.[58]

As the escape was getting under way, a Japanese column headed by a tank appeared near the warehouse, moving in to block the road. A platoon commander, Yang Yangzheng, manned a machine gun hoping to hold back the Japanese. He only managed a few bursts before the tank fired a shell in his direction. A piece of shrapnel hit the left side of his face. In a daze, he groped for his left eye, and touched only warm, wet tissue. Then he collapsed. Half-conscious, he had the feeling of being grabbed by the arms and legs and being carried by running men. Unable to open his eyes, he heard familiar voices explain that he had made it to the other side of the creek. Then he fainted. When he woke up, he was in a hospital bed. A doctor explained to him that his left eye had been beyond repair. "We had to remove it," the doctor said. Yang Yangzheng understood. He accepted his fate. After all, he was lucky. He was alive.[59] Some 355 other members of the "Lost Battalion" also survived. Miraculously, fewer than 100 died.[60]

———————

A Chinese soldier injured in the battle for Shanghai had roughly a fifty-fifty chance of surviving.[61] Those were tough odds, but he was lucky compared with a compatriot hit by an enemy bullet or shrapnel elsewhere in China during the long war with Japan. Shanghai had better hospital facilities than any other Chinese city at the time, and as the battle progressed, the facilities were gradually expanded as the spacious dance-halls of the downtown entertainment districts, the Vienna Gardens and the Lido, were turned into huge sickbays.

Despite the extra capacity, the hospitals, both old and new, were stretched to the limit since they had to accommodate not just military casualties, but also a growing number of civilians who had fallen victim to the indiscriminate air war waged over Shanghai.[62] Besides, transportation was a growing problem. Even those wounded just a few miles from the metropolitan area had to undergo an excruciating ordeal before reaching a hospital bed. A soldier injured south of Wusong Creek would have his wounds dressed in a rough fashion by his comrades and would then be made to wait for transportation back to Shanghai. The ensuing bumpy ride, along narrow, shell-torn roads, took place under the cover of darkness, with no headlights on. A trip that would normally last 80 minutes routinely took five hours.[63]

Transportation could only happen at night because Japanese aircraft deliberately machine-gunned and bombed anything that bore the Red Cross. The official explanation given by Japanese spokesmen was that ambulances had been commandeered to carry war material to the front, while there were also reports of private companies using the Red Cross on their trucks as extra insurance against air attack. However, foreign observers suspected that the real reason for the Japanese practice was different. After all, hospitals were places "where soldiers were refitted for war." Whatever the reason, it soon became well known that the Red Cross offered no special protection, and ambulance crews realized that they were better off covering the markings on the sides of their vehicles as best they could with mud and boughs of trees.[64]

Inside the hospitals, small things were done to relieve the plight of the injured. Cabaret girls and dancers, out of a job because the war had put an end to much of Shanghai's nightlife, donned uniforms and became nurses overnight. "The vision of a dainty, young girl arranging pink carnations in a jam jar beside a wounded hero gave a much-needed softening touch of beauty," a journalist reported from a makeshift hospital. "Another soft-voiced creature was relating the day's news to an interested group, while others were busy feeding canned fruits, which they had brought, to those unable to feed themselves."[65] Sadly, the Chinese supreme commander, the ascetic Chiang Kai-shek, would have none of this, and banned the female visits to the hospitals whenever he got wind of the practice.[66]

Beyond the immediate reach of the Shanghai ambulances, in the area around Luodian for example, the conditions could be as bad as anywhere in China. It was not unusual for those who suffered non-lethal wounds to die because their units failed to provide them with rudimentary care in a timely fashion. It was a situation that in most other armies would have caused widespread consternation, but many soldiers in the Chinese military seemed to consider it the natural order of things. The Chinese as a nation were used to hardship, and the tenacity of the injured soldiers was a source of admiration and wonder among foreign observers. "Often pain-racked, with gory bandages, they are singularly cheerful and uncomplaining even when facilities are inadequate," wrote a correspondent for the *North China Daily News* after visiting a field hospital.[67]

Some Chinese units simply left those injured to their own devices. If they could, the wounded would get up and try to limp back in the hope of finding someone who would help them in their agony. Some officers with severe injuries managed to crawl aboard trains bound for Nanjing, where they arrived, driven almost mad with thirst, with bandages that had not been changed for a week.[68] Others roamed the countryside behind the front, living ghosts with nowhere to go. Falkenhausen suggested in a report in late October that these stragglers should be returned to their respective units, instead of causing confusion and clogging up transportation routes in the rear areas.[69]

Being abandoned could actually sometimes be an advantage, considering the alternative. Missionaries in northern China reported how 200 seriously injured soldiers had been placed inside a barrack, which had then been set ablaze, not by the Japanese but by their own. There was nothing that could be done for them, the Chinese officers responsible for the atrocity said with a shrug.[70] The medical service was "without a doubt the most sinister chapter of the Chinese Army," the German war correspondent Lily Abegg wrote.[71] Few would dispute that verdict

Contemporary foreign observers tried to explain the callousness by referring to traditional culture, arguing that inherited norms did not call for help for those injured in war.[72] Others pointed out that China was so populous and the pool of manpower so large that it made no sense to treat the injured rather than recruit new soldiers.[73] Perhaps to a large extent, the shortcomings of military medicine were simply a reflection of the poor state of the medical profession in general in China.

In the late 1930s the country had one doctor for every 45,000 inhabitants. By contrast, the number in the United States was one for every 800. Only a small number of the nation's trained physicians decided to join the army, since the pay was one tenth of what they could make as civilians. Those who did enter came under such heavy mental strain from the suffering that surrounded them that they wanted out as quickly as possible. The consequence was that the average Chinese dressing station and divisional hospital was overseen by medics who, in the words of American journalist Theodore H. White, "would not be employed as soda jerks in American pharmacies."[74]

The doctors were not helped by widespread ignorance in the rank and file, especially outside of the elite German-trained divisions. In these second-rate divisions, which had been recruited overwhelmingly among China's huge rural population, superstition thrived. "The soldiers had contacted herb doctors all their lives," White wrote. "Hygiene was a mystery to them, and they believed in charms and ancient remedies." They ignored the doctors' advice to boil water before drinking it, and got it straight from the paddy field. Sick soldiers ate from the same shared pot of rice as everyone else. They used the bandages from their first aid kits to swab out the barrels of their rifles.[75]

Military medicine in the Japanese armed forces was a somewhat different matter, at least during the initial phase of the war in Asia. Each Japanese soldier was paired with a combat buddy who, if he was injured, would dress his wound and bandage it. If this was not possible, the injured soldier would be sent back to the company dressing station just behind the frontline. More serious cases would end up in field hospitals at battalion or regimental level.[76] An uncertain fate awaited them there. Initially, the hospitals that the Japanese Army was able to take over in the Shanghai area suffered from a severe lack of resources. Medical officer Aso Tetsuo, who arrived towards the end of the battle, was assigned to a facility where there were 100 patients to every doctor, and all the medical personnel had to share one portable boiling-water sterilizer between operations. The sick and injured soldiers were lying shivering on the floor, still in their blood-covered uniforms, unable to take a bath.[77]

At least they were not ignored like their counterparts in the Chinese Army. Japanese soldiers invalided home received a hero's welcome. American journalist John Goette described what happened when two 10,000-ton hospital ships arrived at the Japanese port of Mori. On the dock were long rows of civilians—officials, students and priests—all holding paper flags. As the returning soldiers were carried through the streets in buses and ambulances, every man and woman stopped and bowed deeply. Weeks and months of recovery lay ahead. Surgeons would restore damaged arms and legs. Instructors would teach them trades that could secure an income despite their disabilities. An organization arranged contact with girls willing to marry legless or blinded veterans. "I have seen the wounded of China, America, France and England brought back, but never have I been made conscious of such a surge of gratitude, such a oneness between fighting men and civilians," Goette wrote later.[78]

The Japanese Army's policy towards injured soldiers made perfect sense, given the morale boost it provided to the rank and file. For the same reason, its attitude towards cholera patients was all the more mystifying.

The dreaded disease soon spread among the troops in the Shanghai area, just as it did among the city's civilians. Some units, such as the Amaya Detachment, had their ability to act as a fighting force severely compromised as it decimated their ranks.[79] The army's response was to place the patients inside rope fences and leave them to care for themselves. Nohara Teishin reported how a friend of his contracted cholera and ended up in a pen like this. "Give me water, give me water," the friend begged. Nohara would boil it in a mess kit and hand it to him at the end of a bamboo pole. "When we went into battle, I had to leave him. I don't know how often the medics came to take care of them. I just felt pity for my own friend. Many died. My friend died, too," Nohara recalled."[80]

––––––––––––

The withdrawal from Zhabei and Jiangwan was the beginning of the end for the Chinese Army in the Shanghai area. It had moved to a fortified line that stretched along the south bank of Suzhou Creek, before bending north towards the city of Nanxiang, then veering slightly north-northwest and running all the way to the Yangtze. Suzhou Creek offered excellent conditions for defense as it formed a natural barrier of up to 150 feet across, with steep seven-foot banks on either side.[81] But once this line was lost, there would be no other line to move back to. Losing Suzhou Creek would mean losing Shanghai. Losing Shanghai would in turn be construed as a decisive defeat not just by the Chinese public, but by the whole world. "Therefore," German advisor Borchardt wrote, "the Chinese command was placing all its bets on holding the position as long as possible without risking the annihilation of units that would be essential for continuing the war."[82]

The Japanese planned their main attack directly south across Suzhou Creek, in order to seal off the troops inside Shanghai, but first they needed to create the necessary room for maneuver. For this reason, and in order to secure their right flank, they launched a major attack against Nanxiang on October 28, following a route along the railway from Shanghai. Benefitting from the usual intensive assistance from aircraft and artillery, the Japanese managed to penetrate the Chinese frontline with little difficulty. However, they did not take Nanxiang, and overall it was less of a victory than it looked, as the Chinese had organized a deep defense, preparing a two-mile band of obstacles and barriers east of the city. In another advance, which veered south, the Japanese engaged in a short battle before taking the town of Zhenru, of importance in part because it housed a radio station that transmitted most of Shanghai's telephonic and telegraphic communications with the outside world.[83]

At noon on October 30, the Japanese renewed their attack on Nanxiang, this time with a greater force than the day before, spearheaded by 30 tanks. They gained little ground and suffered heavy casualties, as Chinese units equipped with anti-tank weapons were waiting for them along the few roads that allowed armored movement.[84] It was evident that continued attacks west would be extremely costly, and Matsui Iwane decided to temporarily halt the advance and instead focus on the more important crossing of Suzhou Creek. Time was of the essence, as he believed the Chinese defenders south of the creek were temporarily weakened after the withdrawal from Zhabei and were still waiting for resupplies of weapons and ammunition.[85]

In preparation for crossing Suzhou Creek, for several days the Japanese had been assembling a small fleet of vessels commandeered from Shanghai's civilian population, ranging from motorboats and sampans to simple bamboo barges.[86] As early as October 31, the 3rd Japanese Infantry Division, at the eastern end of the Suzhou Creek front, launched several crossings. In one of the attacks, carried out late in the afternoon near the village of Zhoujiaqiao, Japanese soldiers were able to reach the southern bank. They were immediately met by enfilading fire from Chinese machine guns and suffered serious losses. They also had to defend themselves against Chinese reserves, which had been summoned after a few hours to eliminate the threat. Nevertheless, they were able to keep their narrow foothold.[87]

A parallel attempt by the same division a little further downstream, closer to the edge of the International Settlement, failed miserably despite an impressive display of Japanese material superiority. Engineers laid a mile-long smokescreen across the creek, while a dozen three-engine bombers protected by fighters constantly hovered over the battlefield, keeping an eye out for targets.[88] A small landing party was able to cross the creek, but the moment it set foot on the other side, it was met by a strong artillery barrage, and a Chinese counterattack pushed them back into the creek. Foreign military observers speculated that this attack was reconnaissance in force rather than a serious attempt at crossing the creek in this sector. It seemed unlikely that the Japanese would seek battle so close to the International Settlement, since they would have been forced to carry out operations in heavily built-up areas.[89]

On November 1, three battalions of the 9th Japanese Division attacked in small boats across Suzhou Creek near the place where the Chinese front-line bent north, and succeeded in establishing a bridgehead on the other side. That day and the following two days, the division managed to pour a large number of troops across, and eventually controlled an area stretching about half a mile along the south bank of the creek. On the following day, the Chinese made a determined effort to eliminate this growing threat. They made significant gains, but even so, failed in their mission to completely wipe out the Japanese landing party. This was in part because the Chinese were unable to use their significant artillery resources to their full extent. At the start of the day's battle, 60 feet had separated the trenches of the opposing forces, and a barrage targeting the Japanese was just as likely to hit Chinese lines.[90]

———————

"Poison gas!" The horrified cry was passed down the Chinese ranks. The dense white cloud drifted lazily across the creek, towards the lines of entrenched defenders, who had no equipment to protect themselves against chemical agents. It was just before dawn on November 3, the start of the fourth day of the battle for Zhoujiaqiao. The exhausted Tax Police Division troops had been engaged in numerous battles with the Japanese, but in spite of appalling losses, they had not succeeded in wiping out the bridgehead. Rather, the Japanese had built a pontoon bridge across Suzhou Creek, and had been able to take and hold a small two-storey building near the bank known as "the red house."[91]

The Tax Police Division's commander, Huang Jie, had become a nervous wreck, weighed down by fatalism after Chiang Kai-shek had threatened to court-martial any officer who allowed the Japanese to move to the south bank of the creek. The sight of the ominous cloud was the last straw, and even after it was established it was not poisonous gas but a smoke screen, Huang Jie was a spent force. Yet another Japanese assault was just minutes away, and he was in no shape to lead the defense. "It's over. It's all over," he said matter-of-factly. He grabbed his sidearm and lifted it to his temple. Sun Liren, another senior Tax Police officer, was standing nearby and stopped him. "General, please go back," he urged him. "We'll take care of this."

The battle lasted until 4:00 p.m. By then, the battalion which had taken the brunt of the Japanese onslaught was no longer a coherent unit. Its commander had died, as had all but one of its company commanders, and more than half its platoon commanders. Out of an original strength of 600 men, 200 remained. This was not what the Tax Police Division had expected when it was pulled out of the area south of Wusong Creek late the previous month. They had thought the Dachang position, with its strong defenses, could hold for at least a month or two, more than enough time for the fatigued troops in the rear to rest and get back in shape. Warnings from some concerned officers that the enemy could be at Suzhou Creek within three days and that proper care should be taken to deploy the troops along the creek had fallen on deaf ears.

Therefore, when the Japanese did take Dachang and then marched to the banks of Suzhou Creek, many units of the Tax Police Division were taken by complete surprise. One of the regimental commanders had been so confident that nothing would happen that he had gone to the International Settlement to enjoy life in the dancehalls. When word had reached him of the attack, he had not been able to find his own regiment. Disorganized shooting, more a confused melee than an actual fight, had continued near Suzhou Creek long after dark. A regiment held in reserve had been sent towards the bank to intercept the attackers, only to lose its way and wind up in the crossfire between Chinese and Japanese lines. For a few terrible hours, in near-complete darkness where no one could distinguish friend from foe, the regiment had suffered massive casualties, many due to friendly fire.

On the evening of November 3, after the latest Japanese attempt to cross the creek, the Tax Police Division's commander ordered Sun Liren to rest. However, Sun Liren felt he had one task left to do. The pontoon bridge that the Japanese had built across Suzhou Creek was still largely intact, even though the Chinese had tried repeatedly to destroy it. They had launched a frontal attack. It hadn't worked. An attempt to send a swimmer downstream with explosives had also ended in failure. In the end, they had prepared large rolls of cotton, readily available form nearby textile mills, soaked them in gasoline and rolled them downhill towards the bridge, but they had been stopped by Japanese barbed wire.

For his last attempt, Sun Liren had requisitioned a number of sea mines. He planned to float them downhill and detonate them when they were level with the bridge. If this plan was to have any chance of succeeding, he needed the cooperation of engineers. Unfortunately, the engineers he ordered to participate in the late-night mission had not been trained by him, and even though they were below him in rank they felt no inclination to exert themselves for the sake of an officer they did not know. They worked slowly, and by dawn they still had not pushed the mines into the water. In the faint morning light, they made visible targets standing near the bank. A Japanese position nearby spotted them and opened fire. Sun Liren was hit, but he was one of the lucky ones. When soldiers from the Tax Police Division found him later, they had to drag him from under a pile of dead bodies. Doctors found 13 bullet wounds in his body. The battle of Shanghai was over for him.

In the struggle for Suzhou Creek, the Chinese committed the same error over and over again, according to their German advisors. With a few exceptions, lack of independent thinking on the part of junior Chinese commanders prevented them from immediately reacting aggressively to Japanese crossings. This gave the Japanese time to dig in, and subsequent Chinese counterattacks only succeeded after several costly failures, if at all. In addition, the Chinese artillery lacked flexibility and was not trained to adjust plans at short notice, or to choose the ordnance most suitable for the situation at hand. As a result, the Germans argued, "the enemy was given sufficient time to set up a good defense, and even if later Chinese attacks with better support did result in significant successes, they never ended in the complete annihilation of the enemy force that had crossed the creek."[92]

The Japanese, however, were equally frustrated, and no one more so than their commander Matsui Iwane. Even if the 9th Division had made significant advances, the 3rd Division remained stuck in a narrow strip of land south of the creek. Hopes of a quick, decisive push southeast to trap the remaining troops in Shanghai and Pudong had not materialized. Not for the first time, the Japanese general was left to ponder how his lofty ambition had collided with harsh reality in the battlefields around Shanghai.

November 3 was the birthday of Emperor Meiji, the 19th-century ruler who had brought greatness to modern Japan. Matsui reminded himself of how he had originally hoped he would be able to celebrate the festival as the conqueror of Shanghai. That had turned out not to be the case, and the long, drawn-out battles west of the city had come as an especially unpleasant surprise. "Now we've finally won a small piece of land south of Suzhou Creek, but the south of Shanghai and all of Pudong remains in enemy hands," he wrote. "That the festival is happening under conditions such as these is a source of boundless humiliation."[93]

––––––––––

Japanese planners in Tokyo had long been concerned that operations in the Shanghai area were not proceeding at all as they had expected when they first started sending troops to the city in August. Even the dispatch of three extra divisions had resulted in only limited progress, and the Army General Staff had started considering whether a more fundamental strategic change was needed in China. The basic question was whether to prioritize the campaign in the north or the battles in the Shanghai area. Japan did not have resources for both, and it had to make a choice. In early October, the officers in the Japanese capital decided that Shanghai must be dealt with first.

This conclusion was partly triggered by fears that the Soviet Union would attack Japanese possessions in northeast Asia, perhaps even before New Year. If this were to happen at a time when a large portion of Japan's military was still bogged down in the Shanghai area, the result could be catastrophic. It was preferable to resolve the situation near the city in a speedy fashion and be ready to meet the Soviets if they did decide to attack. An extra bonus, as far as some Japanese officers were concerned, was the chance to wipe out once and for all dozens of Chinese divisions, the core of Chiang Kai-shek's army, at a time when they were helpfully amassed in and around Shanghai, lined up for elimination.[94]

In an order issued on October 9, the Army General Staff established the 10th Army, the unit designed to tilt the balance in Shanghai. It consisted of the 6th Infantry Division, on deployment in north China at the time, as well as a brigade of the 5th Infantry Division, referred to as the Kunizaki Detachment, and finally, from the home islands, the 18th and 114th Infantry Division.[95] To command the new army, Tokyo picked General Yanagawa Heisuke, a 58-year-old veteran of the Russo-Japanese War who had retired from active service a year earlier, but was called back to active duty. He was particularly suited to the job, since two decades earlier he had been a military attaché in Beijing and an instructor at the city's army college.

The 10th Army was a formidable force, and while it was being formed, the Japanese planners discussed where to deploy it. They agreed it would have to land behind Chinese lines. Therefore, there were only two possible landing sites: either the south bank of the Yangtze, roughly in the same area where the landing in late August had taken place, or the north bank of Hangzhou Bay. The problem with landing on the Yangtze was that the Chinese had expected a move like this ever since the hostilities of 1932 and had built up robust defenses on both banks, including coastal batteries that could cause serious problems for any landing force, no matter how well protected.[96]

Hangzhou Bay posed other difficulties. The area was not at all suitable for a large amphibious operation. The flat shore meant there was a broad inter-tidal zone and a fast-running tide, and there was no quiet period when flow changed to ebb. In other words, there was nothing approaching a fixed coastline, and disembarking the troops, a difficult maneuver at the best of times, would be rendered even harder. The terrain beyond the beaches was also far from ideal for a large, modern army. Like other areas near Shanghai, it was crisscrossed by rivers and creeks, and there were hardly any good roads. Still, all this was made up for by one consideration: a landing here would come as a near total surprise to the Chinese. That settled it. Hangzhou Bay was their choice.[97]

Once the decision to land in Hangzhou Bay had been made, representatives of the army command arrived in Shanghai to consult with local officers. The information they received was that the area was heavily fortified and that there would be significant logistical problems. Even so, they insisted on going ahead with their plan. Matsui Iwane was his usual contrarian self, at least when communicating with his diary. "It would probably be much easier if they landed on the banks of the Huangpu and Yangtze

Rivers," he wrote.[98] He thought the operation depended on too many uncertain factors, dismissing it as the typical product of staff officers with no idea about the real conditions in the field. "This plan gives me the impression of a bunch of young people at play," he wrote in his diary.[99]

If Matsui ever voiced his doubts, they were ignored. The 10th Army was to land before dawn on November 5. The Kunizaki Detachment was to lead the way, taking possession of a stretch of coastline east of the town of Jinshanwei in the middle of the night. It was to be followed by the 6th Division, with the 18th Division on its right flank and 114th Division on its left. All units were to move north to the Huangpu River at a brisk pace and cross it. A major objective north of the river was the city of Songjiang, a transportation hub for both rail and road. Finally, in the flat countryside west of Shanghai they were to link up with Japanese units marching south, sealing off as many Chinese soldiers as possible.[100]

Success hinged on catching the Chinese unawares, and therefore secrecy was paramount for the 10th Army as it prepared for its mission. The commanders remembered an old saying, "if you want to cheat the enemy, first you must fool your own men," and they decided to follow it. Prior to the embarkation of the 6th Division, they handed out maps of Qingdao, a port city in northern China, to give the impression that this was the target of the operation. If there were a leak anywhere, the information that would be passed on would be wrong.[101]

The convoy carrying the 6th Division left waters off the Korean peninsula on November 1, heading south. The next day it linked up with another convoy carrying troops of the 18th and 114th Divisions from Japan. It had become a sizeable fleet of nearly 200 vessels, and even greater care had to be taken to avoid detection. There were strict bans against turning on any light, and radio silence was enforced at all times. As the ships approached Shanghai they sailed in a long arc out to sea, only steering back towards land as they were level with Hangzhou Bay. The soldiers, who were now informed of their real objective, were filled with excitement, and more than a little apprehension. As they crowded the dark decks, they could see the vague, looming silhouette of the great continent they had set out to conquer.[102]

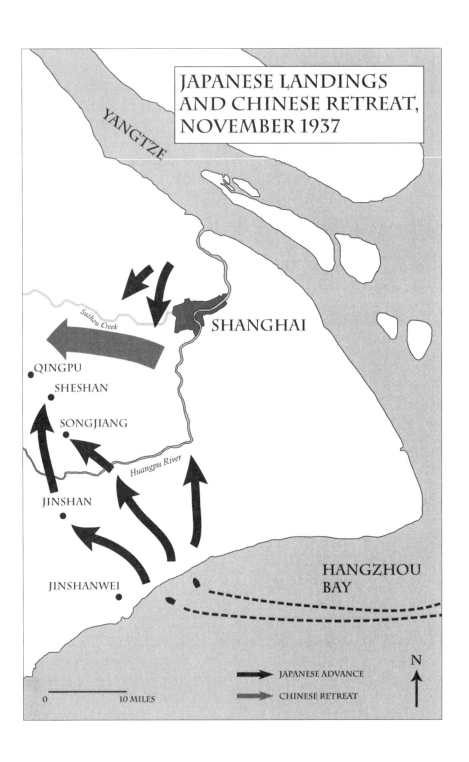

JAPANESE LANDINGS
AND CHINESE RETREAT,
NOVEMBER 1937

YANGTZE

Suzhou Creek

SHANGHAI

QINGPU

SHESHAN

SONGJIANG

Huangpu River

JINSHAN

JINSHANWEI

HANGZHOU
BAY

N

0   10 MILES

JAPANESE ADVANCE

CHINESE RETREAT

CHAPTER

8

···

Collapse

NOVEMBER 5–11

TAMAI KATSUNORI[1] WISHED TO BE A GOOD-LOOKING CORPSE. IF HE were to die in battle, he did not want to be found with an ugly, black fringe around his chin. The stubble he was carrying was the result of days on board the transport headed for the China coast, during which the 30-year-old corporal and other soldiers of the 18th Japanese Infantry Division had let their beards grow. Those who had shaved had been forced to pay a penalty of 50 yen. It had just been a silly game to kill time that would otherwise have been spent needlessly on thoughts about what was ahead. Now he no longer wanted to play the game. It was hours before dawn, and an officer had just been to the quarters he shared with his 13-man squad informing them that the landing was imminent. As he got to work with his razor, others did the same. They all wished to be handsome in death.[2]

"In the boats!" Tamai and his men had ascended to the deck when the order was passed around in lowered voices. As they stared into the night, all they could see was complete darkness. Still, they knew the coastline was just a few miles away, and that a well-armed enemy might be lying in wait. It was important to maintain the element of surprise right until the last moment. Despite their efforts to avoid any sound, the metallic ring of swords, rifles and helmets could be heard as the soldiers, weighed down by their equipment, scrambled clumsily into the landing craft. They sat down uncomfortably, almost on top of each other, in the cramped space. It was so dark that Tamai could not make out any familiar faces. Each soldier was sitting, blinded and mute, all alone with his own overpowering fears.

As the boat started making its way towards the shore, two red lights indicating the landing zone shone out to sea, like malevolent eyes. The faint light of day intermingled with the complete darkness and revealed dozens of other boats moving slowly through the black water. The soldiers felt how the current coming in from the ocean to the right constantly threatened to throw them off course, and how the landing craft operator was struggling to keep steering for the predetermined target area. They were wondering when the enemy would hear the noise of their engines and start firing, and they knew the thin-skinned boat would offer no protection. However, nothing happened. "There is no one in there!" someone exclaimed.

Long before the vessel had reached the shore, it hit the shallow ground. Tamai's squad jumped over board, landing in knee-deep, ice-cold water. They started a long cumbersome slog in sticky mud, feeling grateful that the enemy remained absent at the moment they were at their most vulnerable. As they crossed the water's edge and walked onto the wide, flat beach, they suddenly were surprised by a salvo from the left. All fell flat on the ground and continued the advance, wriggling through the gray muck towards the bank, which they could see ahead of them. As they slowly wormed their way forward, the fire from the invisible enemy grew more intense, and a soldier was hit through the thigh. Suddenly, the company commander appeared from behind, walking briskly with drawn sword as if on a parade ground. Tamai and his men felt silly, lying flat on their stomachs. They got up and followed him.

They made it to the bank and took cover behind it. The Chinese defenders who had been shooting at them appeared to have been in positions just above them, but they had fled at the sight of the mass of soldiers appearing out of the morning mist. Only then did Tamai notice how strange they all looked. Covered in mud from top to toe, and with anxiously rolling, bloodshot eyes, they resembled demons. They moved inland in a loose formation across treeless fields, before again taking cover behind a small elevation in the ground. A soldier handed around a bottle of carbonated cider. It tasted so good it almost hurt. The heightened danger sharpened the senses. The colors became brighter.

They heard gunfire ahead and moved up, joining a group of Japanese soldiers that had surrounded a cluster of houses on a hilltop, occupied by the Chinese. The defenders fired furiously, apparently directed by an observer standing behind one of the windows. Tamai ordered his machine gunner to fire. He raked the houses, which disappeared in a cloud of dust and splintered wood. When the dust settled, the Chinese were no longer firing and the soldier in the window had disappeared. "It is odd how the sound of one's own guns can be such sweet music," Tamai thought. "When the enemy is firing, the explosion and the whistle of the bullets seem ugly and vicious in the extreme. But when it is your own fire that you hear, it sounds pleasant, almost friendly."[3]

The rest of the day went by in a confused succession of events, as the soldiers moved around with no precise idea of what they were heading for; marching down narrow paths, around small plots of cultivated land and across creeks and canals. When they passed undamaged houses, they set them ablaze to ensure that they were not used to hide snipers or store ammunition. Sometimes the burning buildings burst in huge explosions, showing them that their fears had been well founded. Yet the only Chinese soldiers Tamai saw up close during the first day of fighting were the corpses of infantrymen, lying where they had been killed.

All the civilians had left, almost. In the middle of the day's ceaseless activity, Tamai passed a farm building with an old woman sitting in front. Near her was a wrinkled old man, and in her lap she had a small girl, possibly her grandchild. As the old woman saw Tamai point his bayonet at her, she trembled with fear. The girl pressed her face to the woman's bosom. "I'm sorry, but why didn't you run away in time?" Tamai asked in Japanese. She did not know his language, but he felt she somehow understood. Then he saw what was behind her—wide fruit fields and sheaves of freshly harvested rice stacked in tall piles. The old couple had stayed behind to protect their home and their land. Tamai could not bear the sad expression on the woman's face. He walked on.

———————

The landing on the north shore of Hangzhou Bay, which Tamai had participated in, was a success. The surprise was as complete as the Japanese planners could have possibly hoped. They transported a fully equipped

invasion force of thousands of infantrymen to China's doorstep and remained unseen and unheard until the last moment. The Kunizaki Detachment, the advance unit, moved into its landing craft as scheduled at 3:00
a.m. on November 5 and headed towards its appointed portion of coastline. Meanwhile, the rest of the 10th Army waited in tense anticipation on
board ships anchored two miles from the coastline. The lack of any sound
from the shore suggested that the detachment had met no resistance, but
no one could know for sure, as radio silence was maintained to the last.
Then finally, the detachment signaled with light projectors that the landing
had gone according to plan.[4]

The soldiers of the second wave waiting in their vessels could start the
approach. Navigation was difficult, because of the mist and the current.
As a result, several units got mixed up in the first confused hours after the
landing. The rough sea also meant that landing craft took longer than expected to make the return trip to the transport vessels to pick up more soldiers. This was a problem, since speed was essential. The 10th Army had
planned for the invasion force to move quickly from the landing zone and
occupy the area beyond before the Chinese had time to launch a counter-
strike. Each Japanese soldier brought rice for one week and as much ammunition as he could carry. They were not going to be slowed down by a long
and cumbersome supply train. Mobility was the key.[5]

Every man in the invasion force was wearing shoes, or rather thick
socks with rubber soles. This even including the officers who had been
ordered to leave their tell-tale high boots behind on the transport ships,
along with any decorations revealing their ranks. The danger posed by
Chinese snipers was simply too great, and it was deemed much safer for
them if, from a distance, they looked indistinguishable from the men they
commanded.[6] However, on the first day of the landing, it hardly mattered.
Apart from scattered resistance near the shore, the Chinese attempted only
two minor counterattacks. One took place on the left flank and did nothing to delay the march to the north. The other, on the right flank, had
similarly limited success, and the Chinese were forced to pull back ahead
of the Japanese.[7]

The need to remain undetected for as long as possible had prevented
the Japanese ships from launching artillery barrages in preparation for the
landing. Still, their absence was not significant as the Japanese did not

encounter major opposition at the coastline, and once they moved inland, they were able to count on the navy's heavy guns dealing with the scattered pockets of resistance they came across. As the morning progressed and the mist over the shore cleared, aircraft from offshore carriers also started bombarding the Chinese defenses.[8] A Chinese air squadron appeared over the landing site, seemingly by coincidence, and repeatedly flew at low height over the troops and their transport vessels, but did not strafe the Japanese or drop any bombs. It appeared that they had just been on a training flight, and none of the planes carried ammunition. One of them was even shot down while leaving the area.[9]

The lack of a decisive Chinese response was the result of several factors. Just as had happened two and a half months earlier at the Yangtze estuary, the Chinese commanders had not arranged air reconnaissance over Hangzhou Bay, and therefore failed to detect the Japanese naval buildup. And even if the Chinese defenders had received a few hours' extra warning, it is not clear what they could have done. Preliminary defenses had indeed been prepared along the shore during the course of the preceding months, as the Japanese landing parties found out, but they were nowhere near the more robust state of the fortifications up north closer to Shanghai. It was easy to get the impression that the troops had been lulled into a false sense of security after months of inaction. Zhang Fakui, who was nominally in command of the defending units, was criticized by the German advisors for not having done enough to ensure they stayed alert. The Chinese troops had become "a sleeping army," as the Germans dismissively stated.[10]

On top of this, the Japanese attacked at a time when the defense of the area was particularly weak. Throughout the previous months, troops had been continuously moved from Hangzhou Bay closer to Shanghai, where all the actual fighting had been taking place. In the late fall, the defense of the bay area had been in the hands of just two Chinese divisions, the 62nd and 63rd, and even that meager force had been reduced to half its size. In the last days of October and first days of November, Zhang Fakui had moved the 62nd Division to the Pudong area, leaving the task of covering the entire stretch of coastline to the 63rd, assisted by three artillery batteries[11] and a few underwhelming units from the local militia.[12] The Japanese struck so soon after the coastal defense had been thus weakened that years later the Chinese commanders still did not rule out the possibility that traitors in their midst had informed the Japanese about the changing conditions in the landing zone.[13]

By mid-morning of November 5, more than 3,000 Japanese soldiers had already landed, and the number increased by the hour. From early on, the situation was so serious that only swift and decisive action gave the Chinese generals any hope of preventing disaster. However, just when they should have thrown everything behind an all-out effort to push the Japanese back into the sea, they decided to play the waiting game. The consensus at the Third War Zone command center in Suzhou in the early hours of the day was that the landing had been carried out by weak forces in an attempt to divert attention away from more important operations that would take place elsewhere in the near future.[14]

Albert Newiger, one of two senior German advisors attached to the Third War Zone staff, immediately saw the grave danger posed to the Chinese flank by the new development and argued that the threat should be eliminated immediately. He explained how a failure to do so would jeopardize the entire Chinese Army in Shanghai. As he knew the area around Songjiang, the immediate Japanese objective, from tactical walks with students from the Central Military Academy prior to the war, he offered to help lead a counterattack with the available Chinese forces in the area. The response that Newiger received was not at all encouraging. The staff officers in Suzhou sought to give an exaggeratedly upbeat interpretation of the situation on the north shore of Hangzhou Bay, hinting that the German might be overreacting. Even if he were not overreacting, they argued, the Chinese troops present in the area were not of a good enough quality to carry out an attack.[15]

It appeared to Newiger and other German advisors that the Chinese high command, including Gu Zhutong, had already moved mentally to the next stage—full-scale retreat from the Shanghai area. The Germans agreed that this might be the only feasible option left for the Chinese, but what they failed to understand, in Newiger's view, was that a retreat was a military operation like any other, and needed to be carefully planned. Most importantly, the flanks had to be secured to make for an orderly withdrawal, rather than a mad stampede for the rear. For this exact reason, even if a consensus was gradually emerging to abandon Shanghai, it was still necessary to defend the southern flank. That meant moving aggressively against the force that had landed at Hangzhou Bay. The Germans thought it was simple logic. But no one was listening.[16]

Newiger had long had his doubts about the efficiency of decision making at the top level in the Chinese Army, but he had finally lost whatever illusions he might still have had. Fear of espionage caused the senior commanders to change positions two to three times a day, resulting in constant interruptions in the kind of meticulous staff work needed to make an army operate properly. Repeated Japanese air attacks further complicated life at the headquarters. The location of the air-raid shelters reserved for the senior officers was known only to a tiny group of people—another symptom of the pervasive fear of spies and assassins. However, the consequence was that the key officers were often nowhere to be found, hidden away in secret bunkers, when their presence was needed the most. By contrast, neither Newiger nor his fellow advisor on the Third War Zone staff, Lieutenant Klaus von Schmeling, was offered any particular protection against air attack. On the contrary, they were assigned quarters in a building with no basement. Perhaps it was a not-too-subtle indication of the Germans' rapidly declining status.[17]

Despite this, what bothered Newiger the most was the fundamental apathy that he felt had set in at the headquarters. In the end, he could keep quiet no longer and approached Chiang Kai-shek himself. He found that by now, not even the supreme commander seemed eager to act at the moment of crisis. That was the last straw. Newiger asked to be pulled from the Third War Zone and allowed to return to Nanjing. "I left with a sad feeling of missed opportunities and in the realization that the events had been larger than the people in charge," he wrote in brief memoirs prepared for his German subordinates after returning home.[18]

———

"Duty is heavier than a mountain, death is lighter than a feather." Sone Kazuo, the young officer who had been goaded by his men into decapitating a prisoner, remembered the old saying well. It had been part of the ethical code guiding the soldiers and sailors of the Japanese Empire for more than 50 years, and every recruit for several generations had been supposed to make it his own personal philosophy. As for himself, he felt no connection to those words as he stood 50 yards north of Suzhou Creek, watching another unit getting ready to cross. The officer commanding the unit was the aggressive type that many privates disliked intensely—prepared to defend Japan's honor, and promote his own career, to the last man. As he stood there toasting with cold sake, his bombastic words sounded ominous in all their perverted ambition. "Your lives have all been entrusted to me," he said, as he lifted his glass, facing the expressionless soldiers who were about to make a dash across the creek. "It is my hope that we can die together for this glorious cause."[19]

Sone Kazuo should perhaps have felt detached. After all, he was not going to the creek at that moment. It was no good. He knew that any time he might be among the unlucky ones sent across the 150 feet of heavily defended water. He tried to come to terms with the fact that he could soon be killed, but it was not easy. He was only 22 years old and felt far too young to die. Too many thoughts, and too little to do. The lack of activity made the wait even worse, not just for Sone Kazuo, but for everyone around him. Some were visibly nervous and could think of nothing to busy themselves with that could take their minds off the imminent attack. Others wrote letters home. The format they followed was roughly the same: "Dear Mom and Dad. Everything is quiet here. Please don't worry." Sone Kazuo couldn't help thinking that some of the letters would arrive at the same time as the telegram informing the parents that their son had died for the emperor.

Finally, the dreaded order arrived. It was the turn of Sone Kazuo's company to attack across the river. It was evening when they were told, and they had a few hours to get ready before the early morning attack. It was the equivalent of being ordered "over the top" on the Western Front during the Great War. As part of the army's ritual, Sone Kazuo drank a cup of wine with the rest of his unit. He was not used to alcohol and felt a burning sense in his throat. He had mixed feelings. On one hand, he did not want the danger. On the other hand, a voice inside him told him to just forget everything and get it over with.

Before dawn on the next day, they moved to the riverbank. A line of engineers appeared, wearing only helmets and loin cloths. They had the worst deal of anyone. They had to step out into the river, braving enemy fire, and hold up the planks that the attacking soldiers were to run across in order to get to the other side. "Hey engineers, make it easy for us, will you?" the infantrymen said as they passed. They got no replies from the grim-faced, half-naked men. The engineers were protected by the darkness as they stepped into the cold water, and they avoided becoming the targets of enemy fire. As dawn broke, their man-held bridge stretched all the way to the other side.

The infantry started crossing in single file, and they immediately attracted fire from Chinese defenders on the other side, who had a better view of what was happening. Some of the soldiers were hit and fell into the water. From a distance, it almost looked as if they had simply tripped by accident. Much sooner than he would have liked, it was Sone Kazuo's turn to run onto the primitive bridge and into the murderous fire. He saw machine gun bullets hit the surface of the water nearby, whipping up small geysers of white foam. He instinctively felt like stopping but he told himself that if he did not keep moving forward he would be an even easier target.

Suddenly, he felt a violent blow to his belly, like a punch. He lost his balance, as if an invisible hand had pushed him into the water. He tried to wade back to the part of the gangway where he had stumbled, but he was dragged back to the bank by medics. As they looked him over on dry land, they could not immediately detect any injury. Investigating a bit further, someone found a bullet stuck in his uniform. It had bounced off a piece of metal and failed to penetrate him. That was his lucky ticket out, at least for the day. He was sufficiently bruised that he was not thrown back into the attack. Anyway, it did not really matter anymore. The battle around Suzhou Creek was coming to an end. The fate of Shanghai was being sealed. All along the front Japanese soldiers were encouraged when they saw a huge balloon hovering under the sky with a banner showing that help had arrived: "One million Japanese soldiers have landed at Hangzhou Bay."[20]

One million soldiers was an absurd exaggeration, meant to boost the morale of the Japanese soldiers and intimidate their Chinese adversaries. In reality, of course, the landing force was far smaller. Just as important, after the initial surprise at the light and scattered resistance, the Japanese troops at Hangzhou Bay faced considerable logistical challenges. Disembarkation was a more prolonged affair than planned, partly due to the fog that had been the ally of the Japanese on the first day, but had now turned against them. Once the materiel was eventually unloaded on the shore, it was often stuck there. Due to a lack of good roads, guns and other heavy equipment could not be easily transported inland and were not immediately available to assist the troops in battle.

Thus, when the 6th Infantry Division, the 10th Army's spearhead, made its way north through a maze of paddy fields, it looked like an army transported from the 19th century into the 20th. In front of the headquarters company was the divisional commander, Tani Hisao, short and bespectacled, astride his warhorse. He was followed by his senior staff officers, who were also mounted. Behind them came long rows of soldiers, the bayonets of their long Arisaka rifles gleaming in the pale autumn sun, like a steel forest on the move. It was an army of conquest almost Napoleonic in its lack of modern technology, stripped down to the bare essentials to facilitate movement in the difficult terrain.

Since times immemorial, the locals had used the waterways that cut through the land for all major traffic. For the men of the 6th Division, they posed not means of transportation but rather obstacles, and in many cases they had to double back after suddenly encountering another impassable body of water, hidden behind tall unharvested rice fields. On different occasions, they had somewhat better luck, finding primitive bridges made by the farmers. Usually they were so narrow that they allowed crossing in single file only. The horses were not used to the delicate balancing act, and some slid whinnying and kicking into the water. In the end, the soldiers had to unload the equipment from the animals' backs and carry it across the streams themselves.[21]

Still, all things considered, it was almost like a peacetime maneuver. Enemy resistance was weak and sporadic, and despite the natural obstacles they chanced upon along the way, the divisions made brisk progress. By the evening of November 5, less than 24 hours after the first unit had landed, they had already moved three miles inland. Before noon the following day, they stood at a ferry port on the Huangpu River, as a group of more than 100 soldiers forced their way to the other side, clearing the path for a the continued attack towards Songjiang. Meanwhile, the left flank of the Japanese landing force was engaged for the first time in more severe fighting, but still managed to make headway. The Japanese momentum seemed unstoppable.[22]

In their desperation, the Chinese resorted to another throwback to the age of Napoleon: scorched earth tactics, such as they used up north in Zhabei. To the extent that time allowed, they burned every building and every field, destroyed the harvest, killed the animals and poisoned the wells. Nothing was to be left to the victors. It was a method that made sense against an enemy that traveled light and expected to live off the land. What most military men ignored was that the ones who had to ultimately pay the price were the locals who saw their homes, family property for generations, reduced to ashes. After sunset, when the Japanese made camp for the night, they saw dozens of small fires all along the horizon.[23]

From early in the day on November 7, General Tani Hisao's column picked up even more speed, as the terrain became less unpredictable with fewer creeks to slow down the advance. The Japanese could see from their maps that they were getting close to Jinshan, the seat of the county they had invaded. As they approached a hilltop, they heard the sound of rifles and machine guns. It appeared that a Japanese unit was engaged in a firefight. Tani Hisao spurred on his horse and galloped up the hill, where he was met by soldiers of one of the division's brigades, which had moved ahead of the rest of the landing force. Tani jumped off his horse and swiftly shook hands with the brigade commander. "I can see you're really busy," the general said.

From the hilltop, Tani Hisao was able to immediately get a view of the situation as it had evolved. Below was the town of Jinshan. Large parts of it were engulfed in black smoke. The Japanese vanguard was advancing west through the streets, driving the Chinese ahead of them at a distance of 300 to 400 yards. As they retreated, the Chinese set fire to as many buildings as they could in the brief time they had left. The battle lasted a few hours, ending when the Japanese were in control. Further advances that day were out of the question. The Chinese had set up strong positions near a bridge just west of the town and dominated the only route of advance from there. Besides, the troops needed rest.

It was a town half consumed by flames that the 6th Division moved into, but the members of Tani Hisao's staff were lucky. They found a single intact building, and quarters for the night. The prospect of a hot meal and a night under a roof—much-coveted comforts for soldiers in the field— raised the mood of everyone, from general down. But as they were sitting down to eat, a loud cry echoed through the narrow streets: "Fire! Fire!" It was arson. The headquarters company had to quickly evacuate and move to the eastern part of Jinshan. The division had only been in China for three days, but it had already got its first taste of the constant lingering uncertainty that had been the lot of armies of occupation since ancient times.[24]

––––––––––––

Once the Chinese command had been persuaded that the invasion at Hangzhou Bay was not an act of deception, but marked the main Japanese effort, it sent all available forces to the south to contain the rapidly multi- plying threat. The problem was that they had almost no troops to spare. The 62nd Infantry Division, which had only just left the bay area for Pudong, received orders to return at maximum speed. It was an obvious choice, since it was well acquainted with the landing zone after having manned the coastal defenses for months. However, the drawback was that once it had departed from Pudong, the district was left with virtually no regular troops to resist the Japanese encroaching from the north and west.[25]

The Chinese commanders dispatched a total of seven divisions and one independent brigade to the landing area.[26] On paper, it was a force roughly twice as big as the Japanese opponent, but in reality it was far infe- rior. Some of the units had been through lengthy periods of battle and were no longer at full combat strength. They were sent south with no time to prepare, and in many cases, morale was taking a beating from the con- stant flow of bad news from the front. Further undermining the Chinese response, the divisions ordered towards Hangzhou Bay were forced to use exactly the same poor road network that slowed down the Japanese, and therefore they mostly arrived in the combat zone too late to have much of an impact.[27]

Once the chance to push the Japanese back into the sea had passed, the next best option was to seek to stop them at Huangpu River. It was a significant natural barrier, but its defensive potential was not exploited to the utmost, and there were no fortifications prepared beforehand along its banks. In addition, in a fateful Chinese oversight, large numbers of civilian vessels of all sizes and forms were left on the south bank of the river, giving the Japanese an easy means of transport to the other side. Faced with the constant stream north of the better equipped and more experienced Japanese soldiers, in several instances the Chinese defenders simply gave up and retreated without a fight.[28]

Reacting to the menace in the south, the Chinese commanders committed the same mistake that they had made in several earlier crisis situations. They picked troops newly arrived in Shanghai and threw them directly into battle, regardless of the fact that they were exhausted after a long trek from a different part of China and had little idea about the local conditions, leaving them no chance of reaching anything like maximum efficiency. The 107th and 108th Divisions, that made up the 67th Army, had just reached the Shanghai area from Henan province in central China, when they were ordered on November 8 to move south. They were to hold the strategic city of Songjiang until November 11 at least, they were told.[29]

The Chinese commanders might have had no other choice but to send the 67th, but the results could have been easily predicted. Although the two divisions fought hard to keep Songjiang, they were no serious match for the Japanese, and as early as November 9, they were withdrawing from the almost surrounded city. While making a river crossing during the retreat, the army commander Wu Keren was assassinated by a group of plainclothes men. The hitmen—whether they were Japanese soldiers or local traitors who had been paid off to do the job was never determined—made him the only general to lose his life in the entire Shanghai campaign.[30] Following this blow, the 67th Army ceased to be an efficient fighting force and in the end simply fled the battlefield. As was the case with many other lower-quality units in the Chinese military, the rank and file had never been encouraged to seize the initiative themselves, and the corps did not survive losing its commanding officer.[31]

Amid the chaos and confusion of the landing zone, many Chinese officers came to the conclusion that the battle of Shanghai was lost and they concentrated on salvaging whatever equipment could be saved before it was too late. Three artillery batteries posted along the north shore of Hangzhou Bay tried to put up a fight on the morning of November 5, but after a few hours of non-stop firing it seemed that they had made no difference whatsoever. Artillery officers in Pudong, hoping to preserve the artillery for later in the war, applied for permission to pull it out of the danger zone. Permission was granted, and late at night on the day of the landing, 32 trucks arrived near Hangzhou Bay and evacuated the three batteries along with their manpower, leaving behind only 200 mules and horses.[32] As the Chinese front along Hangzhou Bay crumbled, even a retreat could be considered a small triumph.

———————

Chiang Kai-shek was in a state approaching nervous breakdown when the full extent of the Japanese landing at Hangzhou Bay became clear to him. On the evening of November 5, he had more than 20 telephone conversations with Gu Zhutong, each time speaking in a more panicky voice. "Is there a fight?" he asked. "The artillery is bombarding us heavily," Gu Zhutong replied. "There are airplanes, warships."[33] Late the same evening, Chiang conferred with Chen Cheng and appeared to accept the latter's view that the time had come to abandon the positions south of Suzhou Creek. Nevertheless, political considerations prevented him from announcing his decision to his commanders right away. He wanted the Brussels Conference to get underway, and did not wish the participants to consider China a lost cause. Some generals also believed that he hoped to carry on the struggle until November 13, so he could at least win a minor propaganda victory by saying that China held out for a full three months.[34]

Despite this variety of motives, on the evening of November 8, the commanders of the Third War Zone agreed that the only realistic option left was a general withdrawal to a defensive line at Suzhou, further west of Shanghai. Chiang was insistent that this move was something more honorable than a mere rout. "This is a strategic retreat, and the enemy should know that we are not pulling out because we have no fight left in us," he wrote in his diary on the day the decision was made.[35] Not only the Japanese view, but also the views of the powers meeting in Brussels were a concern. On the other hand, in the critical last days of the battle, he also repeatedly emphasized in his diary the need to preserve China's ability to wage war in the long term. He came around to that conclusion in a much belated fashion, after having worn out all his best divisions in and around Shanghai.

Privately, Chiang was despairing at the turn the battle had taken and agonizing over mistakes committed by the Chinese. With slightly paranoid anger, he blamed his officers for the impending defeat and, with growing frequency, demanded courts-martial against acts of delinquency, real and imagined. He blamed the lack of preparedness of the Chinese defense at Hangzhou Bay on Zhang Fakui. "This is all because of negligence on Zhang Fakui's part in the defense of the area. It's such a pity!" he wrote in his diary.[36]

In a sign that Chiang was becoming increasingly unhinged, his threats to put senior officers in front of a firing squad became even more frequent than before. At one point during the last feverish days before Shanghai fell, Chiang called Zhang Fakui, demanding to talk to Sun Yuanliang, the commander of the 88th Division. Sun Yuanliang was nowhere to be found, and a search was launched. Eventually, he was tracked down at the Paramount, one of the ballrooms in the International Settlement which continued their business despite the hostilities. Chiang Kai-shek was livid: "Damn Fool! Shoot him!" Zhang Fakui was used to this kind of spur-of-the-moment death sentence, and he did not carry it out. He was never asked to account for this, and Sun Yuanliang, too, soon found himself back in Chiang's good graces.[37]

Shortly afterwards, on the night between November 8 and 9, Chiang issued a fateful order to the head of the Shanghai police Cai Jianjun. He was to stay in Nanshi, the southern Chinese part of the city, and fight while the rest of the army moved west. The command, passed on by Zhang Fakui, sounded suspiciously like a suicide mission. When Cai refused, Chiang's reply was brief and resolute: "Shoot him." Again, Zhang Fakui deliberately failed to implement the order, and in the end Cai survived the battle.[38] In both cases, the officers threatened with execution were considered protégés of Chiang's, which added to his sense of betrayal when they disappointed him. At the same time, the close personal ties probably also made it easier for him to forgive them once his fury had run its course.[39]

While eager to assign blame to everyone around him at a time when the catastrophe in Shanghai was still unfolding, Chiang was later able to view the defeat with greater equanimity, even in public forums. In a speech delivered a year after the fall of Shanghai, he frankly described the failure to predict the landing in Hangzhou Bay as a mistake that had caused huge losses for China, and he ultimately accused himself of negligence. "It's a responsibility that I, as supreme leader, should take upon myself! I truly ask forgiveness of the motherland!"[40]

––––––––––––

Some Chinese soldiers in the area north of Hangzhou Bay barricaded themselves in isolated villages and tried to resist the invasion force. But for the majority of soldiers in the Japanese 6th Division, the opponent was like an army of ghosts, an elusive enemy of shadowy figures far in the distance that were constantly withdrawing ahead of them. They rarely stopped to fight, and never attained any tangible form. That said, in one particular location the two sides clashed in spectacular fashion, resulting in one of the bloodiest battles of the entire Shanghai campaign. That place was Sheshan, a couple of lonely hills reaching a height of up to 320 feet in the middle of an otherwise flat and featureless landscape. Possession of the twin hills was essential for the control of the area west of Shanghai, as the main road between the two major cities of Songjiang and Qingpu went right between them.

Two buildings gave the hills a special character. One was a French Catholic church known as the Sheshan Basilica. Built from dark red bricks, it towered over the lush greenery covering the hill, and looked older than it actually was, having been recently rebuilt and reopened only in 1935. The other building was a modern observatory, set up by western missionaries. In different ways, both were examples of two of the main influences exercised by the West on China over the preceding century—religion and science. Be that as it may, what happened on the slopes and in the valleys of the hills on the night between November 9 and 10 was a repeat of an age-old confrontation between two ancient Asian civilizations.

A company moving in advance of the 6th Japanese Division arrived near the Sheshan hills at dusk on November 9. They saw a long column of vehicles heading west along the road. It was the Chinese Army on the run. After the convoy had passed, the company hastily set up a roadblock at a bridge over a narrow creek. One platoon was placed at the head of the bridge, with the other two spreading out on either side to beat back the Chinese if they attempted to evade the roadblock by fording the creek. After waiting for a short period, soldiers from an outpost placed down the road returned reporting a column of at least 300 Chinese infantrymen moving west, heading for the bridge. Soon afterwards, Chinese scouts appeared but the Japanese managed to intercept them before they had time to return and warn the main force about the danger ahead.[41]

At 7:30 p.m., well after dark, the Japanese spotted the first Chinese appearing in the distance. With bated breath, they waited until the column was just 50 yards away, and then they opened fire. The first rows of Chinese fell like pins. Those who were not hit moved forward, some stepping on top of those already killed or injured. The usual slaughter ensued. After several minutes of incessant firing, the Japanese machine gun malfunctioned. The Chinese grasped the opportunity and rushed without hesitation towards the bridge. With shaking hands, the Japanese machine gun crew struggled to get the weapon working. It was a race against time, and the Japanese won it by a few seconds. Just before the first Chinese reached the bridge, the machine gun fired again, chopping up the closest enemy soldiers at nearly point-blank range.

The Japanese company commander ordered mortar crews to fire at the Chinese column pressing towards the bridge. The shells exploded in and around the dense, gray mass of men, causing numerous casualties. Shortly afterwards, the machine gun ran out of ammunition. This time the Chinese managed to get to the bridge, and a fierce bayonet fight commenced. At the same time, about 100 Chinese infantrymen attempted to circumvent the roadblock, wading across the river at some distance from the bridge. They walked right into one of the two Japanese platoons posted on the flanks. The Japanese bayoneted every single Chinese soldier and pushed them back into the water. Still, the Chinese kept coming. The Japanese company commander, watching the struggle at some distance, felt that it was only a matter of time before his soldiers would buckle under the strain. For a brief moment, it appeared that the battle was hanging in the balance. Then the Chinese seemed to lose vigor, and suddenly, as if by command, they retired back into the night. The Japanese remained in control of the bridge, at least for the time being.

As the evening progressed, more soldiers from the Japanese 6th Division arrived below the hills, including the commander, Tani Hisao. The headquarters company was waiting in the dark at the side of a road when a burst of machine gun fire forced everyone to fall flat on the ground. The

Chinese were back, but rather than opting for the road and suicide, they had filtered through the surrounding countryside, and were firing from positions on the periphery of the Japanese position. As bullets flew from all directions, a Japanese war correspondent crawled over to the division's chief of staff and asked: "We're in trouble, aren't we?" "Oh, that's nothing," the officer replied. "This kind of thing often happens in battle. If you want to catch the tiger, you have to enter the tiger's den, eh? There's nothing to be afraid of."[42]

Possession of the two hills was crucial, especially after dawn when the valley would be bathed in daylight, and anyone with control of the highest points would have an overwhelming tactical advantage. A group of Japanese soldiers advanced up the slope of the hill crowned by the French church and the observatory. Salvoes rang through the darkness, but no one knew who was firing. When they reached the top, the Japanese were greeted by a French priest standing at the gate of the church. The officers talked to him in their halting English, while troops fanned out to clear the hill of Chinese soldiers. They tried to explain what they were doing and that they would leave soon. "I know exactly what's going on," the priest said, interrupting them. "I was a captain in the Great War."[43]

Once the hill had been secured, the Japanese soldiers escorted their division commander to a building on its slopes, hoping to keep him out of danger. A company was posted in positions at the top of the hill to keep it in Japanese hands. "No smoking, no talking. Be quiet when you walk," officers warned the privates. Despite the extreme danger, many of the soldiers gave in to exhaustion. They had been marching for days, catching just a few hours of sleep here and there, and unsurprisingly dozed off. The company commander, a giant who towered over his men, went from position to position, brusquely prodding the soldiers with his sheathed sword.[44]

In the pitch-black night, chaos and confusion reigned, and friend and foe became hard to distinguish as both milled around in the dark forest on the hillside. A guard searched the area around the building where the division commander was hiding when he suddenly stumbled upon two sleeping Chinese, still clutching their rifles. He and other guards led them away and killed them.[45] A few hours before dawn, a Japanese machine gun squad was climbing the slopes of the observatory hill. The squad commander sensed that there were too many men in the squad. He turned around and made a count, and discovered that the last two in the group did not belong. "They are Chinese!" a private exclaimed. "Bastards," the squad commander yelled, striking the head of the first Chinese with his rifle butt. They killed the two enemy soldiers before unceremoniously kicking their bodies down the slope.[46]

As the sun rose over Sheshan, division commander Tani Hisao staggered out of the building where he had been holed up during the night. He walked over to a machine gun nest that offered a good view of the landscape below. His uniform smattered in mud and his broken glasses held up crudely with a piece of string, he peeped down. "What a lot of people," he mumbled. The battlefield was littered with bodies, the vast majority of them Chinese. Some were lying on the road, others in the ditch on either side or scattered throughout the surrounding rice fields. There were hundreds.[47]

A Japanese officer descending the hill to inspect the scene noticed something stirring inside an untidy and bloody pile of corpses. A Chinese soldier crawled out, got on his feet and, when he saw he was surrounded by enemies, drew his gun and shot himself. "He is an enemy, but he has made himself worthy of admiration," the officer said with an approving nod of his head.[48] A little distance away, men from the division went to a stream to fetch water for their rice. The surface was covered with a tangled mass of dead bodies, but if the Japanese soldiers cared, they did not show it. They were hungry, and they had to eat.[49]

The Chinese retreat from Shanghai began in an orderly fashion. At 10:00 a.m. on November 9, the last soldiers to pull out marched in neat rows past St Ignatius Cathedral and its thousands of refugees, heading southwest out of the city they had been fighting for over a period of nearly three months. On their way out, they burned down major properties that could be of potential use to the city's new masters, including factories, coal yards and even a number of foreign homes. With particular glee, they also set fire to the huge Toyoda Cotton Mills, for years a symbol of Japan's growing presence in the Yangtze Delta.[50] Initially, the withdrawal looked as if it would be as disciplined as the withdrawals that had taken the Japanese aback time and again during the previous months. It was not to be.

The Japanese were in hot pursuit, and by noon they had taken possession of Hongqiao Airfield, the scene of the shooting that had unleashed the battle in August. They were determined to impose maximum damage on the weakened enemy. Planes took off incessantly from aircraft carriers anchored off Shanghai, machine-gunning roads tightly jammed with retreating infantry. The Japanese Air Force also bombed bridges and train stations, shelled already battered transportation networks, and destroyed telephone and telegraph lines. With communications interrupted, save for the odd field radio, the Chinese were at a severe disadvantage. Runners were sent out to scattered units but were killed or got lost. Some deserted.[51]

Coordination became next to impossible, and for the first time in the campaign, a pull-out disintegrated into a mad stampede with each individual soldier consumed by the hope of personal survival. As everyone was struggling to get out at the same time, the result was a slowdown, in some cases paralysis. Once panic started spreading among the troops, there was nothing the officers could do to rein it in. Earlier withdrawals had been of a more limited tactical nature. This time the operation was of an entirely different magnitude and difficulty, as hundreds of thousands of troops were forced to move along a narrowing strip of land between the two Japanese pincers. It was something the staff officers had never been trained for.[52]

None of the Chinese were under any illusion about what would happen to them if they fell into Japanese hands. As the battle seemed lost, deserters acting alone or in small groups were scrambling for ways to gain entry into the foreign areas. Some achieved safety by forcing their way at gunpoint. Others pretended to be civilians. A foreign correspondent watched how one Chinese soldier standing under a bridge over Siccawei Creek on the border of the French Concession threw away his rifle and revolver and took off his tunic and pants. He then jumped into the foul-smelling stream only dressed in white underwear, and waded across the waist-deep muck, to be let in by the French guards on the other side.[53]

Senior Chinese officers, who did not expect their rank to offer them any special protection if they were caught by the Japanese, were forced to resort to similar methods. Ye Zhao, a general who had arrived in Shanghai with his south Chinese troops earlier in the battle, was retreating with his staff when he came across a deserted farm building west of the city. There he helped himself to a set of used peasant clothes. Shortly afterwards, he was overtaken by the advancing Japanese, who had no idea of his true identity and impressed him as a porter. That way he was able to survive and eventually escape back to Shanghai.[54]

Zhang Fakui also escaped along chaotic roads to Qingpu, but could go no further without specific orders. He was preparing to stay there and had quietly reconciled himself with the thought that he would be taken prisoner by the Japanese. He phoned Gu Zhutong, the deputy commander of the Third War Zone, at the same time as Gu was talking to Chiang Kai-shek on another phone. Chiang overheard Zhang Fakui asking where to go next, and on the spur of the moment ordered him to move further to Suzhou. "That's why I say that although Christians should not believe in fate, sometimes it is really all a matter of fate," Zhang Fakui said, looking back.[55]

The Japanese were approaching Nanshi, the southern and predominantly Chinese part of Shanghai, and it was time for a last reckoning before the district fell. A group of Chinese who had been found guilty of spying on behalf of the Japanese were lined up in the afternoon sun and executed by firing squad. An officer, a dapper dresser who seemed to have spent most of his time far behind the front, went from body to body and delivered a shot to the back of the head of each convict. Hundreds of onlookers—men, women and children—watched in silence.[56]

As the government packed up and prepared to leave, it urged the residents to carry on the fight, and in particular pay attention to enemies in their midst. "People should guard against the activities of traitors and puppets, and the best way to do it is to build a solid spiritual Great Wall," said a ranking official before departing.[57] The people of Shanghai did take matters into their own hands, sometimes with fateful consequences. A 31-year-old Chinese who had returned from studies in Germany and had retained a foreign appearance was attacked by a mob believing him to be Japanese. When he produced a Chinese ID card, he was accused of being a spy. He was beaten with two wooden sticks, and even though police ran to his rescue, they could not save him in time. He died on his way to hospital.[58]

The haste of the Chinese Army's retreat came as a shock to many civilian residents of Shanghai. They had thought the city could be held for months, perhaps even indefinitely. Instead, it fell in the course of a few hectic days, leaving no time to flee anywhere. Thousands of desperate men and women, weighed down by their belongings, turned up at the bridges leading to the French Concession, begging on their knees to be let in. They were met by French police, reinforced by tanks, who ordered them to turn around. When they would not listen, they commanded local Chinese in their employ to drive the crowd away. "Old and young and mothers carrying infants were ruthlessly clubbed or beaten back with long bamboo poles," wrote *The New York Times'* correspondent Hallet Abend, who watched the pitiful scene. "At one bridge a railing collapsed under the crowd's pressure and forty women and children fell shrieking into Siccawei Creek. Five or six were drowned."[59]

The impending victory had whetted the Japanese Army's thirst for blood. Chinese, whether in uniform or not, faced an uncertain future if they had the bad luck of running into an adrenaline-pumped band of enemy soldiers. An English architect experienced what that meant first-hand. He had been driving his car west of Shanghai on a necessary errand, helping a Japanese soldier start his truck on the way. Eventually, he had taken in a terrified Chinese family of seven desperate to escape the unsafe countryside and get to the International Settlement.

On the way back, his car was stopped by a Japanese roadblock. The soldiers opened the doors and tried to drag out the panic-stricken Chinese. When the car owner stepped out, brandishing his passport and hoping to talk his way out of the predicament, he was faced with a six-foot-tall Japanese who pointed a revolver at his heart. Out of the corner of his eye, he saw a Japanese infantryman shoot an injured Chinese lying by the roadside. It looked like the end. However, at the last moment, the Japanese truck driver whom the Englishman had helped earlier turned up and argued his case. He was allowed to move on with the Chinese family.[60]

It was clear that left to the mercy of the Japanese armed forces, everyone in conquered Shanghai was in danger. The safety district envisaged by Jacquinot was needed, and it was needed urgently. By early November, the Japanese Consul General Okamoto had received a reply from Tokyo. It agreed to the plan. The local army and navy commanders also gave their consent after receiving reassurances that no Chinese military personnel

A Japanese poses next to a Chinese gun after the fall of the fortress of Wusong. The Wusong artillery constituted severe challenges for the Japanese north of Shanghai in the initial stages of the battle. *Author's collection*

"You can figure how close we were to the fighting," wrote the American sailor who took this photo. The snapshot is through a porthole in the heavy cruiser USS *Augusta*, which was anchored in the port of Shanghai almost throughout the entire battle. An American sailor was killed when a Chinese shell exploded near the vessel. *Author's collection*

Above: As the fighting intensified and threatened to spill over into the International Settlement, the foreign powers sent reinforcements to their garrisons. Here US troops are lined up on the bank of the Huangpu River. A swastika flag is flying over German property in the background. *Author's collection*

Left: Japanese soldiers search a Chinese civilian in the countryside near Shanghai. Men of fighting age such as this person ran a severe risk of being executed. *Author's collection*

Above: The French Concession was guarded by both conscripts from the homeland and troops from the colonies, including Indochina. They were especially active towards the end of the battle, when large numbers of refugees sought safety in the foreign zones. *Author's collection*

Right: Civilians became casualties from the first day of the battle. Here a Chinese woman is receiving medical treatment from a US Navy doctor. *Author's collection*

Right: The Japanese army waged the war in China with extreme brutality. Its soldiers rarely took any prisoners. Like their German counterparts, they often documented their own misdeeds with the camera. In this photo, not from Shanghai, a platoon poses in front of a just-decapitated person. It is not possible to determine from the clothes that the corpse is wearing if he was a soldier or a civilian. *Private collection*

Bottom left: A group of Chinese civilians have been detained and are now awaiting questioning by the Japanese. Some of the captives seem to be mere boys. *Author's collection*

Bottom right: A Japanese Type 89 medium tank outside a partly destroyed government building in the northern outskirts of Shanghai, middle of September 1937. Japan had an advantage in armor but was never fully able to utilize it because of the difficult, water-rich terrain near the city. *Courtesy Asahi Shimbun.*

Japanese artillery on the move during the attack on Yanghang, September 1937.
Courtesy Asahi Shimbun

The autumn rain caused tanks and other heavy wheeled equipment to become bogged down. But the cavalry could still move. October 1937, when this photo was taken, saw a stalemate reminiscent of the static warfare on the Western Front two decades earlier. *Courtesy Asahi Shimbun*

Opposite page, top & bottom: Like the Germans discovered in Russia, the Japanese in China eventually realized that rain and mud could be formidable enemies. By October 1937, the bright sun of August had given way to chilly and damp weather. *Courtesy Asahi Shimbun*

Below: Japanese soldiers simulate an attack across a creek near Shanghai, October 1937. The photographer's position, well above the protective embankment, shows that this photo is posed. *Courtesy Asahi Shimbun*

Above: Japanese infantrymen in their trenches north of Suzhou Creek on November 1 1937. Engineers have prepared a smokescreen and the soldiers are ready to go over the top. They are carrying as little gear as possible for the sake of mobility. The lack of composition gives the photo an immediate feel like few others from the Shanghai battle. *Courtesy Asahi Shimbun*

Opposite page, top & bottom: The creeks and canals of the countryside around Shanghai were a net advantage for the defense and posed serious logistical problems for the Japanese attackers. October 1937. *Courtesy Asahi Shimbun*

Japanese soldiers march into Nanshi, the southern predominantly Chinese part of Shanghai, in early November 1937. Parts of the district were just as devastated as Zhabei further up north, which had been subject to deliberate arson by retreating Chinese. *Courtesy Asahi Shimbun*

Top left: Japanese infantry prepare to move into the last unoccupied part of Chinese Shanghai. The city appears deserted. The advance of the Japanese Army in the last part of the battle set off large refugee streams as word spread of its ruthless treatment of civilians in areas under its control. *Courtesy Asahi Shimbun*

Bottom left: A Japanese soldier's grave near Shanghai. The Japanese army preferred to cremate its dead, but the high fatality rates in the battle often made a hasty burial, or no burial at all, a preferable method. This grave, however, seems to have received special care and attention. *Author's collection*

Below: Japanese infantry cross Suzhou Creek in November 1937. The creek was the last major obstacle the Japanese army faced before conquering Shanghai. Engineers have laid a pontoon bridge across. When time was of the essence, the engineers would step out into the water and hold up the planks, allowing the soldiers to run across in single file. *Courtesy Asahi Shimbun*

The Japanese invasion force has invited Western journalists to visit its positions near Wusong. The cameraman is Harrison Forman, shooting footage for the "March of Time" newsreel service. He covered major parts of the war in Asia and was also present in Poland at the time of the German attack in 1939. *From the American Geographical Society Library, University of Wisconsin-Milwaukee Libraries*

Shanghai's new rulers: Japanese marines inspect items belonging to two Sikh men. *From the American Geographical Society Library, University of Wisconsin-Milwaukee Libraries*

would enter the zone.[61] Jacquinot reiterated that reassurance publicly. "It is purely and simply what it is called, a district of safety for the non-combatants," he said.[62]

The district, known as the Jacquinot Zone, opened formally at 5:00 p.m. on November 9, 1937, on the northern edge of the Chinese city.[63] It immediately became home to an estimated 100,000 refugees. Jacquinot saw it as a revolutionary step. "It might, with advantage, be copied elsewhere for instance in Europe," he declared.[64] Newspaper commentators were equally enthusiastic. "Even in the most difficult and delicate circumstances produced by the heat of battle, scope is still left for the observance of the laws of humanity and the sanctity of the pledged word," the *North China Herald* wrote in an editorial.[65] It did, in fact, become a model for the protection of civilians in other urban battles.[66] For Jacquinot himself, the main legacy was the Shanghai zone, which remained in operation until 1940 and shielded large numbers of people from the arbitrary cruelty of the Japanese victors. "The Japanese have not gained entry here," he told a visitor with a mixture of defiance and pride. "And the only flags that fly over this place are the French flag and the standard of the Red Cross."[67]

November 11 was the 19th anniversary of the end of the Great War. For Shanghai's expatriate community the day should have been an opportunity to reflect on the horrors of past wars and unite in the hope that they would never happen again. Instead, it was a reminder that armed conflict was still very much part of the human condition. The annual parade on the Bund took place as in previous years, but sandbags had to be removed at the foot of the War Memorial to make room for wreathes.[68] The military orchestra's solemn music was mixed with the sound of gunfire as south of the Settlement, Shanghai saw its last great urban battle. There, pockets of Chinese resistance held out, determined to make the conquest of the city as hard as possible for the Japanese.

Between five and six thousand Chinese soldiers were left in Nanshi after three days of fighting. From early on the morning of November 11, the Japanese moved in for the kill. Their artillery started a furious and indiscriminate artillery barrage against the densely populated urban area.[69] American reporter Edgar Snow and other foreign correspondents were following the battle from the relative safety of the French Concession, across Siccawei Creek. The Japanese tanks proceeded cautiously down narrow roads, rolling a few feet before unleashing their guns and then hastily backing up. The infantry also moved from cover to cover, mindful of Chinese snipers hiding in the buildings along the alleys and in the stilted huts erected on top of the city's canals.

Most residents had fled the advancing Japanese, and the combat appeared to unfold in a ghost town. But there were a few almost surreal examples of civilians going on living their lives in the middle of whistling bullets and exploding grenades. In a sampan, a group of Chinese were eating rice as if nothing out of the ordinary was happening. Suddenly, a machine gun salvo cut across the boat, and the occupants speedily hid under the matting. Whether they were killed or not, Snow, who watched the scene, would never find out.

The Japanese were still facing the same terrain difficulty that had beset them for three months—waterways. As they moved through Nanshi, they were constantly slowed down by the need to set up pontoon bridges across canals in order to move from one block to the next.[70] The French wanted no part of the fight and saw to it that the border with the Chinese district was clearly marked off as a non-combatant area. This was done by means of thousands of small Tricolors, leftovers from the July 14 Bastille Day, planted by police.[71]

The Chinese made one of their last stands in full view of spectators inside the French Concession. It was an unequal encounter. The Japanese rolled their tanks up and fired at the Chinese positions over a distance of no more than 60 yards. The Chinese were also exposed to intensive air raids and eventually they were pushed back. Once the situation appeared completely hopeless, a Chinese soldier carried a wounded comrade north across the Siccawei Creek into the French Concession, evading the hail of bullets that the Japanese sent after him. The French guards, who did not conceal that their sympathies were with the Chinese, helped the two soldiers up the bank. This incident encouraged the other Chinese to follow suit, and soon dozens of soldiers poured across the border into the French sector, handing over their weapons. They had become internees, a French sop to the now-powerful Japanese, but they had avoided almost certain death at the hands of their enemy.[72]

Not all the Chinese soldiers escaped that way. Some moved further east to a position that was also close to the southern edge of the French Concession, near a water tower which served as a landmark for that part of town. It was a doomed position. It offered even less protection than the one the Chinese defenders had left, while enabling the Japanese to jump from building to building during their advance. The encounter was short and deadly. After a few minutes the Chinese knew they had lost, and in full view of the Japanese, they abruptly turned around and dashed for the French Concession, scrambling over the barbed wire at the border.[73] Before entering they abandoned their weapons and equipment in big piles, leaving souvenir hunters among the foreign observers to have a field day. The French commander arrived at the scene and praised the Chinese soldiers for their bravery while giving them his personal assurance that they would not be handed back to the Japanese.[74]

Casualties during the final skirmish could have been much worse, but one last tragedy was still waiting to happen. Edgar Snow looked around and noticed a small red pool on the ground in front of him. "Is this paint or blood?" he asked. It was just below the water tower, which had served as a good vantage point for watching the battle. Curious, Snow started ascending the winding staircase to the top. On the way up, he met a group of people walking down carrying a lifeless body. It was Pembroke Stevens, a British journalist. He has been shot through the head and the groin. It was his blood Snow had seen. He was already dead. In his buttonhole, he wore a red poppy, in remembrance of Armistice Day.[75]

The battle across Siccawei Creek was drawing to an end. The victorious troops moved through the last unoccupied streets of Chinese Shanghai, weeding out the few remaining pockets of resistance. As in Zhabei, the defenders attempted to set fire to buildings in a bid to leave as little as possible for the army of occupation. Thick smoke rose over the district, reducing visibility dramatically, and spectators inside the French Concession had to judge the progress of the battle from the sound. As the machine gun fire gradually died out, it was replaced by triumphant shouts of "Banzai!" At 3:34 p.m., the Rising Sun flag was hoisted over the last Chinese stronghold in Nanshi. The battle of Shanghai was over.[76]

CHAPTER

9

· ·

Aftermath

ANYONE APPROACHING SHANGHAI TOWARDS THE END OF 1937 WOULD have been dumbfounded by the terrible destruction that had been wrought on the area during the course of three months of war. When Robert Guillain, a French journalist, arrived from Japan aboard the passenger ship *Nagasaki Maru* in early November, he was struck by the blackened ruins of Wusong, greeting him as silent testimony to the just-ended battle. "The entire town and the villages all round it had been horribly destroyed, burned and razed to the ground by the bombing. Astonished, I realized the savagery of modern war. In the surrounding countryside, even the smallest farm building had been shelled and consumed by fire. The trees had been blown to shreds. For mile after mile the scene along the riverbank was one of ruins and scorched earth, dotted with the charred skeletons of trees and signposts."[1]

German correspondent Wolf Schenke knew Shanghai from before the war. It was a changed city that met him on his return on November 12.[2] A walk through the nearly empty streets of Hongkou confronted him with "the most sinister atmosphere" he had ever felt anywhere. The buildings were mostly gone. Smaller structures had been turned into heaps of rubble. Telephone wires had been blown apart by the shock waves of the explosions and were hanging limply just above the heads of the passing pedestrians or were lying on the ground. "What life, what crowds had been on the Broadway before! Now the rain poured incessantly from low-hanging clouds on the fully deserted streets. The only sign of life was in the form of Japanese military aircraft flying past at high speed and of Japanese sentries wrapped in long raincoats who were standing at the corners with fixed bayonets."[3]

In a city where hardly a single street had escaped harm, the district of Zhabei was the epicenter of devastation. The immediate vicinity of the North Train Station had been reduced to a sinister lunar landscape, the gutted buildings standing like rugged moon cliffs. The asphalt roads were riven by deep fissures, similar to those caused by earthquakes. Liliane Willens, the young Jewish Russian girl, was taken by her father on a tour of the area after the fighting had ended and the blaze extinguished. She was overwhelmed by the comprehensive destruction. "I suddenly understood that wars meant the killing of real people, not death toll statistics printed in newspapers and mentioned on the radio," she wrote in her memoirs.[4] It was no wonder that even the expatriates who had gradually become used to the artillery were in a state of shock. Rarely before in the history of human conflict had a major city been subject to this level of destruction.

Chinese officials attempted to put a positive spin on the battle before leaving the city and heading for Nanjing. It was important to let people know that their sacrifices had not been in vain. "What has been learned in Shanghai in the past 90 days," Mayor Yu said, "could very well be turned into good use for the whole nation in the war of resistance. The confidence of the people of Shanghai in a final victory cannot fail to have been shared by their brethren throughout the country."[5] He was speaking as if the war was over in Shanghai, and it was true that the big war had come to an end. However, a small, low-intensity conflict continued to brew, and would claim many more lives in the months and years ahead.[6]

As early as spring 1938, reports emerged of armed Chinese bands forming in the countryside around Shanghai. Residents of the foreign areas frequently heard shooting on the fringes of the city. In August of that year, guerrillas were able to hoist the Chinese flags for a few hours in the suburbs. In the spring of 1939, the threat had become so pronounced that the Japanese military began constructing a system of fortifications at Wusong.[7] Meanwhile, the civilian population had not only the war to worry about. The withdrawal of the government left a vacuum that was taken over by mafia-style gangs. "There was nothing they would not do and no evil they would not commit, with the result that good people vanished without a trace and bandits arose in great number, committing murders and rapes every day," an anonymous resident wrote in a letter to the remnants of the municipal government.[8]

In late 1937, the Japanese could not know what would happen that far in the future. They thought they had won. On December 3, Matsui Iwane's army staged a victory parade through the unoccupied International Settlement, which was their right as one of the governing powers. It was a serious misjudgment. Japanese civilians and *ronin* were commandeered to act as jubilant masses lining the route, waving national flags. Some foreigners felt provoked. A number of fistfights broke out between Japanese and western residents. When the parade passed by the Great World Amusement Center where hundreds had died on "Black Saturday," a Chinese man jumped to his death from the top of a building, shouting as he fell: "Long Live China!"[9]

When the parade moved down Nanjing Road, the accompanying police grew tense. This was the most risky part. Suddenly, a grenade was thrown from a window. It exploded, injuring four Japanese soldiers and one British police officer. Matsui's battle-hardened veterans immediately fanned out to find and kill the assassin, but it was a Chinese police officer who shot him dead.[10] The parade had become the fiasco that most had expected. It did nothing to ingratiate Japan with the people of Shanghai, and it showed that the Japanese would never be able to control even this small corner of China, let alone the vast country in its entirety.

The battle for Shanghai had turned out to be the bloodiest international battle in Asia since the Russo-Japanese War earlier in the century, and it was largely Chinese blood that had been spilled. By late October, the Japanese estimated that China had suffered 250,000 military casualties fighting for the city.[11] In the months after the end of the battle, the Chinese put the number at 187,200.[12] Some even estimated that it was as high as 300,000.[13] No matter the exact figure, the result of the battle was carnage of catastrophic dimensions, which hit Chiang Kai-shek's best German-trained divisions with disproportionate severity. China took a beating that it would not recover from fully until 1944, after massive American aid.

The high casualty rate was the result of a combination of factors. Many Chinese soldiers went into the battle fully expecting to die. Their willingness to throw themselves into suicidal attacks against well-fortified positions pushed fatality rates far higher than they would otherwise have reached. Chinese tactics also contributed to the casualty rate. Their use of their numerical superiority to counterbalance Japan's material edge led to what was in essence a contest of flesh against steel. In a rather grim sense, the approach did have some logic to it, but nevertheless it was in stark contrast to the Chinese commanders' reluctance to sacrifice any of their expensive imported equipment. At the same time as they were willing to squander their very best formations with almost complete abandon, they protected key weaponry to the point of not using it. The elite 87th and 88th Divisions were nearly used up in a few days of intense fighting in late August, while the Pudong artillery kept its activity close to a minimum for the entire three months for fear of attracting Japanese air raids.

One must question what Chiang Kai-shek got in return for this massive sacrifice. The answer depends on what he set out to achieve, and there is no consensus on this, partly because he was in all likelihood prompted into action by a mixture of motives. If his main objective was to lure the Japanese away from the north, where they had won a series of easy victories, the Shanghai battle was a Chinese success. As the autumn of 1937 progressed, the Japanese commanders were forced to increasingly divert their attention, along with men and materiel, to the tactically much more complex area around Shanghai, where their technical superiority counted for less than on the north Chinese plain. However, moving the war to the center of China came with its own risks. It jeopardized the nation's economic heartland, which was also close to its political capital in Nanjing, and ultimately invited a Japanese occupation that would last for nearly eight years.

If Chiang Kai-shek was also motivated by a wish to attract foreign attention, it is less obvious whether he got what he wanted. He certainly had the opportunity to wage war in front of an audience of thousands, assembled in the International Settlement and French Concession, as well as in front of the rest of the world who could follow the conflict via the media. Shanghai was already home to dozens of foreign correspondents before the war broke out, and with the onset of hostilities, many more arrived by steamship to report on the evolving conflict. For three long months, Shanghai was on the front pages of the world's major newspapers. The Chinese also proved adept at propaganda, getting maximum mileage out of, for example, the "Lost Battalion's" desperate and militarily futile fight in Zhabei in late October. Still, none of the great powers was ever tempted to step in and offer any kind of substantial support to China. Even the Brussels conference turned out to be of no direct help to the Chinese cause.

It was not just the Western world that was interested in the conflict, but also the Soviet Union. Chiang Kai-shek held high hopes that Moscow could provide help, and historical records seem to suggest that Soviet diplomats deliberately goaded him on with vague promises of support. China fought in order to invite Soviet entry into the war against Japan. Even so, the end result may have been the exact opposite. Because China entered into war with Japan, the Soviet Union didn't have to. Any attack that Japan might have launched against the Soviet Union was made impossible, at least in the medium term, by the need to subdue the Chinese giant, who might have been weak, but was a giant nonetheless. The Soviet Union did start providing material aid to China—the first of nearly 300 Russian attack and bomber aircraft arrived in mid-October[14]—but it was a poor substitute for a real ally. Also, while the Soviet Union emerged as a reluctant partner for China, China lost the robust assistance it had received from the Germans.

––––––––––

The Germans played a key role in Shanghai in 1937. Every major Chinese unit had at least one German advisor attached to it. This was reflected at several different levels. Chiang's strategic decision to make a stand in Shanghai appears to have been heavily influenced by Falkenhausen's views. Similarly, the chief German advisor seems to have had a considerable impact on China's tactical choices. His opinions about the need to hold on to the town of Luodian, or to concentrate most of the fighting during the dark hours, also coincided with actual Chinese behavior in the field. German officers further down the hierarchy lent a hand in the fight against Japan, whether it was because they felt loyalty towards China or because they simply craved a chance to test their skills in actual battle. It must be considered a little miracle that, as far as can be judged from the sources, no German lost his life in Shanghai.

Despite their enthusiasm, the Germans gradually discovered that their influence was waning. Chiang Kai-shek and his commanders started ignoring their opinions. They did not listen when the Germans suggested launching surprise assaults against weak areas along the Japanese line, or proposed organizing speedy counterattacks against landing forces before they had built up critical mass. More seriously, Chiang held on to Shanghai long after it made any sense, militarily or politically, to do so, at a time when the Germans would have considered it more opportune to cut losses and withdraw in an orderly fashion to better positions in the rear. The German must have come to realize what was meant when it was said that Chiang's stubborn fury was both "his greatest strength and his greatest fault."[15] Chiang had accepted the initial German proposal to fight for Shanghai, and he was determined to see it through to the end, at whatever cost to his men.

The Germans left China and returned home mostly during the course of 1938, just in time for the war in Europe. They seem generally not to have put their China experience to any particular use. The lessons they had learned about urban warfare were apparently largely ignored, however useful they might have been in Stalingrad in the winter of 1942 and 1943, or in countless other European cities. Instead, they all had fairly conventional experiences during the war. Falkenhausen headed the military government in Belgium from 1940 to 1944 and was put on trial after the war mainly for his role in the execution of Belgian hostages. He was returned to Germany and released in 1951. He died in 1966, at the age of 87. Chiang Kai-shek remained grateful for his German chief advisor's services and provided assistance to him, mostly in the form of money, in the post-war years.[16]

One German, at least, ended up with a story stranger than fiction. That was Robert Borchardt, the officer whose Jewish ancestry had put his officer career in limbo. Back in Germany, he left the army but wrote the bulk of an after-action report, *Die Schlacht bei Shanghai*, or *The Battle at Shanghai*, for the German High Command. In the meantime, his father had been interned in Dachau concentration camp, before being released and emigrating to the United Kingdom. But even though Robert Borchardt had been given good reasons to hate the Nazis, he ended up fighting harder for them than most.

When war broke out, he accepted an offer to return to the armed forces. Promoted to the rank of captain, he was involved in setting up Sonderverband 288, a unit that was to have operated in North Africa and the Middle East in an unconventional role similar to that of the Long Range Desert Group, the British commando force. The Sonderverband never came to fulfill its original purpose, but was attached to the Afrika Korps as a standard combat unit. Borchardt was put in charge of an armored reconnaissance company and received the Knight's Cross in August 1941. This made him one of the highest decorated Germans of Jewish descent during the war. Later, he had a simple explanation for why he had fought for a regime that had murdered millions of people like him. "I served because I wanted to prove Hitler's racial nonsense wrong," he said. "I wanted to prove that people of Jewish descent were indeed brave and courageous soldiers."[17]

Even if the Chinese did most of the suffering in and around Shanghai in 1937, the battle also turned out far costlier for the Japanese than any of the proud empire's generals and admirals had foreseen. By November 8, the total number of Japanese military casualties in the battle was 9,115 dead and 31,257 injured.[18] The Japanese forces benefited from crushing superiority in artillery and air power, but this could not make up for the fact that the soldiers on the frontline had to pay the price for their superiors' consistent arrogant underestimates of Chinese strength and will to fight. The dispatch of reinforcements happened in a piecemeal fashion, and Matsui and the field commanders never felt they had quite enough men at their disposal to bring about a quick and decisive end to the campaign.[19]

Nevertheless, as the battle for Shanghai approached its end, Matsui gained confidence that he had build up enough momentum to deal a blow to Chiang Kai-shek from which he would never recover. In an interview with a German reporter in late October, Matsui had said that after taking Shanghai the Japanese Army would march on to the political capital of Nanjing if necessary.[20] He was a man with keen political instincts, who knew that it was always better to ask forgiveness after the fact than seek permission before. "I never asked orders from my government," he told a group of journalists. "Everything that is happening here is taking place under my entire responsibility."[21]

It is doubtful that the Japanese would have continued to Nanjing without an aggressive general like Matsui in charge. During the first days after the fall of Shanghai, they merely pursued the retreating Chinese columns. This was a sound tactical move, and did not necessarily imply any wider-ranging strategic decision to go all the way to Nanjing. Yet, after the Japanese staged another surprise amphibious landing on November 13, this time on the south bank of the Yangtze River, it seemed there was very little shielding the Chinese Army from complete collapse. On November 15, Japanese commanders in the Shanghai area decided to head for Nanjing and bring an end to the war once and for all.[22]

On its way to the Chinese capital, the Japanese divisions marched across a once-prosperous and densely populated area, whose silk products had once made their way to the markets of ancient Rome. They turned it into a deserted and blackened wasteland where the only living creatures were stray dogs "unnaturally fattened by feasting on human corpses."[23] The soldiers routinely massacred whatever civilians they came across, sometimes as a form of entertainment after a long day on the road. On rare occasions when individual soldiers questioned the need for this harshness, the officers explained that it was retribution for fierce resistance offered by the Chinese Army.

Kurosu Tadanobu, a soldier of the 13th Japanese Division, described what happened when his artillery unit entered a village and set up camp for the night. "We'd take all the men behind the houses and kill them with bayonets and knives," he said. "Then we'd lock up the women and children in a single house and rape them at night. I didn't do that myself, but I think the other soldiers did quite a bit of raping. Then, before we left the next morning, we'd kill all the women and children, and to top it off, we'd set fire to the houses, so that even if anyone came back, they wouldn't have a place to live."[24]

By December 1937, the Japanese Army arrived at Nanjing. Whatever prestige it might have won due to its military prowess in Shanghai and beyond, was completely erased by the ensuing orgy of rape and murder that seemed to have no end, but rather escalated as if the sight of blood whetted the Japanese appetite for more. Days turned into weeks. It became the infamous "Rape of Nanjing." An unnamed foreign resident of the city described what life under Japanese occupation meant. "At noon a man was led to headquarters with head burned cinder black—eyes and ears gone, nose partly, a ghastly sight. I took him to the hospital in my car where he died a few hours later. His story was that he was one of a gang of some hundred who had been tied together, then gasoline thrown over them and set afire."[25]

Robert O. Wilson, an American surgeon at Nanjing's University Hospital, described the horrors he witnessed in a letter to his family dated December 18, 1937: "Two girls, about 16, were raped to death in one of the refugee camps. In the University Middle School where there are 8,000 people the Japs came in ten times last night, over the wall, stole food, clothing, and raped until they were satisfied. They bayoneted one little boy, killing him, and I spent an hour and a half this morning patching up another little boy of eight who [had] five bayonet wounds including one that penetrated his stomach."[26]

Matsui appears to have been horrified when he realized the extent of the atrocities committed by his troops. According to one report, he subsequently subjected his senior officers to a personal reprimand that surprised everyone in attendance by its severity.[27] It did not, however, save him from the gallows. He was sentenced to death by the International Military Tribunal for the Far East and hanged in Tokyo's Sugamo Prison in December 1948. Tani Hisao, the bespectacled commander of the 6th Infantry Division, was sent back to China after the war to answer for crimes committed by his troops. He was executed in Nanjing in April 1947.

That was years into the future. In December 1937, as a young girl, Liliane Willens had only hazy ideas about what was going on in Nanjing. Kept in the dark by her concerned parents, she nevertheless saw the ghastly pictures in the local newspapers. The "Japanese dwarfs" were very, very bad, she was told by Old Amah, her Chinese nanny. Then the woman explained ominously how war had broken out in China every five years, first 1927, then 1932 and now 1937. In five more years, the Japanese would attack again, she said.[28] She was almost correct. Four years and one month after the last shot rang out in Shanghai, the first shot was fired over Pearl Harbor. Only then did China's lonely struggle become a world war.

······································

Order of Battle

Names of commanders are given, in parentheses, down to division level for the Japanese side, and down to army level for the Chinese side. Please note that there was some organizational inconsistency in the deployment of Chinese forces in the Shanghai area. In principle, divisions were grouped into armies, which in turn were grouped into army groups. However, the army level was sometimes skipped, in which case the divisions went into battle under the direct command of the army group. As a result, in certain cases in the order of battle below, divisions are listed as placed on the same organizational level as armies. This is not meant to reflect any necessary equivalence between divisions and armies in terms of manpower strength or combat value.

JAPAN

FORCES IN SHANGHAI, AUGUST 13, 1937

Third Fleet (Hasegawa Kiyoshi)
    8th Cruiser Division (Nagumo Chuichi)
    11th Gunboat Division (Tanimoto Umataro)
    1st Torpedo Squadron
    3rd Torpedo Squadron
    Shanghai Special Naval Landing Force (Okawachi Denshichi)

JAPANESE REINFORCEMENTS, DISEMBARKING FROM AUGUST 23, 1937

Shanghai Expeditionary Force (Matsui Iwane)

3rd Division (Fujita Susumu)
    5th Brigade
        6th Regiment
        68th Regiment
    29th Brigade
        18th Regiment
        34th Regiment
11th Division (Yamamuro Monetake)
    10th Brigade
        12th Regiment
        22nd Regiment
    22nd Brigade
        43rd Regiment
        44th Regiment

JAPANESE REINFORCEMENTS, DISEMBARKING FROM SEPTEMBER 22, 1937

Attached to Shanghai Expeditionary Force:
    9th Division (Yoshizumi Ryosuke)
        7th Brigade
            7th Regiment
            35th Regiment
        18th Brigade
            19th Regiment
            36th Regiment
    13th Division (Ogisu Ryuhei)
        103rd Brigade
            14th Regiment
            65th Regiment
        26th Brigade
            116th Regiment
            58th Regiment
    101st Division (Ito Masaki)
        101st Brigade

101st Regiment
149th Regiment
102nd Brigade
103rd Regiment
157th Regiment
Shigeto Detachment (Shigeto Chiaki)

Japanese reinforcements, disembarking from November 5, 1937

10th Army (Yanagawa Heisuke)
6th Division (Tani Hisao)
11th Brigade
36th Brigade
18th Division (Ushijima Sadao)
23th Brigade
35th Brigade
114th Division (Suematsu Shigeharu)
127th Brigade
128th Brigade
Kunizaki Detachment (5th Division's 9th Brigade)
6 Heavy Artillery Brigade

CHINA

Chinese Forces as of September 6, 1937

Third War Zone (Feng Yuxiang)

8th Army Group (Zhang Fakui)
28th Army (Tao Guang)
62nd Division
55th Division
63rd Division

45th Independent Brigade
45th Independent Artillery Brigade

9th Army Group (Zhang Zhizhong)
  Right Wing (Sun Yuanliang)
    72nd Army (Sun Yuanliang)
      88th Division
      Peace Preservation Corps
  Left Wing (Wang Jingjiu)
    71st Army (Wang Jingjiu)
      87th Division
    78th Army (Song Xilian)
      36th Division
    61st Division
    20th Independent Brigade

15th Army Group (Chen Cheng)
  Right Wing (Hu Zongnan)
    1st Army (Hu Zongnan)
      1st Division
      78th Division
    8th Division
    15th Division
    16th Division
    32nd Division
    57th Division
    77th Division
    159th Division
  Central Wing (Luo Zhuoying)
    18th Army (Luo Zhuoying)
      11th Division
      67th Division
      60th Division
    54th Army (Huo Kuizhang)
      14th Division
    98th Division

4th Army (Wu Qiwei)
  59th Division
  90th Division
  66th Learning Brigade
Left Wing (Liu Heding)
  39th Army (Liu Heding)
    56th Division
  74th Army (Yu Jishi)
    51st Division
  6th Division
  37th Independent Brigade

CHINESE FORCES AS OF OCTOBER 21, 1937

Third War Zone. (Chiang Kai-shek, deputy commander: Gu Zhutong)

Right Wing (Zhang Fakui)
  8th Army Group (Zhang Fakui)
    28th Army (Tao Guang)
      62nd Division
    55th Division
    63rd Division
    45th Independent Brigade
    2nd Independent Artillery Brigade
    Artillery Learning Batallion
  10th Army Group (Liu Jianxu)
    45th Division
    52nd Division
    126th Division
    37th Independent Brigade
    11th Brigade (temporary)
    12th Brigade (temporary)
    13th Brigade (temporary)
    Ningbo Defense Command

Central Wing (Zhu Shaoliang)
   9th Army Group (Zhu Shaoliang)
      8th Army (Huang Jie)
         61st Division
         Tax Police Division
      71st Army (Wang Jingjiu)
         87th Division
      72nd Army (Sun Yuanliang)
         88th Division
         Peace Preservation Corps
      78th Army (Song Xilian)
         36th Division
      3rd Division
      18th Division
      Songhu Defense Command
   21st Army Group (Liao Lei)
      1st Army (Hu Zongnan)
         1st Division
         78th Division
         32nd Division
      19th Division
      26th Division
      135th Division
      171st Division
      173rd Division
      174th Division
      176th Division

Left Wing (Chen Cheng)
   15th Army Group (Luo Zhuoying)
      76th Army (Tao Zhiyue)
         16th Division
      18th Army (Luo Zhuoying)
         11th Division
         67th Division
         90th Division

15th Division
77th Division
39th Army (Liu Heding)
56th Division
74th Army ((Yu Jishi)
51st Division
58th Division
34th Independent Brigade
44th Division
60th Division
Jiangsu Peace Preservation Regiment
16th Artillery Regiment
Two artillery companies
19th Army Group (Xue Yue)
2nd Army (Li Yannian)
9th Division
20th Army (Yang Sen)
133rd Division
134th Division
25th Army (Wan Yaohuang)
13th Division
66th Army (Ye Zhao)
159th Division
160th Division
Learning Brigade regiment
69th Army (Yuan Zhaochang)
57th Division

Reinforcements late October to early November 1937

Attached to 9th Army Group:
46th Division
154th Division
Attached to Right Wing:
67th Army (Wu Keren)

107th Division
108th Division
79th Division
Training Brigade
Attached to 15th Army Group:
98th Division

Attached to 19th Army Group:
54th Army (Huo Kuizhang)
14th Division
33rd Division
105th Division

Attached to 21st Army Group:
48th Army (Wei Yunsong)
170th Division
172nd Division

Sources: Cao Jianlang, *Zhongguo Guomingdangjun jianshi, [A Brief History of the Chinese Nationalist Forces]*, Beijing: Jiefangjun chubanshe, 2009; *Riben haijun zai Zhongguo zuozhan [The Japanese Navy's War in China]*, Tianjin: Tianjin shi zhengxia bianyi weiyuanhui, 1991.

Notes

PROLOGUE

1. Zhang Fakui. *Reminiscences of Fa-k'uei Chang: Oral History, 1970–1980*. Columbia University Libraries, Oral History Research Office, p. 490. This document is based on a series of interviews Zhang gave in the 1970s.

2. Snow, Edgar. *The Battle for Asia*. Cleveland OH: The World Publishing Company, 1941, p. 45.

CHAPTER ONE: THREE CORPSES

1. The account of the situation at Hongqiao Aerodrome on the night between August 9 and 10 is based mainly on reports in the Shanghai-based *North China Daily News* (hereafter cited as *NCDN*), as well as *The New York Times* and other western media. Details have also been gleaned from *Shin Shina gensei yoran* [The Current Situation in China]. Tokyo: Toa Dobunkai, 1938, p. 65, quoted in Higashinakano Shudo. *The Nanking Massacre: Facts versus Fiction*. Tokyo: Sekai Shuppan, 2006, p. 11.

2. "Chapei Again Fearful," Associated Press, August 9, 1937, in *The New York Times,* August 10, 1937.

3. Ibid.

4. Li Junsan. *Shanghai Nanjing baoweizhan* [*Defensive Battles for Shanghai and Nanjing*]. Taipei: Maitian chubanshe, 1997, pp. 49–50.

5. *All About Shanghai and Environs*. Shanghai: The University Press, 1934, pp. 1, 39, 41.

6. Dong, Stella. *Shanghai: The Rise and Fall of a Decadent City*. New York: HarperCollins, 2001, pp. 22–23.

7. Fenby, Jonathan. *Generalissimo: Chiang Kai-shek and the China He Lost*. London: Simon & Schuster, 2003, pp. 138–139.

8. Hanson, Haldore. *Humane Endeavour: The Story of the China War*. New York: Farrar & Rinehart, 1939, p. 124.

9. Dong, p. 113.

10. Dong, pp. 109–117.

11. Fenby, pp. 147–148.

12. Jordan, Donald A. *China's Trial by Fire: The Shanghai War of 1932*. Ann Arbor: University of Michigan Press, 2001, p. 47.

13. Abend, Hallett. *My Life in China. 1926–1941*. New York: Harcourt Brace, 1943, pp. 192–193.

14. Jordan, pp. 186–190.

15. Teitler, Geir et al. *A Dutch Spy in China: Reports on the First Phase of the Sino-Japanese War*. Leiden: Brill, 1999, p. 51.

16. Barnhart, Michael A. *Japan Prepares for Total War: The Search for Economic Security 1919–1941*. Ithaca: Cornell University Press, 1987, pp. 27–28, 39.

17. Bix, Herbert P. *Hirohito and the Making of Modern Japan*. New York: HarperCollins, 2001, p. 306.

18. Dryburgh, Marjorie. *North China and Japanese Expansion 1933–1937*. Richmond and Surrey: Curzon Press, 2000, p. 147.

19. Taylor, Jay. *The Generalissimo: Chiang Kai-shek and the Struggle for Modern China*. Cambridge MA: Belknap, 2009, p. 145.

20. Bix, p. 321.

21. Qiao Defu, a 13-year-old farm boy, saw his mother recover a foot-long bayonet from the family's cornfield. "It was gleaming. We used it at home to cut radish leaves," he recalled many years later. "Xuezhan Nanyuan, xuebing sui jiangjun sunqu" ["The bloody battle for Nanyuan: Soldiers followed general into obliteration"], *Beijing News*, July 7, 2005.

22. Dorn, Frank. *The Sino-Japanese War 1937–41: From Marco Polo Bridge to Pearl Harbor*. New York: Macmillan, 1974, p. 42. The incident is recognized by Chinese historians. See, Xiao Yiping et al. *Zhongguo kangri zhanzheng quanshi* [*A Complete History of China's Anti-Japanese War*]. Chengdu: Sichuan renmin chubanshe, 2005, vol. 2, p. 13.

23. Volume 3 of *Defense Exhibits Rejected by the International Military Tribunal for the Far East* (IMTFE).

24. Wilson, Dick. *When Tiger Fight: The Story of the Sino-Japanese War 1937–1945*. New York: The Viking Press, 1982, p. 22.

25. Dorn, pp. 42, 46.

26. Lu, David J. *From the Marco Polo Bridge to Pearl Harbor: A Study of Japan's Entry into World War II*. Washington DC: Public Affairs Press, 1961, p. 17.

27. Bix, p. 322.

28. Kuo Mo-jo. "A Poet with the Northern Expedition," in *Far Eastern Quarterly*, vol. 3, no. 2, February 1944, p. 163.

29. Zhang Fakui, p. 453.

30. Yang Tianshi. "Chiang Kai-shek and the Battles of Shanghai and Nanjing," in Mark Peattie et al. (eds.). *The Battle for China*. Stanford: Stanford University Press, 2011, pp. 144–145.

31. Zhang Fakui, p. 453.
32. Shen Zui. *Juntong neimu* [The Inside Story of the Military Statistics Bureau]. Taipei: Xinrui chubanshe, 1994, p. 70.
33. Wakeman, Frederic E. *Spymaster: Dai Li and the Chinese Secret Service.* Berkeley: University of California Press, 2003, p. 244.
34. Dreyer, Edward L. *China at War 1901–1949.* London: Longman, 1995, pp. 181–185.
35. The Chinese Army was built around the square division, consisting of four regimental units. This had been popular in Europe prior to World War I, but was gradually abandoned by the European powers for the triangular division, made up of three regiments.
36. Ch'i Hsi-sheng. *Nationalist China at War: Military Defeats and Political Collapse, 1937–45.* Ann Arbor: University of Michigan Press, 1982, p. 37.
37. *Die Schlacht bei Shanghai.* Berlin: Oberkommando der Wehrmacht, 1939, p. 5. *Die Schlacht bei Shanghai* (hereafter cited as *DSBS*) was based on the testimonies of former German advisors to the Chinese military, but was mainly authored by Robert Borchardt, one of Germany's earliest experts on tank warfare.
38. Chang Jui-te. "The Nationalist Army on the Eve of War," in Peattie et al. (eds.). pp. 89–90.
39. Chang Jui-te, p. 103.
40. Liang, Hsi-huey. *The Sino-German Connection.* Amsterdam: van Gorcum, 1978, pp. xii, 172.
41. Andersson, Lennart. *A History of Chinese Aviation.* Taipei: AHS of ROC, 2008, p. 108.
42. Andersson, p. 128.
43. Chennault, Claire Lee. *Way of a Fighter.* New York NY: C. P. Putnam's Sons, 1949, pp. 40–41. This was more than an empty threat. Chiang had previously had subordinates executed, even for failures for which they could not reasonably be blamed. See, e.g. Taylor, p. 71.
44. Chennault, pp. 37, 40.
45. Gong Yeti. *Kangzhan feixing riji* [A Flight Diary of the War of Resistance]. Wuhan: Changjiang wenyi chubanshe, 2011, p. 115.
46. Gong, p. 111.
47. Gong, p. 117.
48. Taylor, p. 147.
49. Barnhart, p. 92.
50. Forman, Harrison. *Horizon Hunter.* New York: Robert M. McBride, 1940, p. 207.
51. Zhang Fakui, pp. 454–455.
52. Yang Ji. *Huzhan mihua* [Secret Talk on the Shanghai Battle]. Liming shuju, 1938, p. 37.
53. Zhang Zhizhong. *Huiyilu* [Memoirs]. Beijing: Wenhua chubanshe, 2007, p. 72.

54. Zhang Suwo. *Huiyi fuqin Zhang Zhizhong* [*Remembering My Father Zhang Zhizhong*]. Nanjing: Jiangsu wenyi chubanshe, 2012, p. 85.
55. Zhang Suwo, p. 86.
56. Willens, Liliane. *Stateless in Shanghai*. Hong Kong: Earnshaw Books, 2010, p. 97.
57. *North China Herald*, July 14, 1937.
58. *North China Herald*, July 21, 1937.
59. Farmer, Rhodes. *Shanghai Harvest: A Diary of Three Years in the China War*. London: Museum Press, 1945, p. 37.
60. Alcott, Carroll. *My War with Japan*. New York: Henry Holt, 1943, p. 236.
61. *North China Herald*, July 28 and Aug 4, 1937.
62. Powell, John B. *My Twenty-Five Years in China*. New York: Macmillan, 1945, p. 293.
63. Ristaino, Marcia R. *The Jacquinot Safe Zone: Wartime Refugees in Shanghai*. Stanford: Stanford University Press, 2008, p. 45.
64. *North China Herald*, August 18, 1937.
65. Farmer, p. 37.
66. *North China Herald*, August 18, 1937.
67. Kageyama Koichiro. "Oyama jihen no hitotsu kosatsu—dai niji Shanhai jihen no dokasen no shinso to gunreibu ni ateta eikyo" ["A reconsideration of the Oyama incident: the facts about the trigger of the second Shanghai incident and the impact it had on the Naval General Staff"]. *Gunji shigaku*, vol. 32, no. 3, December 1996.
68. Zhang Fakui, p. 456.
69. Shi Shuo. "Bayaosan Songhu Kanghang jilue" ["Clever stratagems adopted during the 813 Songhu battle"], in *Bayaosan Songhu Kangzhan: Yuan Guomindang jiangling Kangri Zhanzheng qinliji* [*The August 13 Songhu Battle: Personal Recollections from the War of Resistance against Japan by Former Nationalist Commanders*]. Beijing: Zhongguo wenshi cubanshe, 1987, p. 91. This priceless collection of memoirs by key commanders is cited hereafter as *BSK*.
70. Zhongguo dier lishi dang'an guan, *Kangri zhanzheng zhengmian zhanchang* [*The Frontal Battleground in the Anti-Japanese War*]. Nanjing: Fenghuang chubanshe, 2005, vol. 1, p. 329.
71. Zhongguo dier lishi dang'an guan, vol. 1, p. 330.
72. *NCDN*, August 12, 1937.
73. Morley, James William. *The China Quagmire: Japan's Expansion on the Asian Continent 1933–1941*. New York: Columbia University Press, 1983, p. 265.
74. Barnhart, p. 92.
75. Spunt, Georges. *A Place in Time*. New York: G. P. Putnam's Sons, 1968, p. 353.
76. Zhang Fakui, p. 457. Zhang goes on to tell the interviewer that "I cannot say this in my 'Reminiscences of the War of Resistance' [memoirs serialized in the Taiwanese magazine *Lianhe Pinglun* from January 1962 to January 1963] because

we claim that ours was a 'War of Resistance'."

77. Zhongguo dier lishi dang'an guan, p. 335. Zhang Zhizhong's eagerness to fight the battle may have helped give rise to the sensational claim that he was in fact a Communist mole deliberately triggering a war between Chiang Kai-shek's Nationalists and the Japanese. In particular, according to this version of history, Zhang was allegedly the mastermind behind the shooting at Hongqiao Aerodrome. The motive was supposedly to weaken Chiang and set the stage for a Communist revolution. See, Chang, Jung et al. *Mao: The Unknown Story*. London: Jonathan Cape, 2005, pp. 208–209. The best that can be said about this story is that it would be interesting if it were true. However, it is supported by no available evidence whatsoever. See also, Benton, Gregor et al. "The Portrayal of Opportunism, Betrayal and Manipulation in Mao's Rise to Power," in *The China Journal*, no. 55, January 2006, pp. 106–107.

78. Zhang Zhizhong, p. 72.

79. Zhang Zhizhong, p. 75.

80. Chen Yiding. "Yangshupu Yunzaobin zhandou" ["Battle of Yangshupu and Yunzaobin"], in *BSK,* p. 111.

81. Zhang Zhizhong, p. 75.

82. Bruce, George C. *Shanghai's Undeclared War*. Shanghai: Mercury Press, 1937, p. 10.

83. Zhongguo dier lishi dang'an guan, p. 340.

84. Sun Yuanliang. *Yiwan guangnian zhong de yi shun* [*An Instant in a Trillion Light Years*]. Taipei: Shiying chubanshe, 2002, p. 205. See also, Zhang Boting. "Songhu huizhan jiyao" ["Summary of the Songhu Battle"], in *BSK*, p. 132. The decision by the 88th and possibly also the 87th Division to move further than their orders dictated was widely recognized by observers at the time. See, Cao Juren. *Wo yu wo de shijie* [My World and I]. Beijing: SDX Joint Publishing Company, 2011, p. 595.

85. Zhang Fakui, p. 484.

86. Liu Jingchi, "Songhu Jingbei Silingbu jianwen" ["Account of Songhu Garrison Command"], *BSK*, p. 3.

87. Zhongguo dier lishi dang'an guan, p. 341.

88. *NCDN*, August 13, 1937.

89. *NCDN*, August 13, 1937.

90. Yang Ji, p. 4.

91. *NCDN*, August 14, 1937.

92. *NCDN*, August 13, 1937.

93. Morley, p. 266.

CHAPTER TWO: "BLACK SATURDAY"

1. The account of Rawlinson's activities on August 14 is based mainly on Frances

Rawlinson's testimony, written within 24 hours of the events, reproduced *in toto* in Rawlinson, John Lang. *Rawlinson, the Recorder and China's Revolution: A Topical Biography of Frank Joseph Rawlinson 1871–1937*. Notre Dame, IN: Cross Cultural Publications, 1990, p. 1. Other details have been added from a report published by the police in the French Concession: *Rapport sur la catastrophe du 14 Aout 1937*. Shanghai: Services de Police, 1937 and from *History of Air Operations in the First Phase of the China Incident (from July to November 1937)*. Tokyo: Liquidation Department of the Second Demobilization Bureau, 1951, also known as *Japanese Monograph No. 166*. The latter is the part of a series of nearly 200 monographs compiled by the U.S. military in Japan after the war that were based on surviving records and the recollections of former Japanese officers.

2. *Rapport sur la catastrophe*, p. 2; *Japanese Monograph No. 166*, p. 18.
3. Ibid.
4. Rawlinson, p. 756.
5. Zhang Boting with Li Dongfang. "Bayaosan Songhu Huizhan Huiyi' ["Reminiscences of the 813 Songhu Battle"], in *Zhuanji Wenxue*, vol. 41, no. 2, 1982, p. 19., quoting Ji Zhangjian, the former head of the corps. If the story is true, it is a distinct possibility that the *ronin* were not marines in disguise, but the real thing, given the close cooperation between military and *ronin* elsewhere.
6. *NCDN*, August 14, 1937, and *Political Strategy Prior to the Outbreak of War*. Tokyo: Military History Section Headquarters, 1952, also known as *Japanese Monograph No. 144*, p. 29. Zhang Zhizhong claimed in a telegram to Chiang Kai-shek sent on the same day that Japanese soldiers had fired at civilians first, before regular Chinese soldiers opened up retaliatory fire. (See, Zhongguo dier lishi dang'an guan, vol. 1, p. 409.) Given the severe numerical inferiority of the Japanese, it is unlikely that they would deliberately invite attack with such a rash course of action. According to the Japanese correspondent Hayashi Fusao, who visited the Shanghai front some time afterwards, the Japanese commanders were, of course, painfully aware that they were outnumbered and took great care not to provoke the Chinese. See, Long, Jeff E. "The Japanese Literati and 'the China Incident': Hayashi Fusao Reporting the Battle of Shanghai," in *Sino-Japanese Studies*, vol. 15, 2003, p. 32.
7. Similar disagreement reigns over the start of hostilities in 1932. See, Jordan, pp. 42–43.
8. *DSBS*, p. 9.
9. Bruce, p. 10.
10. *NCDN*, August 14, 1937.
11. The bridge derived its name from traditional Chinese astrology, according to which a person's fate can be predicted from eight characters imbued with special significance.
12. Zhang Boting, pp. 132–133.

13. Zhang Boting with Li Dongfang, pp. 18–19. The account, heavily annotated by Li, is based partly on testimony made in the early 1980s by Wu Qiujian, Major Yi's regimental commander, who was then living in Los Angeles. See also, Zhongguo dier lishi dang'an guan, vol. 1, p. 410, and Zhang Boting, pp. 132–133. In nearly all Chinese accounts, the skirmish at the Eight Character Bridge is taken as the "official" start of the war. However, this is a somewhat arbitrary choice, as fighting in Shanghai actually began in the morning.
14. Hsu Long-hsuen and Chang Ming-kai. *History of the Sino-Japanese war (1937–1945)*. Taipei: Chung Wu Publishers, 1972, p. 203; *NCDN*, August 14, 1937.
15. *DSBS*, p. 9; *NCDN*, August 14, 1937.
16. Prussia, assisted by a shifting alliance of smaller German-speaking powers, carried out three successful wars in the third quarter of the 19th century, against Denmark (1864), Austria (1866) and France (1870–1871). Although the formation of the German Empire in 1871 was the result of complex and multi-faceted processes, it can be argued that the three conflicts had been instrumental in creating a sense of common purpose among the politically divided Germans. This at least was how, prior to 1945, many educated Germans looked at their own history.
17. Lee, Bradford A. *Britain and the Sino-Japanese War, 1937–1939: A Study in the Dilemmas of British Decline*. Stanford CA: Stanford University Press, 1973, p. 35.
18. Teitler et al., p. 92.
19. Shi Shuo, p. 102.
20. *DSBS*, p. 10
21. Li Junsan, p. 69.
22. Sun Yuanliang, p. 211. Sun misremembers the date of Huang's death. See, Zhongguo dier lishi dang'an guan, vol. 1, p. 411.
23. Yuan Ying et al., *Koushu Songhu kangzhan* [*An Oral History of the Songhu Battle*], vol. 1, Shanghai: Shanghai Songhu Kangzhan Jinianguan, 2007, p. 98.
24. Xiao Yiping et al., vol. 2, p. 81.
25. Zhang Zhizhong, p. 76.
26. Chennault, p. 42.
27. Fenby, p. 103.
28. Feng Yuxiang. *Wo suo renshi de Jiang Jieshi* [*The Chiang Kai-shek That I Knew*]. Taipei: Jieyou chubanshe, 2007, p. 75.
29. Ge Yunlong. "Feng Yuxiang churen disan zhanqu silingzhangguan jianwen" ["An account of Feng Yuxiang's service as commander of the Third War Zone"], in *BSK,* p. 10.
30. Yang Ji, pp. 37–38.
31. Feng Yuxiang, pp. 75–76.
32. Spunt, p. 354.

33. *DSBS*, p. 9; *NCDN*, August 14, 1937.
34. Verhage, William. "The Bombing of Shanghai," in *Sigma Phi Epsilon Journal*, vol. 35 (1937), no. 2, p. 110.
35. Farmer, p. 42.
36. Shi Shuo, p. 92.
37. *Japanese Monograph No. 166*, p. 20.
38. Oliver, Frank. *Special Undeclared War*. London: Jonathan Cape, 1939, p. 137.
39. Rawlinson, p. 7.
40. Farmer, pp. 45–46.
41. Verhage, pp. 112–113. The description of the scene in Nanjing Road after the blasts is based on a number of sources, including Finch, Percy. *Shanghai and Beyond*. New York: Charles Scribner's Sons, 1953, pp. 255–256; Farmer pp. 44–49; Spunt pp. 357–360; and *NCDN*, August 15, 1937.
42. Finch, pp. 255–256.
43. Spunt, p. 360.
44. *Rapport sur la catastrophe*, Annexe X4.
45. *Shanghai Sunday Times*, August 15, 1937.
46. Powell, p. 301.
47. *Rapport sur la catastrophe*, p. 5.
48. Powell, p. 301.
49. Teitler, pp. 93–95. Dutch spy de Fremery later toured the site in front of the Great World. He had previously been involved in the development of ordinance, and wanted to know what could have caused so many people to die. The result of his investigation was that only a minority had fallen victim to the splinters, and that most had been killed by the gas pressure. He concluded, with cold professionalism, that "thin-walled bombs with as big as possible a payload are to be recommended."
50. Farmer, p. 47.
51. Forman, p. 199.
52. Verhage, p. 114; Reischauer, Edwin O. *My Life between Japan and America*. New York: Harper & Row Publishers, 1986, p. 62.
53. Farmer, p. 48.
54. Alcott, pp. 238–239.
55. *Rapport sur la catastrophe*, p. 17.
56. Chennault, pp. 34–35.
57. Chennault, p. 44.
58. Chennault, pp. 44–45.
59. Chennault, pp. 45–46.
60. Chennault, p. 45.
61. Powell, pp. 300–301.
62. Bruce, pp. 17–18.

63. Powell, pp. 303–304; Teitler, p. 96.
64. Morley, p. 454.
65. *Japanese Monograph No. 166*, pp. 17–18.
66. Peattie, Mark R. *Sunburst: The Rise of Japanese Naval Air Power 1909–1941.* Annapolis: Naval Institute Press, 2002, pp. 106–107.
67. The First Combined Air Group comprised the navy's two first land-based bomber groups, the Kisarazu Air Group and the Kanoya Air Group.
68. Peattie, pp. 104, 106.
69. Some historians have argued that Japan studiously avoided referring to "the China incident" as a war, as that could have triggered an end to American supplies of vital materials under the U.S. Neutrality Act, which prohibited trade with belligerent nations. However, implementing the U.S. Neutrality Act would have hurt China considerably more than Japan. See, Barnhart, pp. 119–121.
70. Bix, p. 323.
71. Abend, p. 270.
72. Yamamoto Masahiro. *Nanjing: Anatomy of an Atrocity.* Westport CT: Praeger, 2000, pp. 40–41.
73. Yoshida Hiroshi. *Tenno no guntai to Nankin jiken.* Tokyo: Aoki shoten, 1998, p. 71.
74. Yamamoto, p. 69.

CHAPTER THREE: FLESH AGAINST STEEL
1. Quoted from Long, p. 36.
2. Quoted from Long, p. 36.
3. Farmer, pp. 56–57.
4. Farmer, p. 59.
5. Farmer, pp. 57–58; Long p. 32.
6. *NCDN*, August 25, 1937.
7. Guo Rugui et al. *Zhongguo Kangri Zhanzheng zhengmian zhanchang zuozhan ji* [*The War of Resistance against Japan: An Account of Frontline Battles*]. Nanjing: Jiangsu renmin chubanshe, 2005, p. 534.
8. *Japanese Monograph No. 166*, p. 26.
9. *Riben haijun zai Zhongguo zuozhan* [*The Japanese Navy's War in China*]. Tianjin: Tianjin shi zhengxia bianyi weiyuanhui, 1991, p. 205.
10. Jiang Zhongzheng (Chiang Kai-shek) (ed.). *Kangri zhanshi: Songhu huizhan* [*The History of the War of Resistance against Japan: The Songhu Battle*]. Taipei: Guofangbu shizhengju, 1962, vol. 3, pp. 267–268.
11. Jiang Zhongzheng (ed.), vol. 3, pp. 267–268. Zhang Boting, the chief of staff of the 88th Division, directly attributes the plan for the operation to the German advisor assigned to the division, but does not name him (Zhang Boting, pp. 135–136). However, Hsin Ta-mo identifies the German advisor assigned to the

88th Division during the battle of Shanghai as Colonel Hans Vetter (Hsin Ta-Mo. *A Review of German Military Advisors' Work in China*, paper delivered at Conference on Chiang Kai-shek and Modern China in Taipei, October 1986, pp. 16, 23).

12. *DSBS,* p. 10.

13. Zhang Fakui, p. 457.

14. Jiang Zhongzheng, p. 268.

15. Chen Yiding, p. 112.

16. Jiang Zhongzheng (ed.), vol. 3, p. 268.

17. *DSBS,* p. 10.

18. *DSBS,* p. 10.

19. Bruce, p. 15.

20. Zhang Fakui, p. 462.

21. Guo Rugui et al., pp. 535–536.

22. Chen Yiding, p. 112.

23. Zhang Fakui, p. 462.

24. Yuan Ying et al., vol. 1, p. 123.

25. Liang, 1978, p. 93.

26. It was not unprecedented for Germans and Japanese to be facing each other in battle. The two nations clashed in a brief campaign over the port of Qingdao in northern China in 1914.

27. Liang Hsi-huey. *Foreign Tributes to Chiang Kai-shek: The Case of Alexander von Falkenhausen,* paper delivered at Conference on Chiang Kai-shek and Modern China in Taipei, October 1986, p. 12.

28. Abandoning the extraterritoriality meant, for example, that German citizens committing crimes inside the foreign areas of Shanghai could be put before a Chinese judge.

29. Liang, 1986, p. 10.

30. Kirby, William. *Germany and Republican China.* Stanford: Stanford University Press, 1984, p. 151.

31. Mohr, E.G. *Sino-German Relations in the Period of Chiang Kai-shek,* paper delivered at Conference on Chiang Kai-shek and Modern China in Taipei, October 1986, p. 12.

32. Martin, Bernd. "The Role of German Military Advisors on the Chinese Defense Efforts against the Japanese 1937–1938," in Pong, David (ed.). *Resisting Japan: Mobilizing for War in Modern China.* Norwalk CT: EastBridge, 2008, p. 68.

33. Mohr, p. 12.

34. Mohr, p. 13.

35. Liang, 1986, p. 11.

36. Liang, 1986, p. 10.

37. Mohr, pp. 13–14.

38. Mohr, p. 13.
39. Mohr, p. 14.
40. Zhang Fakui, p. 477. The dislike appears to have been mutual. The performance of Zhang's units on the Pudong side is repeatedly criticized in *DSBS*, the after-action report written by German officers upon their return home.
41. Liang, 1986, p. 9.
42. Liang, 1986, p. 11.
43. Liang, 1986, pp. 12–13.
44. Liang, 1986, p. 12. Falkenhausen's disappointment with the Chinese reluctance to enter Shanghai's foreign areas shines through in the language of the report issued later for the German High Command.
45. Mohr, p. 18.
46. *NCDN*, August 19, 1937.
47. *NCDN*, August 15, 1937.
48. *NCDN*, August 24, 1937.
49. Bruce, p. 12.
50. Bruce, p. 13.
51. "Weekly Intelligence Summary," August 23, 1937. War Office 5595/9/10.
52. Bruce, p. 14.
53. *NCDN*, August 19, 1937.
54. *North China Herald*, August 18, 1937.
55. "Two Women Are Beheaded For Treason in Shanghai," Associated Press, August 30, 1937.
56. "Shanghai Mobs Kill Suspected Water Poisoners," Associated Press, August 18, 1937.
57. *NCDN*, August 18, 1937.
58. *NCDN*, August 18, 1937.
59. Teitler et al., p. 98; Bruce, pp. 16–17.
60. Bruce, p. 19.
61. For example, on September 8, a shell exploded inside the Chinese staff quarters, injuring four warders. *NCDN*, September 9, 1937.
62. *Riben haijun zai Zhongguo zuozhan*, pp. 205–206.
63. Bix, p. 324.
64. Clifford, Nicholas Rowland. *Retreat from China: British Policy in the Far East 1937–1941*. Seattle WA: University of Washington Press, 1967, p. 23.
65. Guo Rugui et al., p. 536.
66. Chen Cheng. "Chen Cheng siren huiyi ziliao" ["Chen Cheng's personal recollections"], *Minguo Dang'an*, 1987, no. 1, pp. 14–15.
67. *DSBS*, p. 10.
68. Guo Rugui et al., p. 536.
69. Li Junsan, p. 75.

70. *DSBS,* p. 11.
71. Li Junsan, p. 75.
72. Zhang Fakui, p. 461.
73. Song Xilian. "Xuezhan Songhu" ["Bloody Songhu Battle"], in *BSK,* p. 172.
74. Chen Yiding, p. 112.
75. *DSBS,* p. 11.
76. *Riben haijun zai Zhongguo zuozhan,* p. 205.
77. Guo Rugui et al., pp. 536–538.
78. *DSBS,* p. 13. It is no coincidence that the writer of the German report, Robert Borchardt, was a tank specialist, one of the few educated by the *Reichswehr.*
79. Zhang Zhizhong, p. 78.
80. Wu Yujun. "Junmin cheng yiti" ["Army and People Become One"], in *BSK,* p. 199.
81. Fang Jing. "Hongjiang, Baoshan, Yuepu, Guangfu xuezhanji" ["An Account of the Bloody Battles of Hongjiang, Baoshan, Yuepu and Guangfu"], in *BSK,* p. 187.
82. This phrase was coined by the Canadian writer Emily Pauline Johnson in the poem *The Man in Chrysanthemum Land,* written at the end of the Russo-Japanese War.
83. Hanson, p. 120.
84. Alcott, pp. 228–229.
85. Hanson, p. 120.
86. Goette, John. *Japan Fights for Asia.* New York NY: Harcourt, Brace and Co., 1943, p. 39.
87. *Handbook on Japanese Military Forces.* Washington DC: War Department, 1944, p. 9.
88. Dorn, p. 9.
89. Hanson, p. 119.
90. Hanson, p. 120.
91. Hanson, p. 120.
92. Powell, p. 308.
93. Bruce, p. 16.
94. *Japanese Monograph No. 166,* p. 30.
95. This practice was not abolished until early October.
96. *Japanese Monograph No. 166,* p. 30.
97. War Office, 5867/9/20.
98. Fang Jing, p. 186.
99. In fact, Chinese planes were observed over Shanghai as late as October.
100. Fang Zhendong. "Yi cun heshan, yi cun xue," broadcast by Taiwan TV station CTS in 1995 and 1996.
101. *DSBS,* p. 10.

102. Bruce, p. 15.
103. *North China Herald*, September 1, 1937.
104. *DSBS,* pp. 11–12.
105. Guo Rugui et al., p. 536.
106. *DSBS,* p. 12.
107. The Amaya Detachment, named after its commander Amaya Shinjiro, consisted of the 11th Division's 12th Regiment, reinforced with one artillery battalion (Guo Rugui et al., p. 544).
108. *Riben haijun zai Zhongguo zuozhan*, p. 228.
109. The account is based on *Nanjing Datusha Shiliaoji [Collection of Historical Records on the Nanjing Massacre]*. Nanjing: Jiangsu renmin chubanshe, 2005, vol. 60, pp. 116–119. Hereafter cited as *NDS*.
110. War Office, 5595/9/10.
111. Kalyagin, Aleksandr Ya. *Along Alien Roads.* New York NY: Columbia University, 1983, pp. 103–104.
112. Bruce, p. 18.

CHAPTER FOUR: "BANZAI! BANZAI! BANZAI!"
1. The account of Matsui's movements on August 23 and the days immediately before is based mainly on his war journal, published in Chinese translation in *NDS*, vol. 8, pp. 20–199. Entries containing particular information about the landing are on pp. 29–32.
2. Nagumo, born in 1887, later became one the key actors in both the attack on Pearl Harbor and the Battle of Midway. He shot himself in the last stages of the battle for Saipan in July 1944.
3. *NDS*, vol. 8, p. 30.
4. "View From Warship," *NCDN*, August 24, 1937, contains a vivid description of the landing.
5. "View from the Warship," *NCDN*, August 24, 1937. The Dutch spy, de Fremery, uses the same newspaper account in one of his dispatches, but errouneously assumes that it is a description of the parallel landing at Chuanshakou. Teitler, p. 103.
6. Guo Rugui et al., p. 538; *Shina jihen rikugun sakusen, 1, Showa jusan nen ichi gatsu made [Official military history, vol. 86, Army operations during the China incident, part 1: to January 1938]*. Tokyo: Asagumo shimbunsha, 1975, p. 277.
7. Zhang Zhizhong, p. 79.
8. More specifically, the area between Baoshan and Luodian.
9. Zhang Zhizhong, pp. 79–80.
10. Li Guanru. *Tumu dizhu: Guojun dishiba jun zhanshi [Indomitable Power: The War History of the 18th Army Group]*. Taipei: Zhibingtang chubanshe, 2012, p. 74; Zhang Zhizhong, p. 79; Zhongguo dier lishi dang'an guan, p. 419.

11. Teitler et al., p. 104; Zhang Zhizhong, p. 80.

12. Qin Xiaoyi (ed.). *Zhonghua Minguo zhongyao shiliao chubian—Duiri Kangzhan shiqi* [*A Preliminary Compilation of Important Historical Document for the Republic of China—the Period of the War Against Japan*], vol. 2. Taipei: Zhongguo Guomindang zhongyangweiyuanhui dangshiweiyuanhui, 1981, p. 181.

13. Li Guanru, pp. 74–75.

14. Yan Kaiyun et al. "Zhanghuabang, Baiziqiao zhandou" ["The Battles for Zhanghuabang and Eight Character Bridge"], in *BSK*, pp. 203–204; Yuan Ying et al., vol. 1, pp. 141–148.

15. Yan Kaiyun et al., p. 204; Yuan Ying et al., p. 144.

16. Liu, F. F. *A Military History of Modern China, 1924–1949*. Princeton: Princeton University Press, 1956, pp. 91–94. The practice of setting up *Lehr* units dates back at least to the early 19th century in Germany. See, Siegert, Wilhelm. *Geschichte des Lehr Infanterie Bataillons 1820 bis 1896. Mit einem Nachtrag, die Jahre 1897–1906 umfassend von Armin Witthauer*. Berlin: E.S. Mittler und Sohn, 1912. See also, Askew, David. "Defending Nanjing: An Examination of the Capital Garrison Forces," in *Sino-Japanese Studies*, vol. 15, 2003, p. 151, and Zhang Ruide. *1937 nian de guojun*. Taipei: Academia Sinica, 2005, p. 19.

17. Yan Kaiyun et al., p. 204.

18. Yuan Ying et al., vol. 1, p. 144.

19. Yuan Ying et al., vol. 1, pp. 144–145.

20. Yuan Ying et al., vol. 1, p. 145.

21. Yan Kaiyun et al., p. 204.

22. Yan Kaiyun et al., p. 205.

23. Yan Kaiyun et al., pp. 205–206.

24. Ge Yunlong, p. 10.

25. Chen Cheng, 1987, p. 14.

26. Cao Jianlang. *Zhongguo Guomindangjun jianshi* [*A Brief History of the Chinese Nationalist Forces*]. Beijing: Jiefangjun chubanshe, 2009, p. 565.

27. Zhang Zhizhong, p. 82.

28. *DSBS*, p. 15.

29. Guo Rugui et al., p. 539.

30. *DSBS*, p. 16.

31. Forman, p. 208.

32. *DSBS*, p. 16.

33. *DSBS*, p. 16.

34. Qin Xiaoyi (ed.), p. 182.

35. Xue Zhaguang. "Xuezhan Luodian" ["Bloody Battle for Luodian"], in *BSK*, p. 239.

36. *NCDN*, September 4, 1937.

37. *NCDN*, August 27, 1937.

38. *DSBS*, p. 17.

39. Honda Katsuichi. *The Nanjing Massacre: A Japanese Journalist Confronts Japan's National Shame.* Armonk NY: M. E. Sharpe, 1999, pp. 32–36.
40. *NDS,* vol. 8, p. 32.
41. *NDS,* vol. 8, p. 33.
42. *NDS,* vol. 8, p. 32.
43. *NDS,* vol. 8, pp. 33, 36.
44. *NDS,* vol. 61, p. 503.
45. Honda, p. 30.
46. Among the Japanese vessels arriving in Shanghai in late August was the seaplane tender *Kamoi*, built in New Jersey by New York Shipbuilding in 1922. *Riben haijun zai Zhongguo zuozhan,* pp. 238–239.
47. *NDS,* vol. 8, pp. 36, 38; Guo Rugui et al., p. 542.
48. Later in the war, a Russian advisor, Aleksandr Kalyagin, witnessed how personal connections could directly decide life and death. After an air raid on the Chinese headquarters, a general was being dug out of the rubble when a senior guard battalion officer came up and realized that he was from a different faction. "He is not one of ours. Bury him!" the officer said. The Russian observer managed to save the general. See, Wilson p. 10.
49. The following account is based on Guo Rugui. *Guo Rugui huiyilu* [*Guo Rugui's Memoirs*]. Beijing: Zhonggongdang chubanshe, 2009, pp. 76–78.
50. Liu Jingchi, p. 45.
51. *DSBS,* p. 18.
52. Xiong Xinmin. "Yangshupu yu Jiangwan kangzhan" ["The Resistance War in Yangshupu and Jiangwan"], in *BSK,* p. 181.
53. Zhang Fakui, p. 463.
54. Zhang Fakui, p. 464.
55. Zhang Fakui, p. 466.
56. Zhang Fakui, p. 464.
57. Zhang Fakui, p. 464.
58. Teitler et al., pp. 96–97.
59. Snow, p. 47.
60. Willens, p. 101.
61. *NCDN,* August 23, 1937.
62. *NCDN,* August 23, 1937; Bruce, pp. 19–20.
63. Bruce, pp. 22–23. Knatchbull-Hugessen was later invalided back to Britain. He died in 1971.
64. Bruce, p. 24.
65. *China Weekly Review,* September 4, 1937, p. 7.
66. Garver, John W. *Chinese-Soviet Relations 1937–1945: The Diplomacy of Chinese Nationalism.* New York NY: Oxford University Press, 1988, pp. 20–21.
67. The remark was made in a conversation with U.S. chargé d'affaires Loy Hen-

derson. *Foreign relations of the United States, Diplomatic papers, 1937, in Five Volumes, Vol. III, The Far East.* Washington DC: U.S. Government Printing Office, 1954, pp. 498–499.

68. Jiang Zhongzheng (Chiang Kai-shek). *Kunmian ji [Anthology of Encouragement amid Difficulties].* Taipei: Guoshiguan, 2011, p. 569.

69. Wang Shijie. *Wang Shijie riji* [Wang Shijie's Diary]. Taipei: Zhongyang yanjiuyuan jindaishi yanjiusuo, 1992, p. 97.

70. Garver, p. 21.

71. *Foreign Relations of the United States, Diplomatic papers, 1937, in Five Volumes, Vol. III, The Far East,* p. 827.

72. Jiang Zhongzheng, *Kunmian ji,* p. 578.

73. Sun Youli. *China and the Origins of the Pacific War.* New York: St Martin's Press, 1993, p. 90.

74. This view of Chiang's motives for making a stand in Shanghai is not universally accepted. See, Taylor, pp. 147–148. However, it is remarkable that one year later Chiang attempted a similar strategy, when he tried to lure Japan to fight in the south of China in an apparent attempt to entangle the British in Hong Kong in the hostilities. See, Macri, Franco David. *Clash of Empires in South China: The Allied Nations' Proxy War with Japan, 1935–1941.* Lawrence KS: University of Kansas Press, 2012, p. 53.

75. Li Tsung-jen et al., *The Memoirs of Li Tsung-jen,* Boulder, CO: Westview Press, 1979, p. 329.

76. Guo Rugui et al., pp. 543–544.

77. *NDS,* vol. 8, p. 36.

78. The Asama Detachment, named after its commander Asama Yoshio, consisted of two battalions of the 11th Division's 43rd Regiment, reinforced with one company of mountain artillery. See, *Shina jihen rikugun sakusen, 1, Showa jusan nen ichi gatsu made,* p. 277.

79. *NDS,* vol. 8, p. 37.

80. Zhang Zhizhong, p. 81.

81. *NDS,* vol. 8, p. 40; *Shina jihen rikugun sakusen, 1, Showa jusan nen ichi gatsu made,* pp. 277–278.

82. *NDS,* vol. 8, p. 41.

83. *China Weekly Review,* September 11, 1937, p. 30.

84. *NDS,* vol. 8, p. 41.

85. *NDS,* vol. 8, p. 42.

86. Zhang Zhizhong, p. 81.

87. Guo Rugui et al., p. 543.

88. *NDS,* vol. 8, pp. 42, 44.

89. The account of the battle of Baoshan is based on Li Guanru, pp. 89–91.

90. *NCDN,* September 10, 1937.

91. Guo Rugui et al., p. 544.

92. *Japanese Monograph No. 166*, p. 57.

93. *DSBS*, p. 20.

94. *Japanese Monograph No. 166*, p. 67.

95. The Shigeto Detachment, led by Shigeto Chiaki, consisted of five battalions and one company of mountain artillery. See, *Shina jihen rikugun sakusen, 1, Showa jusan nen ichi gatsu made*, pp. 278–279.

96. *Shina jihen rikugun sakusen, 1, Showa jusan nen ichi gatsu made*, p. 279.

97. Fang Jing, p. 187.

98. Guo Rugui, p. 78.

99. *DSBS*, p. 42. The report prepared by former advisors for the German High Command in 1939 contains an appendix with the personal recollections of an unnamed German officer, pp. 42–46. The officer, while not identified, is all but certain to be Newiger. For instance, the anonymous officer describes on p. 43 how he moved to the Chinese high command in late October, accompanied by Lieutenant Klaus von Schmeling, which exactly corresponds with Newiger's movements at the time. Other evidence from the report showing that Newiger was a chief advisor at the Chinese high command from late October onwards is to be found on pp. 48 and 51. See also, Martin, Bernd, p. 76.

100. *DSBS*, p. 43.

101. Hsin Ta-mo, p. 24.

102. *DSBS*, p. 42.

103. *DSBS*, p. 42.

104. Zhang Fakui, p. 507.

105. *DSBS*, p. 42.

106. *Der Spiegel*, May 11, 1970.

107. Rigg, Bryan Mark. *Hitler's Jewish Soldiers: The Untold Story of Nazi Racial Laws and Men of Jewish Descent in the German Military*. Lawrence KS: University Press of Kansas, 2004, pp. 83–84, 358–359.

108. Rigg, p. 314.

109. Rigg, p. 359.

110. The account of Lu Chuanyong's experience in the Shanghai battle is based on Yuan Ying et al., pp. 153–158.

111. The League of Nations 18th session opened on September 13.

112. Guo Rugui et al., pp. 544–545.

113. Qiu Weida, "Diwushiyishi Luodian fangyuzhan" ["The 51st Division's Defensive Battle of Luodian"], in *BSK*, pp. 258–259.

114. "Vigil of Fear Told in Soldier's Diary," Associated Press, October 3, 1937.

CHAPTER FIVE: "RIVERS OF BLOOD"

1. Tiltman's description of his visit to the frontline was published in the *NCDN*

on September 12, 1937.

2. Wang Shijie, p. 100.

3. The Amaya Detachment was strengthened for this assault by the 11th Division's Asama Detachment, which had moved down the Yangtze riverbank in the preceding days and had taken the Shizilin fortress. See, *Shina jihen rikugun sakusen, 1, Showa jusan nen ichi gatsu made*, p. 278.

4. *DSBS*, p. 19.

5. *DSBS*, p. 19; Teitler et al., p. 109.

6. Teitler et al., p. 111–112.

7. Shi Shuo, p. 96.

8. *DSBS*, pp. 19–20.

9. Jiang Zhongzheng. *Kunmian ji*, p. 574.

10. Hsu and Chang, pp. 206–207.

11. Zhang Zhizhong, p. 83; *DSBS*, p. 20.

12. *NCDN*, September 14, 1937.

13. Teitler et al., p. 132.

14. *DSBS*, p. 20.

15. *NDS*, vol. 8, p. 56

16. *NDS*, vol. 8, p. 55.

17. *NDS*, vol. 8, p. 56–57.

18. The casualty numbers are according to Nishimura Toshio, a Japanese officer sent by Tokyo to inspect the Shanghai front. See, Dai Feng et al. *1937 Zhongri Songhu zhanyi* [*The 1937 Sino-Japanese Songhu Battle*]. Taipei: Zhimingtang, 2011, pp. 70–71. Matsui had somewhat lower figures for casualties at the time. See, *NDS*, vol. 8, p. 50.

19. Dai Feng, pp. 70–71; Morley, p. 267.

20. Morley, p. 275.

21. Dai Feng, p. 72.

22. Bix, p. 325; *Shina jihen rikugun sakusen, 1, Showa jusan nen ichi gatsu made*, pp. 278–279.

23. Bix, p. 325.

24. Bix, p. 325.

25. Dai Feng, p. 71.

26. Yuan Ying et al., vol. 2, pp. 46–47.

27. Yuan Ying et al., vol. 2, pp. 47–48. Later in the campaign, Wu's unit was withdrawn to the south and took part in further battles to defend Shanghai. He was seriously injured in both legs during the retreat from the city in November.

28. *DSBS*, pp. 22–23.

29. *DSBS*, p. 23, *NCDN*, September 16, 1937.

30. *DSBS*, p. 23.

31. *Shina jihen rikugun sakusen, 1, Showa jusan nen ichi gatsu made*, p. 279.

32. *NCDN*, September 18, 1937.
33. *NCDN*, September 12, 1937.
34. Yamamoto, p. 42.
35. "Admiration for Chinese Troops," Reuters, September 14, 1937.
36. Farmer, p. 88.
37. Snow, p. 51.
38. Snow, p. 50.
39. Carlson, Evan F. *Evan F. Carlson on China at war, 1937–1941*. Beijing: Foreign Languages Press, 2003, pp. 17–18.
40. Alcott, p. 159.
41. *China Weekly Review*, September 18, 1937, p. 35.
42. Abegg, Lily. *Chinas Erneuerung: Der Raum als Waffe*. Frankfurt a. M: Societäts-Verlag, 1940, pp. 160–161.
43. Abegg, p. 161.
44. Bruce, p. 14.
45. *China Weekly Review*, September 18, 1937, p. 35.
46. The account of the September 18 raid is based on Gong Yeti, pp. 175–179.
47. *NCDN*, September 19, 1937.
48. *NCDN*, September 19, 1937.
49. *Japanese Monograph No. 166*, p. 81.
50. *Japanese Monograph No. 166*, pp. 83–87.
51. *Japanese Monograph No. 166*, pp. 88–90.
52. Gong Yeti, pp. 179–183.
53. Gong Yeti, p. 183.
54. Shen Zui, pp. 69–70.
55. In fact, Dai Li was a complex figure and meant different things to different people. See, Wakeman, pp. 1-11.
56. Shen Zui, p. 70. China's only efficient espionage network in Shanghai had ceased to exist. For the last two months of the campaign, the Chinese were deprived of systematic intelligence about the situation in the enemy camp.
57. Jiang Zhongzheng, *Kunmian ji*, p. 577.
58. Zhongguo dier lishi dang'an guan, vol. 1, p. 387.
59. Dai Feng, p. 76.
60. Dai Feng, pp. 76–77. See also, Benton, Gregor, *New Fourth Army: Communist Resistance along the Yangtze and the Huai 1938–1941*. Berkeley CA: University of California Press, 1999, p. 116.
61. Jiang Zhongzheng, *Kunmian ji*, p. 575.
62. *DSBS*, p. 24.
63. Li Junshan, pp. 78–79.
64. Guo Rugui et al., p. 558.
65. Shi Shuo, p. 96.

66. Zhang Suwo, p. 89.
67. *NCDN*, September 29, 1937.
68. *NCDN*, September 21, 1937.
69. *NCDN*, September 16, 1937.
70. *NCDN*, September 18, 1937.
71. *NCDN*, September 20, 1937.
72. *NCDN*, September 15, 1937.
73. *NCDN*, September 20, 1937.
74. Snow, p. 50.
75. *NCDN*, September 19, 1937.
76. *NCDN*, September 19, 1937.
77. *Christian Science Monitor*, November 4, 1937.
78. Ristaino, p. 60, claims that 500,000 refugees were crammed into the International Settlement by early September. This figure seems too large. The Shanghai Public Health Department reported later that by the end of October, nearly two months later, the number of refugees in the city's 128 camps was 64,189. See, *NCDN*, November 4, 1937. Although it is very likely that large numbers had not been taken in by the camps and were squatting in the streets, it is hard to believe that they would total more than 400,000.
79. Ristaino, pp. 55, 60–61.
80. *North China Herald*, September 15, 1937.
81. *NCDN*, September 19, 1937.
82. *NCDN*, September 15 and 16, 1937.
83. *NCDN*, September 13, 1937.
84. *NCDN*, October 10, 1937.
85. *NCDN*, September 26, 1937.
86. *North China Herald*, October 13, 1937.
87. *Life*, December 20, 1937.
88. *NDS*, vol. 57, pp. 516–517.
89. *DSBS*, p. 25; *NDS*, vol. 8, p. 66.
90. *NDS*, vol. 8, pp. 66–67.
91. *DSBS*, p. 25.
92. *DSBS*, p. 25.
93. *Shina jihen rikugun sakusen, 1, Showa jusan nen ichi gatsu made*, p. 379
94. *DSBS*, p. 24.
95. *NDS*, vol. 8, p. 64.
96. The account of Maebara Hisashi's unit in the Shanghai area is based on *NDS*, vol. 10, pp. 35–36.

CHAPTER SIX: VERDUN OF THE EAST

1. The following account is based on *Huodao Jingfu riji* [*Ogishima Shizuo's Diary*].

Xindian, Taiwan: Lixu wenhua, 2005, pp. 44–56.

2. *Shina jihen rikugun sakusen, 1, Showa jusan nen ichi gatsu made*, p. 379.

3. Hattori Satoshi with Edward J. Drea. "Japanese Operations from July to December 1937," in *The Battle for China*, pp. 172, 512.

4. *Shina jihen rikugun sakusen, 1, Showa jusan nen ichi gatsu made,* p. 380.

5. Chen Cheng, 1987, p. 15.

6. *DSBS*, p. 26.

7. Hattori, pp. 173–174.

8. *DSBS*, p. 26.

9. *NDS*, vol. 8, p. 85.

10. *NDS*, vol. 8, pp. 85–86.

11. Yan Yinggao. "Yu Wenzaobang zhendi gongcunwang" ["Defending the Wusong Creek Front with One's Life"], in *BSK*, pp. 280–281.

12. Contemporary sources often referred to it as the Salt Division because it was funded by the revenues from the government's salt monopoly.

13. Shen Keqin. *Sun Liren zhuan* [*Biography of Sun Liren*]. Taipei: Taiwan xuesheng shuju, 2005, vol. 1, p. 98.

14. Huang Jie. "Wenzaobang, Suzhouhe zhandou" ["The Battles for Wusong and Suzhou Creeks"], in *BSK*, pp. 191–192.

15. *Guijun yu Songhu Kangzhan* [*The Guangxi Troops in the Songhu Battle*]. Shanghai: Shanghai Songhu Kangzhan Jinianguan, 2011, p. 58; *DSBS*, p. 29.

16. Schenke, Wolf. *Reise and der gelben Front*. Berlin: Gerhard Stalling Verlagsbuchhandlung, 1941, p. 246.

17. *Guijun yu Songhu Kangzhan*, p. 58.

18. *DSBS*, pp. 26–27.

19. *DSBS*, p. 43.

20. *NDS,* vol. 61, pp. 504–505.

21. *NDS*, vol. 10, pp. 210–211.

22. *NCDN*, August 26, 1937.

23. *NDS,* vol. 8, p. 46.

24. Teitler et al., p. 147.

25. Zhang Fakui, p. 481

26. *NCDN*, October 31, 1937.

27. *NCDN*, August 25, 1937.

28. Brook, Timothy. *Collaboration: Japanese Agents and Local Elites in Wartime China*. Cambridge MA: Harvard University Press, 2005, p. 93.

29. Teitler et al., p. 147.

30. Abegg, p. 205. Abegg mentions two Soviet volunteer pilots fighting on the Chinese side who parachuted from their burning aircraft and met a similar fate because they were mistaken for Japanese (ibid.). This source must be treated with some caution. While Germany was not a formal ally of the Japanese in

1937, by the time of the publication of the book, they were joined in the Axis. However, it strengthens the credibility of Abegg's account that she contrasts the harsh treatment of Japanese POWs in Nationalist areas with the much more lenient policy in regions controlled by the Communists, pp. 206–207.

31. Kalyagin, p. 228. This was equivalent to between 15 and 30 U.S. dollars at the exchange rate at the time.

32. Shen, vol. 1, pp. 98–99.

33. Shen, vol. 1, p. 99.

34. *DSBS*, p. 26.

35. Farmer, p. 81.

36. Sun Shengzhi. "Pudong paobing xianshenwei" ["The Invincible Might of the Pudong Artillery"], in *BSK*, pp. 228–229.

37. *DSBS*, pp. 30, 47–48.

38. Snow, pp. 46–47.

39. Snow, p. 47.

40. Schenke, pp. 19–20.

41. Alcott, p. 149.

42. See chapter 8. At least one Japanese journalist lost his life in the battle of Shanghai. Iwakura Tomokata, a feature writer for the *Hochi* daily, was killed by a Chinese shell in mid-October. See, *NCDN*, October 16, 1937.

43. The account of Kuse Hisao's participation in the attack on Chenjiahang is based on *NDS*, vol. 60, pp. 184–186.

44. Kuse Hisao spent the next six weeks at a field hospital. He was returned to his unit on November 24 to take part in the assault on Nanjing. *NDS*, vol. 60, p. 187.

45. *Guijun yu Songhu Kangzhan*, p. 53.

46. *DSBS*, p. 25.

47. *Guijun yu Songhu Kangzhan*, p. 54.

48. Liu Weikai. "Luoyang Qiao xuezhanji" ["Account of the Bloody Battle of Luoyang Bridge"], in *BSK*, p. 312.

49. *NDS*, vol. 8, p. 96.

50. *NDS*, vol. 8, p. 97.

51. *NDS*, vol. 8, p. 99.

52. *NDS*, vol. 8, p. 95.

53. *NDS*, vol. 8, pp. 97, 103.

54. *NDS*, vol. 8, p. 103.

55. Associated Press, "China Accuses Japan of Using War Gas," in the *Christian Science Monitor*, October 15, 1937.

56. Zhang Fakui, p. 481.

57. Zhongguo dier lishi dang'an guan, p. 452.

58. Tanisuga Shizuo, a gas specialist, recalled using gas hand grenades in China later

in the war, but it appears from his account that this was a non-lethal type of gas. See, Cook, Haruko Taya et al. *Japan at War.* New York: The New Press, 1992, pp. 44–46.

59. Teitler et al., pp. 138, 146.
60. *NCDN*, September 27, 1937.
61. Teitler et al., pp. 138–139. While de Fremery remained convinced that China did not wage gas warfare, later in the war he became less sure of Japanese innocence in this respect. See ibid., p. 218.
62. This and the following paragraphs are based on *Huodao Jingfu riji*, pp. 58–63.
63. Cook, pp. 31–32.
64. *NDS*, vol. 60, pp. 140–142.
65. *NDS*, vol. 60, p. 140.
66. Quoted from Barnhart, p. 123.
67. Sun Youli, pp. 93–94.
68. Mohr, pp. 18–19.
69. *Guijun yu Songhu Kangzhan*, p. 58.
70. *NDS*, vol. 8, p. 105.
71. *Guijun yu Songhu Kangzhan*, p. 61.
72. *Guijun yu Songhu Kangzhan*, pp. 61–62.
73. *Guijun yu Songhu Kangzhan*, p. 63.
74. *Guijun yu Songhu Kangzhan*, p. 64–65
75. Lan Xiangshan. "Guijun canzhan jianwen" ["Information about the Guangxi Troops' Participation in the War"], in *BSK*, p. 320.
76. Lan Xiangshan, p. 320.
77. *DSBS*, pp. 27–28.

Chapter Seven: The "Lost Battalion"
1. The following account is based on Zhang Boting, pp. 140–142.
2. Zhang Boting's account mistakenly refers to an upcoming meeting of the League of Nations as the rationale for keeping the 88th Division in Zhabei.
3. Zhang Boting was referring to the Chinese habit of repeatedly adding hot water to the same glass of tea in order to make it last.
4. *Shina jihen rikugun sakusen, 1, Showa jusan nen ichi gatsu made*, p. 380; *NDS*, vol. 8, pp. 107–108.
5. *NDS*, vol. 8, p. 108.
6. A similar phenomenon was observed on the Western Front in 1918, when tactical innovations suddenly made mobile warfare possible again after more than three years of positional warfare. Many soldiers reported difficulties adjusting.
7. *NDS*, vol. 8, pp. 108–109.
8. *DSBS*, p. 31.
9. *Christian Science Monitor*, October 22, 1937.

10. *DSBS*, p. 31.
11. Carlson, E. F. *Twin Stars of China*. Beijing: Foreign Languages Press, 2003, p. 27.
12. *Xiangjun yu Songhu Kangzhan* [*The Hunan Troops in the Songhu Battle*]. Shanghai: Shanghai Songhu Kangzhan Jinianguan, 2010, p. 85.
13. Zhongguo dier lishi dang'an guan, vol. 1, p. 399.
14. *Xiangjun yu Songhu Kangzhan*, pp. 85–86.
15. *NCDN*, October 26, 1937.
16. Farmer, p. 85.
17. *DSBS*, p. 32.
18. *Xiangjun yu Songhu Kangzhan*, p. 86; *DSBS*, p. 32.
19. *NDS*, vol. 8, pp. 109.
20. For example, Sun Liren of the Tax Police Division, talked dismissively of "a certain division" which "collapsed the moment it came into touch with the enemy," Shen Keqin, vol. 1, p. 103.
21. *Xiangjun yu Songhu Kangzhan*, pp. 86, 148.
22. Oliver, p. 147.
23. Farmer, p. 85.
24. *The Washington Post*, November 28, 1937.
25. *NCDN*, October 28, 1937.
26. *DSBS*, p. 36.
27. Yang Ruifu. "Gujun fendou siriji" ["Account of the Lone Unit's Four Days of Battle"], in *BSK*, p. 153.
28. *DSBS*, p. 33.
29. *NCDN*, October 28, 1937.
30. *DSBS*, p. 32. The German author also attributes the Japanese failure to act to the peculiar reluctance to engage in night fighting that characterized their conduct in Shanghai. However, this is not entirely convincing given the fact that large parts of Zhabei must have been as light as in the daytime because of the numerous fires.
31. Farmer, p. 85.
32. Farmer, pp. 81–82.
33. Farmer, p. 86.
34. Yang Ruifu, p. 152.
35. Yang Ruifu, pp. 150–152.
36. Yang Ruifu, p. 153.
37. Yang Ruifu, pp. 153–154.
38. Yuan Ying, vol. 1, p. 4.
39. Farmer, p. 86.
40. Yang Ruifu, p. 154.
41. Yang Ruifu, p. 155.

42. Yang Ruifu, p. 157. The Chinese government was keen to achieve maximum propaganda mileage from the defense of the warehouse, turning out, among other things, a major motion picture the year after.

43. Zhang Fakui, p. 481.

44. Li Tsung-jen et al., p. 326.

45. Li Tsung-jen et al., pp. 324, 326.

46. Zhang Fakui, pp. 482–483.

47. *The Washington Post*, November 28, 1937.

48. *NCDN*, October 28, 1937.

49. *NCDN*, October 29, 1937.

50. *North China Herald*, November 3, 1937.

51. Ristaino, pp. 62–63.

52. The account of Yang Huimin's exploits is based on Sun Yuanliang, pp. 225–227.

53. Yang Ruifu, p. 158.

54. Zhang Boting, p. 143.

55. Shanghai Municipal Police files show Yang Hu became a millionaire due to the fortune he amassed as defense commissioner. See, Martin, Brian G. *The Shanghai Green Gang: Politics and Organized Crime 1919–1937*. Berkeley: University of California Press, 1996, p. 168.

56. Zhang Boting, pp. 144–145.

57. *NCDN*, November 1, 1937.

58. Yang Ruifu, p. 163.

59. Yuan Ying et al., vol. 1, p. 5.

60. Bruce, p. 67.

61. Teitler, pp. 147–148.

62. Farmer, p. 78.

63. *NCDN*, September 12, 1937.

64. Farmer, p. 77.

65. *NCDN*, September 14, 1937.

66. Feng Yuxiang, p. 78.

67. *NCDN*, September 14, 1937.

68. Feng Yuxiang, p. 78.

69. Qin Xiaoyi, p. 205.

70. Abegg, p. 166.

71. Abegg, p. 165.

72. Williamsen, Marvin. "The Military Dimension 1937–1941," in Hsiung, James C. et al. (eds.). *China's Bitter Victory: The War with Japan 1937–1945*. Armonk NY: M. E. Sharpe, 1992, p. 148.

73. Abegg, p. 166.

74. White, Theodore H. et al. *Thunder Out of China*. New York: William Sloane Associates, 1946, p. 134.

75. White, p. 138.
76. "Japanese Military Medicine," in *Intelligence Bulletin*. Washington DC: War Department, March, 1946, p. 88.
77. Aso Tetsuo. *From Shanghai to Shanghai: The War Diary of an Imperial Japanese Army Medical Officer 1937–1941*. Norwalk CT: Eastbridge, 2004, p. 22.
78. Goette, pp. 43–45. It is worth noting that this book was published in the United States in 1943, at a time of strong anti-Japanese sentiment, making its claims all the more believable.
79. *NDS*, vol. 8, p. 61.
80. Cook, et al., p. 32.
81. Teitler et al., p. 114.
82. *DSBS*, p. 35.
83. *DSBS*, p. 36; Teitler et al., p. 114; *NDS*, vol. 10, p. 213.
84. *DSBS*, p. 36.
85. *NDS*, vol. 8, p. 113.
86. *DSBS*, p. 36.
87. *Shina jihen rikugun sakusen, 1, Showa jusan nen ichi gatsu made,* p. 381; *DSBS*, p. 37; *NDS*, vol. 8, p. 115.
88. Associated Press, October 31, 1937.
89. Teitler et al., pp. 117–118.
90. *DSBS*, pp. 37–38.
91. The account of the Tax Police Division's actions at Zhoujiaqiao is based on Shen Keqin, vol. 1, pp. 103–106.
92. *DSBS*, p. 38.
93. *NDS*, vol. 8, p. 118.
94. *Shina jihen rikugun sakusen, 1, Showa jusan nen ichi gatsu made,* pp. 385–386.
95. Guo Rukui, p. 570; *Shina jihen rikugun sakusen, 1, Showa jusan nen ichi gatsu made,* p. 388.
96. *NDS*, vol. 62, pp. 13–14.
97. *NDS*, vol. 62, pp. 13–14.
98. *NDS*, vol. 8, pp. 95–96.
99. *NDS*, vol. 8, p. 120.
100. *NDS*, vol. 62, p. 17.
101. *NDS*, vol. 62, p. 16.
102. *NDS*, vol. 62, p. 16.

CHAPTER EIGHT: COLLAPSE

1. Soon after the campaign, Tamai Katsunori published a highly popular account of the Hangzhou Bay landing and the subsequent battles, using the pen name Hino Ashihei.
2. The account is based on Hino's description of the landing in Hino Ashihei.

Wheat and Soldiers. New York: Farrar & Rinehart, 1939, pp. 41–68, supplemented by details from the German translation, *Weizen und Soldaten*. Leipzig: Paul List Verlag 1940, pp. 37–63.

3. Hino, *Wheat and Soldiers*, p. 59.
4. *NDS*, vol. 62, p. 19.
5. *NDS*, vol. 62, p. 17.
6. *NDS*, vol. 62, p. 18. Fear of Chinese snipers had already forced Japanese officers to remove their insignia earlier in the Shanghai campaign. See, Drea, Edward J. *In the Service of the Emperor: Essays on the Imperial Japanese Army*. Lincoln NE: University of Nebraska Press, 1998, p. 98.
7. Jiang Jingguo. *Kangri Yuwu* [*Resisting Japanese Aggression*]. Taipei: Liming wenhua, 1978, vol. 5, p. 63.
8. Jiang Jingguo, *Kangri Yuwu,* vol. 5, p. 63.
9. *DSBS*, p. 48.
10. *DSBS*, p. 48; Jiang Jingguo, *Kangri Yuwu,* vol. 5, pp. 62–63.
11. Sun Shengzhi, p. 232.
12. Cao Jianlang, p. 578; Dai Feng et al., p. 120.
13. Zhang Fakui, pp. 483–484.
14. *DSBS*, p. 45. This type of reasoning in the face of a surprise enemy landing is not unheard of in military history, as the German reaction to the Normandy invasion in June 1944 shows.
15. *DSBS*, p. 45.
16. *DSBS*, pp. 45, 48.
17. *DSBS*, p. 43.
18. *DSBS*, p. 45
19. The account of Sone Kazui's experiences at Suzhou Creek is based on *NDS*, vol. 10, pp. 213–217.
20. *NDS*, vol. 61, p. 576.
21. *NDS*, vol. 62, pp. 19–20.
22. Jiang Jingguo, *Kangri Yuwu,* vol. 5, pp. 64–65.
23. *NDS*, vol. 62, p. 20.
24. *NDS*, vol. 62, p. 21.
25. Dai Feng et al., p. 126.
26. These included the 26th, 55th, 61st, 62nd, 79th, 107th and 108th Infantry Divisions as well as the 45th Independent Brigade. Dai Feng et al., p. 124; Wang Daoping (ed.), vol. 2., p. 148.
27. Dai Feng et al., pp. 124–125.
28. Dai Feng et al., pp. 126–127.
29. Jiang Jingguo, *Kangri Yuwu,* vol. 5, pp. 66.
30. Dai Feng et al., p. 127.
31. Gibson, Michael Richard. *Chiang Kai-shek's Central Army*, unpublished Ph. D.

thesis, George Washington University, 1985, p. 385.

32. Sun Shengzhi, p. 232.

33. Li Junsan, p. 152.

34. Chen Cheng. *Chen Chen Huiyilu—Kanri zhanzheng* [*Chen Cheng's Memoirs: The War of Resistance against Japan*]. Beijing: Dongfang chuhanshe, 2009, p. 38.

35. Chiang Kai-shek, *Kunmianji*, p. 584.

36. Chiang Kai-shek, *Kunmianji*, p. 584.

37. Zhang Fakui, p. 484.

38. Zhang Fakui, p. 485.

39. Chiang Kai-shek did follow through with some of his threats. In early 1938, he ordered the execution of Han Fuju, the military governor of east China's Shandong province, for dereliction of duty.

40. *Jiang Gong sixiang yanlun zongji* [*A Collection of President Jiang's Thoughts and Speeches*]. Taipei, vol. 15, p. 545.

41. The account of the early combat near the bridge at Sheshan is based on *NDS*, vol. 62, pp. 147–149.

42. *NDS*, vol. 62, p. 27.

43. *NDS*, vol. 62, p. 28.

44. *NDS*, vol. 62, pp. 154, 157.

45. *NDS*, vol. 62, p. 29.

46. *NDS*, vol. 62, p. 159.

47. *NDS*, vol. 62, p. 155.

48. *NDS*, vol. 62, p. 29.

49. *NDS*, vol. 62, p. 155.

50. Abend Hallett. "Chinese in Orderly Retreat," *The New York Times*, November 9, 1937; Jiang Zhongzheng (ed.), vol. 3, p. 189.

51. Jiang Zhongzheng (ed.), vol. 3, pp. 189, 191.

52. Carlson, E. F., *Twin Stars of China*, p. 23.

53. Abend, Hallett. "Shanghai French Beat Off Refugees," *The New York Times*, November 10, 1937.

54. Zhang Fakui, p. 489.

55. Zhang Fakui, p. 488.

56. The description is based on a photograph from the Acme news agency, early November 1937.

57. *NCDN*, November 10, 1937.

58. *North China Herald*, November 3, 1937.

59. Abend, Hallett. "Shanghai French Beat Off Refugees," *The New York Times*, November 10, 1937.

60. *NCDN*, November 10, 1937.

61. Ristaino, p. 63.

62. *NCDN*, November 6, 1937.

63. Ristaino, p. 65.
64. *NCDN*, November 6, 1937.
65. *North China Herald*, November 17, 1937.
66. The first time, in Nanjing a few weeks later, was a failure, as the zone became engulfed in the general slaughter that ravaged the city. An attempt in the central Chinese city of Hankou the following year was more successful and probably saved thousands of lives. The concept would go on to be enshrined in a commentary to the 1949 Geneva Convention, which would even honor Jacquinot by name.
67. Ristaino, p. 133.
68. Davidson-Houston J. V. *Yellow Creek: The Story of Shanghai*. Philadelphia PA: Dufour Editions, 1964, p. 155.
69. *Christian Science Monitor*, November 11, 1937.
70. Snow, p. 52.
71. Farmer, p. 90.
72. Carlson, E. F. *Twin Stars of China*. Beijing: Foreign Languages Press, 2003, pp. 23–24.
73. Carlson, E. F., *Twin Stars of China*, p. 25.
74. Snow, pp. 53–54.
75. Snow, pp. 53—54.
76. Bruce, p. 74.

CHAPTER NINE: AFTERMATH
1. Guillain, Robert. *Orient Extreme: Une vie en Asie*. Paris: Arlea/Seuil, 1986, p. 31.
2. Schenke, p. 21. Schenke does not give a date for the arrival, but states it was on the day after the death of Pembroke Stephens.
3. Schenke, p. 15.
4. Willens, p. 104.
5. *NCDN*, November 13, 1937.
6. Soon after leaving Shanghai, Yu Hongjun moved on to a career in economic policy making. Among the posts he would later assume were those of finance minister and central bank governor. In 1949, when Chiang Kai-shek lost control over China to the Communists, Yu fled to Taiwan, where he died in 1960, aged 62.
7. Barnett, Robert W. *Economic Shanghai: Hostage to Politics 1937–1941*. New York NY: Institute of Pacific Relations, 1941, p. 17.
8. Brook, p. 189.
9. Farmer, p. 94.
10. Farmer, pp. 94–95.
11. *NCDN*, October 27, 1937. No reliable estimate of the number of civilian casu-

alties has ever been made.

12. Xu Yongchang. *Xu Yongchang riji* [*Xu Yongchang's Diary*]. Taipei: Zhongyang Yanjiuyuan Jindaishi Yanjiusuo, 1991.

13. Ch'i Hsi-sheng, p. 43.

14. Taylor, p. 149.

15. White et al., p. 46.

16. Liang Hsi-huey, *The Sino-German Connection*, pp. 172–185.

17. Rigg, p. 196; King, Tim. "Secret of Hitler's Jewish soldiers is uncovered," in *The Daily Telegraph*, December 2, 1996. In October 1942, Borchardt, who had advanced to become a major and a regiment commander, was injured at El Alamein and was taken prisoner by the British. He passed through various POW camps in the United Kingdom and Canada, and at some point managed to tell his interrogators that his father was in fact Jewish and lived in England. Borchardt returned to Germany in 1946. "Somebody had to come back to rebuild the country," his wife told him. After the war he had a career in journalism and diplomacy. In the late 1950s and early 1960s he was press attaché to the West German embassy in Washington. He ended his career in intelligence.

18. *Shina jihen rikugun sakusen, 1, Showa jusan nen ichi gatsu made*, p. 387. The figure may be somewhat understated. Matsui in his diary entry for February 7, 1938, after three more months of fighting, mentions "more than 18,000" soldiers having died on the battlefield or from disease. *NDS*, vol. 8, p. 176.

19. Morley, p. 270.

20. *North China Herald*, November 10, 1937.

21. Hanson, p. 118.

22. *Shina jihen rikugun sakusen, 1, Showa jusan nen ichi gatsu made*, p. 416. It appears that Matsui may have wavered slightly in the middle of November on the question of continuing to Nanjing, but he soon changed his mind and supported the drive for the capital whole-heartedly. See, Hattori, pp. 176–177.

23. Farmer, p. 97.

24. Honda, p. 351. Kurosu Tadanobu is not his real name. The author states that for fear of reprisals, the old soldier asked to be identified by a pseudonym only.

25. Timperley, Harold J. (ed.). *Japanese Terror in China*. Freeport NY: Book for Libraries Press, 1938, p. 38.

26. Zhang Kaiyuan (ed.). *Eyewitnesses to Massacre: American Missionaries Bear Witness to Japanese Atrocities in Nanjing*. Armonk NY: M. E. Sharpe, 2001, p. 393.

27. Goette, p. 65.

28. Willens, p. 107.

Bibliography

NEWSPAPERS AND NEWS AGENCIES

China Weekly Review
Christian Science Monitor
Life
North China Daily News
North China Herald
The Daily Telegraph
The New York Times
Washington Post
Associated Press
Reuters

CHINESE-LANGUAGE SOURCES

Cao Jianlang. *Zhongguo Guomindangjun jianshi* [*A Brief History of the Chinese Nationalist Forces*]. Beijing: Jiefangjun chubanshe, 2009.

Cao Juren. *Wo yu wo de shijie* [*My World and I*]. Beijing: SDX Joint Publishing Company, 2011.

Chen Cheng. *Chen Chen Huiyilu—Kangri zhanzheng* [*Chen Cheng's Memoirs: The War of Resistance against Japan*]. Beijing: Dongfang chuhanshe, 2009.

Chen Cheng. "Chen Cheng siren huiyi ziliao" ["Chen Cheng's personal recollections"]. *Minguo Dang'an*, 1987, no. 1.

Chen Yiding. "Yangshupu Yunzaobin zhandou" ["Battle of Yangshupu and Yunzaobin"], in *Bayaosan Songhu Kangzhan: Yuan Guomindang jiang-*

293

ling Kangri Zhanzheng qinliji [*The August 13 Songhu Battle: Personal Recollections from the War of Resistance against Japan by Former Nationalist Commanders*], Beijing: Zhongguo wenshi cubanshe, 1987. Hereafter cited as *BSK*.

Dai Feng et al. *1937 Zhongri Songhu zhanyi* [*The 1937 Sino-Japanese Songhu Battle*]. Taipei: Zhimingtang, 2011.

Fang Jing, "Hongjiang, Baoshan, Yuepu, Guangfu xuezhanji" ["An Account of the Bloody Battles of Hongjiang, Baoshan, Yuepu and Guangfu"], in *BSK*.

Feng Yuxiang. *Wo suo renshi de Jiang Jieshi* [*The Chiang Kai-shek That I Knew*]. Taipei: Jieyou chubanshe, 2007.

Ge Yunlong. "Feng Yuxiang churen disan zhanqu silingzhangguan jianwen" ["An account of Feng Yuxiang's service as commander of the Third War Zone"], in *BSK*.

Gong Yeti. *Kangzhan feixing riji* [*A Flight Diary of the War of Resistance*]. Wuhan: Changjiang wenyi chubanshe, 2011.

Guijun yu Songhu Kangzhan [*The Guangxi Troops in the Songhu Battle*]. Shanghai: Shanghai Songhu Kangzhan Jinianguan, 2011.

Guo Rugui. *Guo Rugui huiyilu* [*Guo Rugui's Memoirs*]. Beijing: Zhonggongdang chubanshe, 2009.

Guo Rugui et al. *Zhongguo Kangri Zhanzheng zhengmian zhanchang zuozhan ji* [*The War of Resistance against Japan: An Account of Frontline Battles*]. Nanjing: Jiangsu renmin chubanshe, 2005.

Huang Jie. "Wenzaobang, Suzhouhe zhandou" ["The Battles for Wusong and Suzhou Creeks"], in *BSK*.

Huodao Jingfu riji [*Ogishima Shizuo's Diary*]. Xindian, Taiwan: Lixu wenhua, 2005.

Jiang Gong sixiang yanlun zongji [*A Collection of President Jiang's Thoughts and Speeches*]. Taipei.

Jiang Jingguo. *Kangri Yuwu* [*Resisting Japanese Aggression*]. Taipei: Liming wenhua, 1978.

Jiang Zhongzheng (Chiang Kai-shek). *Kunmian ji* [*Anthology of Encouragement amid Difficulties*]. Taipei: Guoshiguan, 2011.

Jiang Zhongzheng (Chiang Kai-shek) (ed.). *Kangri zhanshi: Songhu huizhan* [*The History of the War of Resistance against Japan: The Songhu Battle*]. Taipei: Guofangbu shizhengju, 1962, vol. 1-3.

Lan Xiangshan. "Guijun canzhan jianwen" ["Information about the Guangxi Troops' Participation in the War"], in *BSK*, p. 320.

Li Guanru. *Tumu dizhu: Guojun dishiba jun zhanshi* [*Indomitable Power: The War History of the 18th Army Group*]. Taipei: Zhibingtang chubanshe, 2012.

Li Junsan. *Shanghai Nanjing baoweizhan* [*Defensive Battles for Shanghai and Nanjing*]. Taipei: Maitian chubanshe, 1997.

Liu Jingchi, "Songhu Jingbei Silingbu jianwen" ["Account of Songhu Garrison Command"], in *BSK*.

Liu Weikai. "Luoyang Qiao xuezhanji" ["Account of the Bloody Battle of Luoyang Bridge"], in *BSK*.

Nanjing datusha shiliaoji [*Collection of Historical Records on the Nanjing Massacre*], vols. 8, 10, 60, 61, 62. Nanjing: Jiangsu renmin chubanshe, 2005–2010.

Qin Xiaoyi (ed.). *Zhonghua Minguo zhongyao shiliao chubian—Duiri Kangzhan shiqi* [*A Preliminary Compilation of Important Historical Document for the Republic of China—the Period of the War Against Japan*], vol. 2, Taipei: Zhongguo Guomindang zhongyangweiyuanhui dangshiweiyuanhui, 1981.

Qiu Weida. "Diwushiyishi Luodian fangyuzhan" ["The 51st Division's Defensive Battle of Luodian"], in *BSK*.

Riben haijun zai Zhongguo zuozhan [*The Japanese Navy's War in China*]. Tianjin: Tianjin shi zhengxia bianyi weiyuanhui, 1991.

Shen Keqin. *Sun Liren zhuan* [*Biography of Sun Liren*]. Taipei: Taiwan xuesheng shuju, 2005.

Shen Zui. *Juntong neimu* [*The Inside Story of the Military Statistics Bureau*]. Taipei: Xinrui chubanshe, 1994.

Shi Shuo. "Bayaosan Songhu Kangzhan jilue" ["Clever Stratagems Adopted during the 813 Songhu Battle"], in *BSK*.

Song Xilian. "Xuezhan Songhu" ["Bloody Songhu Battle"], in *BSK*.

Sun Shengzhi. "Pudong paobing xianshenwei" ["The Invincible Might of the Pudong Artillery"], in *BSK*.

Sun Yuanliang. *Yiwan guangnian zhong de yi shun* [*An Instant in a Trillion Light Years*]. Taipei: Shiying chubanshe, 2002.

Wang Shijie. *Wang Shijie riji* [*Wang Shijie's Diary*]. Taipei: Zhongyang yanjiuyuan jiandaishi yanjiusuo, 1992.

Wu Yujun. "Junmin cheng yiti" ["Army and People Become One"], in *BSK*.

Xiangjun yu Songhu Kangzhan [*The Hunan Troops in the Songhu Battle*]. Shanghai: Shanghai Songhu Kangzhan Jinianguan, 2010.

Xiao Yiping et al. *Zhongguo kangri zhanzheng quanshi* [*A Complete History of the War Against Japanese Aggression*]. Chengdu: Sichuan chuban jituan, 2005.

Xiong Xinmin. "Yangshupu yu Jiangwan kangzhan" ["The Resistance War in Yangshupu and Jiangwan"], in *BSK*.

Xu Yongchang. *Xu Yongchang riji* [*Xu Yongchang's Diary*]. Taipei: Zhongyang Yanjiuyuan Jindaishi Yanjiusuo, 1991.

Xue Zhaguang. "Xuezhan Luodian" ["Bloody Battle for Luodian"], in *BSK*.

Yan Kaiyun et al. "Zhanghuabang, Baiziqiao zhandou" ["The Battles for Zhanghuabang and Eight Character Bridge"], in *BSK*.

Yan Yinggao. "Yu Wenzaobang zhendi gongcunwang" ["Defending the Wusong Creek Front with One's Life"], in *BSK*.

Yang Ji. *Huzhan mihua* [*Secret Talk on the Shanghai Battle*]. Liming shuju, 1938.

Yang Ruifu. "Gujun fendou siriji" ["Account of the Lone Unit's Four Days of Battle"], in *BSK*.

Yuan Ying et al. *Koushu Songhu kangzhan* [*An Oral History of the Songhu Battle*], vol. 1. Shanghai: Shanghai Songhu Kangzhan Jinianguan, 2007.

Zhang Boting. "Songhu huizhan jiyao" ["Summary of the Songhu Battle"], in *BSK*.

Zhang Boting with Li Dongfang. "Bayaosan Songhu Huizhan Huiyi" ["Reminiscences of the 813 Songhu Battle"], in *Zhuanji Wenxue*, vol. 41, no. 2, 1982.

Zhang Ruide. *1937 nian de guojun*. Taipei: Academia Sinica, 2005.

Zhang Suwo. *Huiyi fuqin Zhang Zhizhong* [*Remembering My Father Zhang Zhizhong*]. Nanjing: Jiangsu wenyi chubanshe, 2012.

Zhang Zhizhong. *Huiyilu* [*Memoirs*]. Beijing: Wenhua chubanshe, 2007.

Zhongguo dier lishi dang'an guan. *Kangri zhanzheng zhengmian zhanchang* [*The Frontal Battleground in the Anti-Japanese War*]. Nanjing: Fenghuang chubanshe, 2005.

ENGLISH-LANGUAGE SOURCES

Abend, Hallett. *My Life in China, 1926–1941*. New York: Harcourt Brace, 1943.

Alcott, Carroll. *My War with Japan*. New York: Henry Holt, 1943.

All About Shanghai and Environs. Shanghai: The University Press, 1934.

Andersson, Lennart. *A History of Chinese Aviation*. Taipei: AHS of ROC, 2008.

Askew, David. "Defending Nanjing: An Examination of the Capital Garrison Forces," in *Sino-Japanese Studies*, vol. 15, 2003.

Aso Tetsuo. *From Shanghai to Shanghai: The War Diary of an Imperial Japanese Army Medical Officer 1937–1941*. Norwalk CT: Eastbridge, 2004.

Barnett, Robert W. *Economic Shanghai: Hostage to Politics 1937–1941*. New York NY: Institute of Pacific Relations, 1941.

Barnhart, Michael A. *Japan Prepares for Total War: The Search for Economic Security 1919–1941*. Ithaca: Cornell University Press, 1987.

Benton, Gregor. *New Fourth Army: Communist Resistance along the Yangtze and the Huai 1938–1941*. Berkeley CA: University of California Press, 1999.

Benton, Gregor et al. "The Portrayal of Opportunism, Betrayal and Manipulation in Mao's Rise to Power," in *The China Journal*, no. 55, January 2006.

Bix, Herbert P. *Hirohito and the Making of Modern Japan*. New York: HarperCollins, 2001.

Brook, Timothy. *Collaboration: Japanese Agents and Local Elites in Wartime China*. Cambridge MA: Harvard University Press, 2005.

Bruce, George C. *Shanghai's Undeclared War*. Shanghai: Mercury Press, 1937.

Carlson, Evan F. *Evan F. Carlson on China at war, 1937–1941*. Beijing: Foreign Languages Press, 2003.

Carlson, E. F. *Twin Stars of China*. Beijing: Foreign Languages Press, 2003.

Cook, Haruko Taya et al. *Japan at War*. New York: The New Press, 1992.

Chang Jui-te. "The Nationalist Army on the Eve of War," in Peattie et al. (eds.).

Chang, Jung et al. *Mao: The Unknown Story*. London: Jonathan Cape, 2005.

Chennault, Claire Lee. *Way of a Fighter*. New York NY: C. P. Putnam's
    Sons, 1949.
Ch'i Hsi-sheng. *Nationalist China at War: Military Defeats and Political
    Collapse, 1937–45*. Ann Arbor: University of Michigan Press, 1982.
Clifford, Nicholas Rowland. *Retreat from China: British Policy in the Far
    East 1937–1941*. Seattle WA: University of Washington Press, 1967.
Davidson-Houston J. V. *Yellow Creek: The Story of Shanghai*. Philadelphia
    PA: Dufour Editions, 1964.
Dong, Stella. *Shanghai: The Rise and Fall of a Decadent City*. New York:
    HarperCollins, 2001.
Dorn, Frank. *The Sino-Japanese War 1937–41: From Marco Polo Bridge to
    Pearl Harbor*. New York: Macmillan, 1974.
Drea, Edward J. *In the Service of the Emperor: Essays on the Imperial Japanese
    Army*. Lincoln NE: University of Nebraska Press, 1998.
Dreyer, Edward L. *China at War 1901–1949*. London: Longman, 1995.
Dryburgh, Marjorie. *North China and Japanese Expansion 1933–1937*.
    Richmond and Surrey: Curzon Press, 2000.
Farmer, Rhodes. *Shanghai Harvest: A Diary of Three Years in the China War*.
    London: Museum Press, 1945.
Fenby, Jonathan. *Generalissimo: Chiang Kai-shek and the China He Lost*.
    London: Simon & Schuster, 2003.
Finch, Percy. *Shanghai and Beyond*. New York: Charles Scribner's Sons, 1953.
*Foreign relations of the United States, Diplomatic papers, 1937, in Five Vol-
    umes, Vol. III, The Far East*. Washington DC: U.S. Government Print-
    ing Office, 1954.
Forman, Harrison. *Horizon Hunter*. New York: Robert M. McBride, 1940.
Garver, John W. *Chinese-Soviet Relations 1937–1945: The Diplomacy of Chi-
    nese Nationalism*. New York NY: Oxford University Press, 1988.
Gibson, Michael Richard. *Chiang Kai-shek's Central Army*. Unpublished
    Ph. D. thesis, George Washington University, 1985.
Goette, John. *Japan Fights for Asia*. New York NY: Harcourt, Brace and
    Co., 1943.
Handbook on Japanese Military Forces. Washington DC: War Department,
    1944.
Hanson, Haldore. *Humane Endeavour: The Story of the China War*. New
    York: Farrar & Rinehart, 1939.

Hattori Satoshi with Edward J. Drea. "Japanese Operations from July to December 1937," in Mark Peattie et al. (eds.). *The Battle for China.* Stanford: Stanford University Press, 2011.

Higashinakano Shudo. *The Nanking Massacre: Facts versus Fiction.* Tokyo: Sekai Shuppan, 2006.

Hino Ashihei. *Wheat and Soldiers.* New York: Farrar & Rinehart, 1939.

History of Air Operations in the First Phase of the China Incident (from July to November 1937) [Japanese Monograph No. 166]. Tokyo: Liquidation Department of the Second Demobilization Bureau, 1951.

Honda Katsuichi. *The Nanjing Massacre: A Japanese Journalist Confronts Japan's National Shame.* Armonk NY: M. E. Sharpe, 1999.

Hsin Ta-Mo. *A Review of German Military Advisors' Work in China.* Paper delivered at Conference on Chiang Kai-shek and Modern China in Taipei, October 1986.

Hsu Long-hsuen and Chang Ming-kai. *History of the Sino-Japanese war (1937–1945).* Taipei: Chung Wu Publishers, 1972.

"Japanese Military Medicine," in *Intelligence Bulletin.* Washington DC: War Department, March, 1946.

Jordan, Donald A. *China's Trial by Fire: The Shanghai War of 1932.* Ann Arbor: University of Michigan Press, 2001.

Kalyagin, Aleksandr Ya. *Along Alien Roads.* New York NY: Columbia University, 1983.

Kirby, William. *Germany and Republican China.* Stanford: Stanford University Press, 1984.

Kuo Mo-jo. "A Poet with the Northern Expedition," in *Far Eastern Quarterly*, vol. 3, no. 2, February 1944.

Lang, John. *Rawlinson, the Recorder and China's Revolution: A Topical Biography of Frank Joseph Rawlinson 1871–1937.* Notre Dame, IN: Cross Cultural Publications, 1990.

Lee, Bradford A. *Britain and the Sino-Japanese War, 1937–1939: A Study in the Dilemmas of British Decline.* Stanford CA: Stanford University Press, 1973.

Li Tsung-jen et al. *The Memoirs of Li Tsung-jen.* Boulder, CO: Westview Press, 1979.

Liang Hsi-huey. *Foreign Tributes to Chiang Kai-shek: The Case of Alexander von Falkenhausen.* Paper delivered at Conference on Chiang Kai-shek and Modern China in Taipei, October 1986.

Liang, Hsi-huey. *The Sino-German Connection*. Amsterdam: van Gorcum, 1978.

Liu, F. F. *A Military History of Modern China, 1924–1949*. Princeton: Princeton University Press, 1956.

Long, Jeff E. "The Japanese Literati and 'the China Incident': Hayashi Fusao Reporting the Battle of Shanghai," in *Sino-Japanese Studies*, vol. 15, 2003.

Lu, David J. *From the Marco Polo Bridge to Pearl Harbor: A Study of Japan's Entry into World War II*. Washington DC: Public Affairs Press, 1961.

Macri, Franco David. *Clash of Empires in South China: The Allied Nations' Proxy War with Japan, 1935–1941*. Lawrence KS: University of Kansas Press, 2012.

Martin, Bernd. "The Role of German Military Advisors on the Chinese Defense Efforts against the Japanese 1937–1938," in Pong, David (ed.). *Resisting Japan: Mobilizing for War in Modern China*. Norwalk CT: EastBridge, 2008.

Martin, Brian G. *The Shanghai Green Gang: Politics and Organized Crime 1919–1937*. Berkeley: University of California Press, 1996.

Mohr, E. G. *Sino-German Relations in the Period of Chiang Kai-shek*. Paper delivered at Conference on Chiang Kai-shek and Modern China in Taipei, October 1986.

Morley, James William. *The China Quagmire: Japan's Expansion on the Asian Continent 1933–1941*. New York: Columbia University Press, 1983.

Oliver, Frank. *Special Undeclared War*. London: Jonathan Cape, 1939.

Peattie, Mark R. *Sunburst: The Rise of Japanese Naval Air Power 1909–1941*. Annapolis: Naval Institute Press, 2002.

Political Strategy Prior to the Outbreak of War [*Japanese Monograph No. 144*]. Tokyo: Military History Section Headquarters, 1952.

Powell, John B. *My Twenty-Five Years in China*. New York: Macmillan, 1945.

Reischauer, Edwin O. *My Life between Japan and America*. New York: Harper & Row Publishers, 1986.

Rigg, Bryan Mark. *Hitler's Jewish Soldiers: The Untold Story of Nazi Racial Laws and Men of Jewish Descent in the German Military*. Lawrence KS: University Press of Kansas, 2004.

Ristaino, Marcia R. *The Jacquinot Safe Zone: Wartime Refugees in Shanghai*. Stanford: Stanford University Press, 2008.

Snow, Edgar. *The Battle for Asia*. Cleveland OH: The World Publishing Company, 1941.

Spunt, Georges. *A Place in Time*. New York: G. P. Putnam's Sons, 1968.

Sun Youli. *China and the Origins of the Pacific War*. New York: St Martin's Press, 1993.

Taylor, Jay. *The Generalissimo: Chiang Kai-shek and the Struggle for Modern China*. Cambridge MA: Belknap, 2009.

Teitler, Geir et al. *A Dutch Spy in China: Reports on the First Phase of the Sino-Japanese War*. Leiden: Brill, 1999.

Timperley, Harold J. (ed.). *Japanese Terror in China*. Freeport NY: Book for Libraries Press, 1938.

Verhage, William. "The Bombing of Shanghai," in *Sigma Phi Epsilon Journal*, vol. 35, no. 2, 1937.

Wakeman, Frederic E. *Spymaster: Dai Li and the Chinese Secret Service*. Berkeley: University of California Press, 2003.

"Weekly Intelligence Summaries," August, 1937. British War Office.

White, Theodore H., et al. *Thunder Out of China*. New York: William Sloane Associates, 1946.

Willens, Liliane. *Stateless in Shanghai*. Hong Kong: Earnshaw Books, 2010.

Williamsen, Marvin. "The Military Dimension 1937–1941," in Hsiung, James C. et al. (eds.). *China's Bitter Victory: The War with Japan 1937–1945*. Armonk NY: M. E. Sharpe, 1992.

Wilson, Dick. *When Tigers Fight: The Story of the Sino-Japanese War 1937–1945*. New York: The Viking Press, 1982.

Yang Tianshi. "Chiang Kai-shek and the Battles of Shanghai and Nanjing," in Mark Peattie et al. (eds.). *The Battle for China*. Stanford: Stanford University Press, 2011.

Yamamoto Masahiro. *Nanjing: Anatomy of an Atrocity*. Westport CT: Praeger, 2000.

Zhang Fakui. *Reminiscences of Fa-k'uei Chang: Oral History*, 1970–1980. Columbia University Libraries, Oral History Research Office.

Zhang Kaiyuan (ed.). *Eyewitnesses to Massacre: American Missionaries Bear Witness to Japanese Atrocities in Nanjing*. Armonk NY: M. E. Sharpe, 2001.

SOURCES IN OTHER LANGUAGES

Abegg, Lily. *Chinas Erneuerung: Der Raum als Waffe*. Frankfurt a. M: Societäts-Verlag, 1940.

Die Schlacht bei Shanghai. Berlin: Oberkommando der Wehrmacht, 1939.

Guillain, Robert. *Orient Extreme: Une vie en Asie*. Paris: Arlea/Seuil, 1986.

Hino Ashihei. *Weizen und Soldaten*. Leipzig: Paul List Verlag 1940.

Kageyama Koichiro. "Oyama jihen no hitotsu kosatsu—dai niji Shanhai jihen no dokasen no shinso to gunreibu ni ateta eikyo" ["A reconsideration of the Oyama incident: the facts about the trigger of the second Shanghai incident and the impact it had on the Naval General Staff"], *Gunji shigaku*, vol. 32, no. 3 (December 1996).

Rapport sur la catastrophe du 14 Aout 1937. Shanghai: Services de Police, 1937.

Schenke, Wolf. *Reise and der gelben Front*. Berlin: Gerhard Stalling Verlagsbuchhandlung, 1941.

Shina jihen rikugun sakusen, 1, Showa jusan nen ichi gatsu made [*Official military history, vol. 86, Army operations during the China incident, part 1: to January 1938*]. Tokyo: Asagumo shimbunsha, 1975.

Siegert, Wilhelm. *Geschichte des Lehr Infanterie Bataillons 1820 bis 1896. Mit einem Nachtrag, die Jahre 1897–1906 umfassend von Armin Witthauer*. Berlin: E.S. Mittler und Sohn, 1912.

Yoshida Hiroshi. *Tenno no guntai to Nankin jiken*. Tokyo: Aoki shoten, 1998.

Index